War Virtually

War Virtually

THE QUEST TO AUTOMATE CONFLICT,
MILITARIZE DATA, AND PREDICT THE
FUTURE

Roberto J. González

UNIVERSITY OF CALIFORNIA PRESS

University of California Press
Oakland, California

© 2022 by Roberto J. González

Library of Congress Cataloging-in-Publication Data

Names: González, Roberto J. (Roberto Jesús), 1969– author.
Title: War virtually: the quest to automate conflict, militarize data, and
    predict the future / Roberto J. González.
Description: Oakland, California: University of California Press, [2022] |
    Includes bibliographical references and index.
Identifiers: LCCN 2021045189 (print) | LCCN 2021045190 (ebook) |
    ISBN 9780520384767 (hardback) | ISBN 9780520384774 (ebook)
Subjects: LCSH: Artificial intelligence—Military applications. | Military
    art and science—Automation.
Classification: LCC UG479 .G66 2022 (print) | LCC UG479 (ebook) |
    DDC 355.8—dc23/eng/20211006
LC record available at https://lccn.loc.gov/2021045189
LC ebook record available at https://lccn.loc.gov/2021045190

31   30   29   28   27   26   25   24   23   22
10   9   8   7   6   5   4   3   2   1

para mis hijos y ahijados

Contents

Contents

Illustrations

TABLES

Terms and Abbreviations

AFRL	Air Force Research Laboratory (US military research lab)
AI	Artificial intelligence
API	Application programming interface, used for developing software apps
ARE	Alternate reality experience
ARG	Alternate reality game
ARL	Army Research Laboratory (US military research lab)
ARPA	Advanced Research Projects Agency (US government agency, 1958–72; renamed DARPA)
AS	Autonomous system
ASM	Autonomous Squad Member (military robot)
ATAK	Android Tactical Assault Kit (US Air Force Research Laboratory smartphone app)
ATM	Automated teller machine
BASIC	Beginners' All-Purpose Symbolic Instruction Code (computer programming language)

BDI	Behavioural Dynamics Institute (nonprofit research organization)
CENTCOM	Central Command (one the US DoD's nine unified military commands)
CIA	Central Intelligence Agency (US government agency)
COIN	Counterinsurgency
CPI	Committee on Public Information (US government agency, 1917–19)
CTTSO	Combating Terrorism Technical Support Office (US government office)
DARPA	Defense Advanced Research Projects Agency (US DoD organization)
DIB	Defense Innovation Board (independent advisory board to US DoD)
DIU	Defense Innovation Unit (US DoD organization)
DIUx	Defense Innovation Unit Experimental (US DoD organization; precursor to DIU)
DoD	Department of Defense (US government department)
DSB	Defense Science Board (US DoD civilian advisory board on science and technology)
EMIC	Emic Training to Improve Cross-cultural Prediction (DARPA program)
ENIAC	Electronic Numerical Integrator and Computer
EOD	Explosive ordnance disposal
FBI	Federal Bureau of Investigation (US law enforcement agency)
FS3	Forensic Social Science Supercollider (DARPA program)
GCP	Google Cloud Platform
GPS	Global positioning system
GSR	Global Science Research (data science company)
HFE	Human factors engineering

HSCB	Human Social Cultural and Behavioral Modeling (US DoD research program)
HTS	Human Terrain System (US Army program)
IARPA	Intelligence Advanced Research Programs Agency (US government agency)
ICE	Immigration and Customs Enforcement (US government agency)
ICRAC	International Committee for Robot Arms Control (nongovernmental organization)
IED	Improvised explosive device
IJOP	Integrated Joint Operations Platform (Chinese state surveillance system)
INSIGHT	Integrative System for Enhancing Fluid Intelligence through Human Cognitive Activity, Fitness, High-definition Transcranial Direct-current Brain Stimulation, and Nutritional Intervention (IARPA-funded research project)
ISAF	International Security and Assistance Force (NATO-led multilateral military alliance in Afghanistan)
ISIS	Islamic State in Iraq and Syria
JEDI	Joint Enterprise Defense Infrastructure (US DoD cloud storage program)
JEDI MIND	Joint Estimation of Deception Intent via Multisource Integration of Neuropsychological Discriminators (IARPA-funded research project)
JSOC	Joint Special Operations Command (US military joint command of SOCOM, Special Operations Command)
MARGARET	Multidimensional Algorithm Generated Anthropological Recording and Ethnographic Tool (DARPA-funded project)
MCWL	Marine Corps Warfighting Laboratory (US military research lab)

MDDS	Massive Digital Data Systems (US Intelligence Community program)
MEMEX	DARPA program
ML	Machine learning
NASA	National Aeronautics and Space Administration (US government agency)
NATO	North Atlantic Treaty Organization (multilateral military alliance)
NGO	Non-governmental organization
NGS2	Next Generation Social Science (DARPA program)
NIST	National Institute of Standards and Technology (US government lab and agency)
NRL	Naval Research Laboratory (US military research lab)
NSA	National Security Agency (US government agency)
NSF	National Science Foundation (US government agency)
NSI	National Security Innovations (defense analytics company)
OCEAN	Openness, conscientiousness, extraversion, agreeableness, neuroticism; also called the "Big Five" personality traits
ONA	Office of Net Assessment (US government office)
PTSD	Post-traumatic stress disorder
QMRR	Quantitative Methods for Rapid Response
RER	Rapid ethnographic research
RMA	Revolution in Military Affairs
SA	Situational awareness
SAIC	Science Applications International Corporation (private company)
SCL Group	Strategic Communications Laboratory (private company)
SOUTHCOM	Southern Command (one the US DoD's nine unified military commands)

TAILOR	Teaching AI (artificial intelligence) to Leverage Overloaded Residuals (IARPA program)
TAK	Team Awareness Kit (US Air Force Research Laboratory smartphone app)
TRUST	Tools for Recognizing Useful Signals of Trustworthiness (IARPA program)
TTP	Tehrik-e-Taliban
UAREHERE	Using Alternate Reality Environments to Help Enrich Research Efforts (IARPA request for information)
UAV	Unmanned aerial vehicle; drone
UGB	Understanding Group Biases (DARPA program)
UTACC	Unmanned Tactical Autonomous Control and Collaboration (military robot)
UX	User experience
VR	Virtual reality
W-ICEWS	Worldwide Integrated Crisis Early Warning System
XDATA	Extracting Data (DARPA program)

Note: Abbreviations that refer to military robots and autonomous weapon systems can be found in table 1 (pp. 27–28). Abbreviations that refer to behavioral modeling and simulation programs can be found in table 2 (pp. 127–29).

1 War Virtually

This book is about the pursuit of a dream—a dream that, over time, may turn out to be a nightmare. It's the story of how a group of scientists and engineers are racing to develop, acquire, and adapt computerized, data-driven technologies and techniques in order to automate war, predict conflict, and regulate human thought and behavior. The advent of artificial intelligence—particularly machine learning—is accelerating the military's relentless drive toward virtual combat zones and autonomous weapons, in the United States and elsewhere. To the outside world, this sounds like the stuff of fantasy, but from the inside, science fiction appears to be on the verge of becoming science fact. At this stage of history, it's still not clear whether the outsiders or the insiders will be correct in their interpretations.

Military planners and policymakers are attempting to harness the latest scientific and technical knowledge to prepare for war, virtually. The technological fantasy of virtual warfare is alluring—even seductive—for it suggests that someday we may conduct wars without soldiers, without physical battlegrounds, and maybe even without death.[1] Although there is no agreed-upon definition for virtual war, as a starting point we might think of it as a confluence of long-term trends, tools, and techniques: war conducted by robotic systems, some of which are being programmed for ethical decision-making; the emergence of Silicon Valley as a major center for defense and intelligence work; algorithmically driven propaganda campaigns and psychological operations (psyops) developed and deployed through social media platforms; next-generation social science models aimed at discovering what drives human cooperation and social instability; and predictive modeling and simulation programs, including some ostensibly designed to foresee future conflict.[2] Although these projects have different historical trajectories, they all have something in common: they're predicated on the production, availability, or analysis of large amounts of data—big data—a commodity so valuable that some call it "the new oil."[3]

In the United States, those undertaking such work are employed in military and intelligence agencies, defense conglomerates and contract firms, university laboratories, and federally funded research centers. The protagonists of the story include computer scientists, mathematicians, and robotics engineers, as well as psychologists, political scientists, anthropologists, and other social scientists. At its core, this book is about how these men and women are attempting to engineer a more predictable, manageable world—not just by means of electronic circuitry and computer code, but also by means of behavioral and social engineering—that is, *human* engineering. Under certain conditions, cultural and behavioral information can become a weapon, what in military terms is called a force multiplier—a way of more effectively exerting control over people and populations.

Given the breathtaking scope of the proposed technologies and their potential power, it's easy to overlook their limitations and risks, since so many of them are still in the realm of make-believe. It's even easier to overlook the serious ethical and moral dilemmas posed by autonomous weapon systems, predictive modeling software, militarized data, and algorithmically driven psyop campaigns—particularly at a time when some observers are warning of an "AI [artifical intelligence] arms race" between the United States and rival powers.[4]

The rush to create computational systems for virtual warfare reveals a fatal flaw that's been with *Homo sapiens* as long as civilization itself: *hubris,* that persistent and terrible human tendency to embrace blind ambition and arrogant self-confidence. The ancient Greeks understood this weakness, and learned about its perils through myths such as the tragedy of Icarus, a young man so enthralled with the power of human invention that he forgot about its limits. But instead of tragedy, our myth-making machinery produces technological celebrities like Tony Stark, Iron Man's brash, brilliant alter ego. There's little room for hubris—much less ethical ambiguity—in the Manichean fantasy worlds of Hollywood superheroes and American politics. But it's important to remember how, in a heavily militarized society like our own, overfunded technology projects and reckless overconfidence can quickly turn to disaster.

UPGRADE

The latest generation of military tools is a continuation of long-standing trends toward high-tech warfare. For example, US scientists have experienced changing patterns of military influence over their work during the course of at least a century. In the early 1960s, as the United States was about to escalate its war in Vietnam, a well-known physicist famously told Defense Secretary Robert McNamara that "while World War I might have been considered the chemists' war, and World War II was considered the physicists' war, World War III . . . might well have to be considered the social scientists' war."[5] By that time, military and intelligence agencies were integrating knowledge from psychology, economics, and anthropology into their tactical missions, provoking controversy and criticism from social scientists concerned about the lethal application of their work.[6]

But what's happening today is broader in scope than anything the military-industrial complex has created before. If you think of the earlier phases of high-tech conflict as versions 1.0, 2.0, and 3.0, then you might say that in the twenty-first century, a major upgrade is under way: chemists, physicists, and social scientists are now working together with roboticists and computer scientists to create tools for conducting data-driven warfare. The advent of War 4.0 is upon us, sparked by the so-called Revolution in Military Affairs—the idea that advanced computing, informatics, precision strike missiles, and other new technologies are the answer to all of America's security problems. In recent years, observers have warned of a drift toward "future war," the rise of "genius weapons," and "T-minus AI."[7]

Like most updates, the latest version of warfare is built upon what came before. More than a half-century ago, the US military launched an advanced electronic warfare campaign targeting enemy convoys traveling across the Ho Chi Minh Trail, a network of roads linking North and South Vietnam. For the Vietcong, the route was a vital lifeline for transporting equipment, weapons, and soldiers. The US military program, dubbed Operation Igloo White, used computers and communication systems to compile data collected by thousands of widely dispersed electronic devices such as microphones, seismic monitors, magnetic sensors, and vehicle ignition detectors. Despite high hopes and a gargantuan price tag, the program was not nearly as effective as its architects had hoped.[8]

Such efforts weren't limited to the collection of hard data—sometimes, they were based on "soft" social science data. A case in point: the Phoenix Program, a brutal counterinsurgency initiative launched by the CIA and the Defense Department in 1968. At about the same time that Operation Igloo White was under way, military officials and intelligence agents were using IBM 1401 mainframe computers to compile ethnographic and demographic information collected by US civil affairs officers. Eventually, they created a database of suspected Vietcong supporters and communists. American advisors, mercenary fighters, and South Vietnamese soldiers then used the computerized blacklist—called the Vietcong Infrastructure Information System—to methodically assassinate more than twenty-five thousand people, mostly civilians, under the aegis of the Phoenix Program. For its users, the computer program magically transformed what would otherwise appear to be a subjective, arbitrary, bloody assassination campaign into a seemingly rational, objective, and antiseptic process of social control.[9]

War 4.0 differs from earlier forms of automated conflict and computerized weapon systems. While it's true that US military personnel used computers as early as 1946, when they programmed ENIAC (the Electronic Numerical Integrator and Computer) to develop better ballistic trajectory charts and hydrogen bombs, today military and intelligence agencies and firms are using not only advanced computational hardware and software, but also vast amounts of data—and from infinitely more sources. The term *big data*, ambiguous as it is, hints at the scale of change. Apart from the expansion of electronic sensors ranging from high-resolution satellites

Figure 1. At the height of the US war in Vietnam, American government agencies and the military used IBM mainframe computers for the Phoenix Program. Photo courtesy of Michigan State University Archives.

and drones to closed-circuit TV cameras, billions of people around the world leave enormous amounts of digital residue behind when using the internet, social media, cell phones, personal fitness trackers, and virtual assistants like Apple's Siri or Amazon's Alexa.[10] Both actual (face-to-face) and virtual (face-to-screen) interactions are subject to closer surveillance than ever before. Military and intelligence agencies don't always have easy access to this data, but many of the corporations that control such information—such as Amazon, Google, and Microsoft—have forged close relationships with the Pentagon and the US intelligence community.

Another difference is that the technologies often rely on algorithms to construct behavioral models for anticipating or even predicting human behavior, in virtual and actual realms. Algorithms provide the means by which large amounts of raw data about our virtual lives can be processed and reassembled as probable outcomes, political preferences, propaganda, or products. If you've ever used Facebook, Instagram, Amazon, Netflix, or Google, you probably have an intuitive sense of how the algorithms work. Unless you're willing and able to opt out by changing your privacy settings—which is typically a cumbersome, confusing, time-consuming process—companies constantly track your internet searches, online purchases, and webpage visits, then feed the data into mathematical formulas. Those formulas, or algorithms, use that data to make calculations, essentially educated guesses about what you might like, and then "recommend" things to you—clothes, shoes, movies, appliances, political candidates, and much more.[11] Algorithms are what fill your news feeds with articles based on your previously monitored online reading or internet browsing habits, and Big Tech firms have built an industry on them by using your data to help their clients target you for online ads. These techniques have helped Facebook, Google, and Amazon dominate the world of digital advertising, which now far eclipses print, TV, and radio ads.[12] When people are transformed into data points, and human relationships become mere networks, the commodification of personal information is all but inevitable without meaningful privacy regulation. What this means in practical terms is that all of us risk having our digital lives become part of the military-industrial economy.

From the perspective of a data scientist, handheld internet-ready digital devices have transfigured billions of people worldwide into atomized data production machines, feeding information into hundreds, if not thousands, of algorithms on a daily basis. The militarization of this data is now a routine part of the process, as suggested by recent reports detailing the Defense Intelligence Agency's use of commercially available geolocation data collected from cell phones.[13] Military and intelligence agencies can use such data not only for surveillance, but also to reconstruct social networks and even to lethally target individual people. A dramatic case occurred in September 2011, when, in a joint drone operation authorized by the Obama administration, CIA and US military personnel assassinated Anwar al-Awlaki—an ardent US-born Muslim cleric—in Yemen. Those who organized the drone strike targeted Awlaki based on the location of his cell phone, which was monitored by the National Security Agency as part of a surveillance program. Two weeks later, a CIA drone attack using the same kind of data killed another US citizen: Awlaki's sixteen-year-old son, Abdulrahman al-Awlaki.[14]

Although Awlaki was intentionally assassinated by US forces, other Americans—and many thousands of civilians in Afghanistan and other parts of Central Asia and the Middle East—have been inadvertently killed by drones.[15] These cases foreshadow a major flaw in the latest iteration of automated war: the imprecision of the technologies, and the great margins of error that accompany even the most sophisticated new weapon systems. In their most advanced form, the computerized tools make use of artificial intelligence, such as iterative machine learning techniques. Although proponents argue that the weapons perform at levels comparable or even superior to humans, they rarely provide conclusive evidence to support their claims. Yet the march to adopt these machines continues apace. The Pentagon's quest to develop AI for military applications has led to the creation of an Algorithmic Warfare Cross-Functional Team, also known as Project Maven. Among its first objectives was to analyze thousands of hours of video footage from drones to produce "actionable intelligence" that might be used to locate ISIS fighters in Syria and Iraq (see chapter 3).[16]

Still another characteristic that differentiates these novel forms of virtual war from earlier attempts is heavy reliance on a stripped-down, portable version of cultural and behavioral knowledge—culture in a box.[17] The problem is that the information is often superficial, shallow, devoid of context. In the world of business, an overly simplistic understanding of cultural dynamics might mean losing potential customers. On the battlefield, it can mean someone getting killed.

PIVOT POINTS

How and when did the shift to virtual war begin? Or, to put it in slightly different terms, how and when did data become a weapon? There are no easy answers to the question, but we can trace several interrelated, incremental changes that began to emerge over the past decade and—little by little—pushed things in this direction. Some of these transformations were technological, some were geopolitical, some were cultural, and some were economic. In addition, billions of people around the world began to communicate and interact with others in substantially different ways—

most significantly, online. It's helpful to think about the quest for an automated battlefield as a kind of convergence, as the end point of these
changes.

Among the most significant factors propelling the trend toward data-
driven warfare is the rapid diffusion of internet-ready smartphones across
the globe, beginning in about 2007.[18] Since the advent of the internet in
1991, *Homo sapiens* had been gradually spending more time online, but
the portability and convenience of smartphones amplified that pattern—so
much so that by 2019, American smartphone users were spending an
average of more than three hours a day on their mobile devices—apart
from the time spent on desktop or laptop computers.[19] During the era of
COVID-19, this undoubtedly increased as people worked, attended
classes, and even socialized in virtual realms. From the perspective of institutions seeking to monitor people's ideas, interactions, interests, or idio-
syncrasies, smartphones, tablets, and other mobile devices have become
powerful tools for collecting huge quantities of data.

To make matters worse, virtual life has been an easy target for spies of
all kinds—and a windfall for intelligence agencies around the world.
Classified documents from the US National Security Administration
(NSA), leaked by Edward Snowden in 2013, revealed the scale of surveillance. The NSA had spied on US citizens and citizens from other countries
by "listening in" through the internet. The agency had stored data in server
farms and then analyzed it, using algorithms to search for patterns. It
would be difficult to overestimate the significance of Snowden's revelation.
"Although the NSA was authorized by the US administration to execute
such global surveillance in order to prevent terrorist attacks, the fact that
the US government spied on its own citizens created a dangerous precedent," wrote a critic.[20]

Another factor that made an impact on the growth of virtual forms of
war—not only in the United States, but also in Europe, Russia, China, and
other regions—was the meteoric rise of the Islamic State of Iraq and Syria,
or ISIS.[21] The group, which sprouted from the ashes of Al Qaeda, grew
rapidly in 2013 and 2014, during a period of extreme political and social
turmoil in the Middle East. The US-led invasion and occupation of Iraq—
and the subsequent fragmentation of Iraqi society—played a leading role
in creating the conditions that allowed ISIS to flourish.[22] For more than

five years, ISIS ruled a self-styled caliphate that seized and maintained political control over large swaths of northern Iraq and southern Syria. Its officials collected taxes, enforced a brutal interpretation of Sharia law, and even issued a new currency: gold and silver dinars.

ISIS launched a sophisticated social media campaign appealing to young people who had faced discrimination, segregation, and harsh treatment as members of minority Muslim communities in many different regions of the world, including North America, Europe, and Central and Southeast Asia.[23] The organization relied on propaganda messages, which included spectacularly violent video clips, to attract recruits, and they were astonishingly effective: by June 2014, approximately forty thousand people from more than eighty nations had affiliated themselves with ISIS in Iraq and Syria, including many Europeans.[24] Nearly five thousand of the recruits were women. Never before had an army relied so heavily on virtual communication as the basis for mobilizing troops. Not surprisingly, American, European, Russian, and Chinese military officials ramped up efforts to counter violent extremists—particularly those claiming to defend Islam—through various forms of cyberwarfare. These projects intensified once attacks by "homegrown" extremists, presumably radicalized in online spaces, began to spread.[25]

The explosion of ISIS onto the world scene led the US military to adopt radically different methods for fighting insurgents. For nearly a decade, American forces in Iraq and Afghanistan had been using a modern interpretation of classic counterinsurgency doctrine. This approach, which was closely associated with General David Petraeus, advocated a return to classic "small wars" techniques developed by David Galula, a French military officer who fought in the Algerian war of independence, and other colonial-era military theorists.[26] Once it became clear that American counterinsurgency efforts were failing, several influential military planners—most notably US Army Lieutenant General Michael Flynn, director of the Defense Intelligence Agency from 2012 to 2014 and US national security advisor for four months in 2017—pushed to pursue a data-intensive strategy, based on easily accessible open-source data and fine-grained "human intelligence" gathered by those in close contact with civilians.[27] Flynn advocated a hybrid approach that might be called computational counterinsurgency, in which social scientists would cooperate with data scientists. At the same time that he was publicly pushing for the military to employ "cultural experts, social experts, archaeologists, [and] anthropologists," he was also working with computer scientists from Johns Hopkins University to trace insurgent networks in Iraq using massive datasets.[28]

Yet another metamorphosis that has pushed war virtually forward over the past decade is a shift in global geopolitics. After the attacks of September 11, 2001, the efforts of the US government had been geared toward protecting the country from Islamic extremism. By 2011, those efforts had begun to shift almost imperceptibly toward a more familiar form of great-power rivalry. As China's economic and political power and influence grew, and as Russia began to reassert itself aggressively on the world stage by invading Crimea and then Ukraine, many observers started to compare the geopolitical landscape to that of previous centuries.[29] However, unlike in previous periods, military officials began preparing to launch and defend against cyberattacks of all kinds: propaganda and dis-information campaigns, malware designed to infect government comput-ers, electronic sabotage of power grids and water treatment plants, and much more.[30] These patterns took shape during the Obama years, and they intensified during the Trump presidency. Other trends that may have played a role include public condemnation of Russian involvement in the 2016 US presidential elections, an escalating trade war with China, and deteriorating diplomatic relations with Iran during the Trump era. American policymakers' pivot toward Russia, China, Iran, and other rival powers has allowed the Pentagon, and the US Congress, to slide back toward a technology-heavy agenda—one focused less on training and edu-cating military personnel than on building machines that will create work for voters living in congressional districts. Think of it as Eisenhower's military-industrial complex, revamped for the twenty-first century.

Taken together, these transformations propelled the trend toward vir-tual war, but they didn't guarantee it. US defense and intelligence agencies are expansive bureaucracies with competing interests and points of view, and they've never been monolithic. Although technology firms and military contractors jumped at the chance to promote high-tech solutions for a dan-gerous world, not all military and intelligence officials were convinced that these tools would work. Some who were less tech-savvy resented the idea that they might be asked to radically change their ways. Others were worried about the safety of military troops. Still others were concerned about the possibility that innocent civilians might be inadvertently killed, or that the use of such technologies might spiral out of control.

But perhaps most important of all were in-house turf wars. The Pentagon and the armed services are sprawling organizations, with factions vying for power and influence. For example, in the 1980s and 1990s, when the Pentagon's Office of Net Assessment began articulating the Revolution in Military Affairs (known as the RMA within the Defense Department)—a doctrine that, as mentioned above, oriented the military toward technology-based solutions—it soon became clear that the "revolution" would rely heavily on airpower, and not just as a means of supporting infantry troops, but as an offensive force in its own right. As US Army and Marine Corps leaders began to worry that their budgets might be cut in order to increase funding for the air force—and as some began to doubt whether the proposed changes would ever work—they launched a bureaucratic counter-revolution, pushing the Pentagon's civilian leadership to back away from the idea. After 9/11, when the United States went to war with global networks of insurgents armed with relatively simple technologies such as improvised bombs, automatic rifles, and grenade launchers, the RMA lost steam.[31] But now, in a period characterized by rapid technological change, cyberwarfare, and the rise to power of rival nation-states, the machinery of computerized combat is once again lumbering forward. Some of those working within military and intelligence circles oppose the shift, but for now, its momentum seems too overwhelming to stop.

DUALITY

It's worth stepping back for a moment to consider the ambiguity of automated data-collection systems and algorithmic techniques. These technologies are a good example of the dual-use nature of scientific research, a persistent kind of polarity in which "theoretical developments are transformed into commercial products or military applications."[32] The idea of dual use often refers to the imaginary divide separating theoretical knowledge from applied work, but it can also describe what happens when technologies developed for military purposes are adopted for commercial use—or vice versa. David Price, who has spent nearly three decades researching the militarization of American social science, reminds us that "some scientific developments like the radar, the internet, GPS navigation systems, walkie-talkies, jet propulsion engines, night vision, and digital photography were initially introduced as military applications and later took on dual civilian uses" during the twentieth century.[33] In other words, tools originally designed for battlefield use by the US military were eventually commercialized, then adopted by millions of civilian consumers.

Dual-use processes aren't just unidirectional. Sometimes, technologies or techniques developed primarily for civilian use or commercial markets are militarized, as in the case of internal combustion engines, or even weaponized, as in the case of dynamite. There are other instances in which dual-use technologies emerge as the result of a two-way exchange of ideas and products between civilian and military institutions, through a symbiotic process of give and take. In many cases, dual-use technologies represent the proverbial double-edged sword, capable of promoting the safety and well-being of people and also of causing them harm.

The power of dual-use technologies was on full display during the first few months of the global coronavirus pandemic. In early 2020, as people worldwide struggled to find ways to slow the spread of the pathogen, the Singaporean government rapidly responded to the crisis. A centerpiece of the country's strategy was TraceTogether, a smartphone app that uses Bluetooth wireless signals to enable contact tracing—a process in which epidemiologists seek to control the spread of a disease by identifying and testing people who have been exposed to infected individuals. Other Asian countries, including South Korea, Hong Kong, and China, used similar software. Although it has a long history, contact tracing had nearly always been done by humans, typically through phone calls, site visits, and interviews. Never before had public health officials used automated cell phone apps to collect data on human movement—certainly not on such a sweeping scale.[34] In essence, the programs were designed to monitor millions of people, all in real time.

Within weeks, as the number of COVID-19 cases began surging in the United States, technology giants Google and Apple—normally fierce rivals—publicly announced that they were joining forces to create their own contact-tracing software that would be hardwired into the operating systems of billions of mobile phones. The tool would allow people with coronavirus to report their infection to a public health app, which would then notify other phones that had come into close contact with the infected person's device.[35]

While news outlets often heralded these developments as an example of the tech industry prioritizing the public interest, some critics began to worry about the potential misuse of such programs. The prospect of two of the world's most powerful tech firms coming together to create a powerful surveillance tool quickly led to grave concerns over data privacy. Other companies—including military contract firms specializing in counterterrorism software and spyware—began offering their services and products to government agencies in the early stages of the pandemic. Take, for example, the Israeli company NSO Group, best known for its controversial Pegasus cell phone spyware, which enables users to hack into smartphones and read text messages, track calls and phone location, and collect passwords. NSO began working with officials from a dozen countries in the Middle East, Europe, Southeast Asia, and South America to track potential COVID-19 carriers. According to Bloomberg Law, "the system, initially developed for counterterrorism, uses algorithms and government-provided data" for the program.[36] Palantir, a controversial technology company that had previously assisted the National Security Agency in implementing its wide-sweeping data dragnet—and helped the US Immigration and Customs Enforcement agency deport undocumented immigrants—reportedly discussed the possibility of using its web-based apps with government officials from the United States, the United Kingdom, France, Germany, Austria, and Switzerland.[37]

Although executives at Google, Apple, and other tech firms have assured the public that contact-tracing apps will include strong privacy protections, transparency, and user consent, critics point to just how easily authoritarian, militarized societies can harness private data to control their own citizens. Clemson University computer engineering professor Richard Brooks notes that "emergency powers quickly become normal operating procedures" over the long term. Brooks, who over the course of his career has received funding from the Air Force Office of Scientific Research, the Army Research Office, the Office of Naval Research, and the Defense Advanced Research Projects Agency, adds: "If the ability to track social contacts exists to stop a contagion, I can guarantee you it will be used to track the spread of dissent."[38]

Take China, for example. At about the same time that Singapore released TraceTogether, the Chinese government began requiring its citizens to download Alipay Health Code, a software program that assigns the user a color-coded symbol to determine whether he or she should be quarantined or allowed to enter public spaces. A green code allows the user to travel without restrictions, but yellow and red codes require one- and two-week quarantines, respectively. Although it's not entirely clear, it appears that the program relies on data from COVID-19 cases and government travel records on individual citizens.

The app was created by Alibaba, a Chinese internet company that is often compared to Amazon. Alipay Health Code shares data with the police, "setting a template for new forms of automated social control that could persist long after the epidemic subsides."[39] China's state news agency, Xinhua, reported that law enforcement officials were involved in the development of the program. The system has the capability of tracking people's movements over time, since every time a person's code is scanned—for example, at a health center or a subway entrance—his or her location is sent to computer servers. The same basic technology, which is essentially a GPS-enabled tracking system harnessed to social network analysis tools, supplemented with government databases, is therefore capable of serving both public health officials and military intelligence agencies.

As troubling as these scenarios sound, the fact is that millions of Chinese citizens have *already* been subjected to sophisticated forms of mass surveillance, and then detained en masse with the help of internet technologies. For instance, in 2014, the Communist government began using the internet and mobile technologies to crack down on Uyghurs, an ethnic minority group concentrated in the country's westernmost province of Xinjiang. Uyghurs, who are mostly Muslims, have been under siege for decades by the government, which has attempted to colonize Xinjiang with ethnic Han Chinese. Beginning in 2014, the military began using a popular social media program, WeChat, as a surveillance tool for monitoring communication between Uyghurs.[40]

At about the same time, the Chinese government rolled out facial recognition technology to scan Uyghurs at police checkpoints and entrances into supermarkets, shopping centers, and hospitals. By systematically collecting data from smartphones, computers, cameras, and sensors, the government assembled a mammoth database of suspected Islamic extremists. Surveillance techniques played an essential role in the widespread persecution and imprisonment of the Uyghur people. By 2018, a human rights panel from the United Nations estimated that more than a million Uyghurs were being held in a "massive internment camp shrouded in secrecy."[41]

Earlier that year, Human Rights Watch released a detailed report describing a mobile phone app used by Chinese police and military forces in Xinjiang province. The app, called the Integrated Joint Operations Platform (IJOP), sounds like something out of an Orwell novel. As the report explains,

> authorities are collecting massive amounts of personal information—from the color of a person's car to their height down to the precise centimeter—and feeding it into the IJOP central system, linking that data to the person's national identification card number. . . . [T]he system is tracking the movement of people by monitoring the 'trajectory' and location of their phones, ID cards, and vehicles; it is also monitoring the use of electricity and gas stations of everybody in the [Xinjiang] region.[42]

The system is supplied by Xinjiang Lianhai Cangzhi Company, a subsidiary of China Electronics Technology Group Corporation, a state-owned military contractor. In March 2016, the company publicly announced that it had secured a major government contract to develop a program that would monitor citizens' behaviors in order to predict terrorist attacks.

Both surveillance and contact-tracing apps share certain features—particularly the real-time collection of positional data from users' cell phones—and they process the information rapidly with a form of automated social network analysis, a method developed by psychologists and anthropologists in the mid-twentieth century.[43] These techniques can be used for dramatically different purposes—purposes that are polar opposites in terms of their effects on the security and well-being of humans. On one hand, as we have seen in Singapore and South Korea, they can potentially be used as a means of improving public health in the midst of an infectious disease outbreak, by helping epidemiologists track patterns of human interaction.[44] On the other hand, the same basic technology can be used for mass surveillance, thereby eroding individual privacy. For example, some South Koreans expressed grave concerns over their government's decision to publicly post information about the travel histories of confirmed COVID-19 patients in the early months of the pandemic.[45] More troubling still is the Chinese case, in which an authoritarian state uses surveillance apps to repress minority groups and dissidents.

It would be a mistake to assume that the United States is immune to such techniques. In fact, big data analytics has become an essential tool for law enforcement agencies throughout the country—perhaps a predictable outcome in a society where police departments in many cities have come to resemble military combat brigades, in terms of both size and equipment. Across the United States, nearly eighty fusion centers—in which federal, state, and local law enforcement agencies share intelligence information and technology—employ facial recognition software, programs for automatically monitoring social media platforms, and other advanced surveillance tools.[46] It's not an exaggeration to say that policing in some US cities resembles a form of computer-based counterinsurgency, a technologically complex, militaristic approach to population control that relies on repressive tactics, overwhelming force, and winning "hearts and minds" to snuff out insurgents and dissidents (see chapter 6). If American police departments sometimes look and act like occupying armies, it's partly because their officers have undergone the same training and use many of the same weapons of war.[47]

Those weapons are supplemented by a vast array of dual-use analytical tools, some of which are provided to law enforcement agencies by companies that are household names. As noted by technology scholar Ramesh Srinivasan,

> Amazon has made it so inexpensive and easy to buy almost anything. . . . The Chinese Alibaba is no different. . . . [But] what about Amazon's facial recognition technology being sold to military contractors, the police, and the Immigration and Customs Enforcement (ICE) agency? Are we okay with these sorts of transactions, similar examples of which we can find involving every powerful tech company?[48]

At the heart of these contradictions is the idea of *data*—particularly its potential uses and misuses, as it circulates from one domain to another.

Figure 2. Police in military gear confront protesters in Ferguson, Missouri, following the 2014 killing of Michael Brown, an African American teenager shot by a white officer. Photo courtesy of Jamelle Bouie/CC-BY-2.0.

THE GIFT

Data is, at least in literal terms, a gift. The word is derived from the Latin *datum*, meaning "that which is given." It entered the English language in the mid-seventeenth century as a philosophical term for things known, or assumed, to be facts. The idea of "taking something as given" suggests a close connection between gifts, facts, and data. So too does the use of the term *dato* ("fact" in Spanish; "given" in Italian) in some Romance languages today.

Originally, the word *data* had nothing to do with numbers, but by the late 1800s it often meant numerical or statistical facts. During the 1940s, some scientists began using the word to describe specific kinds of information: storable, transmittable numbers used for computer-based operations. The use of the term exploded during the second half of the twentieth century, alongside the rapid development of computers. In popular culture, the concept even took a humanoid form when the popular TV series *Star Trek: The Next Generation* introduced the character Data—an eloquent pale-skinned robot—in 1987.

Since the concept of data is so ubiquitous today, it's easy to forget its origins, and the relevance of gift-giving as a framework for thinking about data. *Financial Times* editor Gillian Tett notes that "while the definition of data has evolved beyond all recognition, the original meaning reveals a bigger truth. What drives our modern cyber-economy is not just bytes and numbers but . . . a massive system of exchanges. Silicon Valley is partly based on oft-ignored barter trades of personal information for services between internet users and tech companies."[49] Anthropologist Kadija Ferryman, who researches the social and ethical implications of health information technologies, underscores the importance of this perspective: "When we think about data this way, as a gift, we can understand the social dynamics at play in today's data collection projects."[50]

Cultural research on gift-giving—what social scientists often call reciprocal exchange—can provide insight into these ideas. In his classic 1922 book *The Gift*, sociologist Marcel Mauss used examples from so-called primitive societies in Melanesia, Polynesia, and the Northwest Coast of America to illustrate the obligatory nature of giving and receiving gifts. He made numerous observations that are remarkably relevant to the idea of data as a gift—such as the notion that gifts are endowed with magical power. Mauss suggested that in small-scale societies that rely heavily on exchange of goods without the use of money, the giver has an enduring bond with the gift, even after it has been exchanged. Thus, Mauss wrote, "the objects are never completely separated from the men who exchange them."[51] As an example, he described the significance of gift-giving among the seafaring Trobrianders, who inhabit islands east of New Guinea. They make dangerous maritime journeys to trade beautifully ornate shell necklaces and armbands with their counterparts living on other islands. These luxury gifts are imbued with the essence, the spirits, of those who cared for them in the past. These items can never be bought or sold—they're literally priceless to the Trobrianders.

We can take this idea and use it to better understand what's happening with data today. Personal data, which you share with tech companies in exchange for seemingly free products and services such as email accounts, search engines, and chat platforms, is tightly connected to and identified with who you are. In other words, your data contains within it a vestige of your soul, of your identity. In the words of cultural anthropologist Rebecca Lemov, "Big data is people . . . they are 'faint images of me' . . . lending ghostly new life to the fruits of algorithmic processing."[52] But even though personal data is a gift that bears an existential and spiritual connection to a real person, it's not priceless. In fact, it's worth money, and Big Tech aggregates it to make even more money through ads. Digital advertising sales are by far the biggest source of revenue for Google, Facebook, Twitter, and many other Silicon Valley firms.

Much of the resentment and outrage directed toward the tech industry by consumers in recent years might be understood in these terms. When users of Facebook and Amazon began to fully understand how these and other tech companies were commercializing their personal data by using it to sell targeted advertisements, many of them began to view it as a kind of betrayal. It's one thing to use an individual's personal information to recommend products and services to him or her—but it's quite another to use the data to push ads. Once personal data is monetized, it slips out of the realm of the gift and into the marketplace. It's no longer a gift, it's a commodity.

BREAKOUT

By now, you've probably guessed that this book is not merely a description of the latest high-tech weapons and gadgets being developed by the Pentagon's mad scientists or Silicon Valley's computer programmers. Instead, the objective is to begin exposing some of the root causes driving the kinds of technological developments and ideas highlighted throughout the following chapters. Another goal is to unearth the sometimes irrational, even magical, thinking that underlies what superficially appear to be coldly objective scientific activities. As an anthropologist, I'm especially interested in exploring the *cultural underpinnings* of virtual war and its technologies.

At this point, I should come clean and admit that I'm something of a closet engineer—in fact, I studied engineering for four years, before being smitten by the social sciences. Although I was fascinated by courses in thermodynamics, materials science, and fluid mechanics, it was oddly unsettling to undergo the rigidly narrow training process. At my university, engineering professors never asked students (who were more than 90 percent male) to think about the moral or ethical implications of their work. Safety concerns were typically reduced to a simple number, the so-called safety factor, and social responsibility was mentioned nowhere in the curriculum. For me, leaving engineering school was more than a relief—it was an escape, a mental breakout that allowed me think more openly about the world and my place in it.[53]

And yet, even as an anthropologist, I haven't been able to shake off my fascination with technology, its complex effects, its unintended consequences. Over the course of my career, as I have studied the culture of militarization—a mightily powerful but often invisible force that permeates nearly every aspect of American life—I've come to understand that many of the mundane artifacts we use every day originated in the laboratories of military and intelligence agencies. Computers, the internet, jet engines, microwaves, transistors, solar panels—all these and more began as innovations created by or developed for the military.

To fully appreciate the ways in which virtual technologies are needling themselves into the fabric of everyday life, it isn't enough to understand just the technical side of the process. Cultural influences play a significant part in the development and deployment of these tools—and in efforts to critique and even resist them.

For example, research on robotics and autonomous weapon systems centers on improving artificial intelligence—but it's also about getting humans to place their faith in the machines (as we'll see in chapter 2). Although it is true that combat troops will sometimes anthropomorphize machines, including robots, it's also the case that military training, particularly combat training, typically instills a spirit of self-sacrifice, brotherhood, and unwavering trust among soldiers, a willingness to lose one's life for others in the platoon.[54] Given this centuries-old tradition, how can troops be expected to experience the same kinds of sentiments toward robotic, automated systems? What kinds of behavioral engineering might be needed to transform soldiers' mistrust in machines? Do social scientists, particularly psychologists, have the ability to fix this "problem"—if indeed it can even be fixed? These questions lie at the heart of chapter 2.

Chapter 3 looks at the increasingly tight, symbiotic relationship between the Pentagon, the CIA and other spy agencies, and Silicon Valley's technology firms. The region's tech industry wouldn't exist without the largesse of military and intelligence agencies. Enormous contracts from the US Defense Department went to regional military contractors like Lockheed Martin, Ford Aerospace, FMC, and Westinghouse in the 1970s and 1980s. By the end of the Cold War, the top defense firms in the region had secured more than $11 billion in defense contracts, producing everything from missile launchers to spy satellites. Despite this fact, many continue to believe that Silicon Valley's economic success is solely the product of unfettered entrepreneurship—even as a new generation of companies and start-ups, many of them specializing in robotics, geospatial technologies, artificial intelligence, and cloud computing, receive lavish funding from the Pentagon and CIA. Some of these firms employ social scientists as ethnographers, "user experience" researchers, and experts who might help create new kinds of human-centered systems. The chapter ends with a discussion of a significant phenomenon: nascent movements among rank-and-file engineers and programmers who oppose the repressive deployment of dual-use technologies.

Chapter 4 examines a relatively new way of conducting psychological warfare or psychological operations—psyops for short. It recounts the story of a now defunct private British defense contractor, SCL Group, that specialized in "behavior change" techniques with a range of applications, from advertising to politics to military propaganda. The company was reportedly involved in more than a hundred political campaigns in over sixty countries around the world. Nearly a decade ago, the American subsidiary of the company, Cambridge Analytica, began harvesting piles of big data collected from social media sites—without the consent of users. A company insider, who later became a whistleblower, claimed that social scientists were deeply involved in the company's projects, which were eventually used to further polarize an already divided American electorate through social media and online advertising. Some have referred to this as an example of how data can become weaponized. The chapter ends with a discussion of how Cambridge Analytica represents only the tip of the iceberg, and why it's important to understand the ways in which data analytics is changing political processes on a global scale by facilitating mass manipulation.

Chapter 5 delves into the intriguing world of DARPA, the Defense Advanced Research Projects Agency. The enigmatic organization, which is sometimes called the Pentagon's own research and development center, has recently launched several social science big data initiatives, including a program designed to use immense online datasets in order to better understand what causes communities to disintegrate into "a chaotic mix of disconnected individuals." By tracing the career of an anthropologist who eventually became a DARPA program manager, responsible for helping to oversee multimillion-dollar research projects, the chapter illuminates the processes by which social science can easily become militarized, and the problems inherent in these processes.

Chapter 6 explores the world of predictive modeling and simulation: a series of ambitious, long-term initiatives launched by the Pentagon, defense contractors, and federally funded research centers. These projects, which are often conducted in partnership with university-based laboratories, are designed to compile gargantuan amounts of information from online sources and then use that data to detect potential hot spots of political instability and conflict. Despite criticisms and doubts about whether the software works as advertised, many companies have been developing predictive modeling programs in close collaboration with US military and intelligence agencies, often for use by local law enforcement officials. The chapter poses larger questions in the context of scientists' concerns over artificial intelligence and long-term human survival in a world of accelerating technological change.

Chapter 7 concludes the book by taking a hard look at what's at stake: the integrity of our democratic society and the viability of *Homo sapiens* as a species. It includes a critique of algorithmic bias—a problem that goes way beyond virtual warfare—and offers some thoughts about the importance of addressing the phenomenon of big datasets that reflect the inequalities and prejudices of the societies that produce them. I also propose ways that concerned government and military officials might take a new approach, by prioritizing *preventive*, rather than *palliative*, national security strategies and by giving *qualitative* data as much weight as *quantitative* data. Finally, I describe how engineers, computer scientists, and social scientists are in a unique position to help inform the broader public about dangerously complex technological systems, and how they can play a leading role in creating a safer, more secure future for us all.

2 Requiem for a Robot

The blistering late-afternoon wind ripped across Camp Taji, a sprawling US military base just north of Baghdad, in an area known as the Sunni Triangle. In a desolate corner of the outpost, where the feared Iraqi Republican Guard had once manufactured mustard gas, nerve agents, and other chemical weapons, a group of American soldiers and Marines were solemnly gathered around an open grave, dripping sweat in the 114-degree heat. They were paying their final respects to Boomer, a fallen comrade who had been an indispensable part of their team for years. Just days earlier, he had been blown apart by a roadside bomb.

As a bugle mournfully sounded the last few notes of "Taps," a soldier raised his rifle and fired a long series of volleys—a twenty-one-gun salute. In 2013, the troops, which included members of an elite army unit specializing in explosive ordnance disposal (EOD), had decorated Boomer posthumously with a Bronze Star and a Purple Heart. With the help of human operators, the diminutive remote-controlled robot had protected hundreds—maybe even thousands—of American military personnel from harm by finding and disarming hidden explosives.[1]

Boomer was a Multi-function Agile Remote-Controlled robot, or MARCbot, manufactured by a small Silicon Valley engineering company called Exponent. Weighing in at just over thirty pounds, MARCbots look like a cross between a Hollywood camera dolly and an oversized Tonka truck.[2] Despite their toy-like appearance, the devices often leave a lasting impression on those who work with them. In an online discussion about EOD support robots, one soldier wrote, "Those little bastards can develop a personality, and they save so many lives."[3] An infantryman responded by admitting, "We liked those EOD robots. I can't blame you for giving your guy a proper burial, he helped keep a lot of people safe and did a job that most people wouldn't want to do."[4] Some EOD team members have written letters to companies that manufacture these robots, describing the bravery shown—and the ultimate sacrifice made—by the machines.[5]

Some warfighters have gone so far as to personalize their droids with what might be called body art. Consider this account, written by an Iraq war veteran:

> I was in Iraq with 1st Battalion 5th Marines. The EOD Techs had a few robots or "Johnny 5s." One particular Johnny 5 had seen so much shit, and survived so many IEDs [improvised explosive devices], that they began tattooing him with sharpies [permanent markers]. You'll notice I said "him," because they did in fact identify with the robots as team members. They sharpied all sorts of "tattoos" on him, even incorporating some of his battle scars into the art. For every blast that he survived, the operators began having him do the raise-the-roof motions with his arms instantly after the blast occurred. It was great. . . . Story has it, that when Johnny finally met his match, each team member took home a tattooed body part.[6]

But while some EOD teams established something like emotional bonds with their robots, others loathed the machines, especially when they malfunctioned. Take, for example, this case described by a Marine who served in Iraq:

> My team once had a robot that was obnoxious. . . . It would frequently accelerate for no reason, steer whichever way it wanted, stop, etc. This often resulted in this stupid thing driving itself into a ditch right next to a suspected IED. . . . [I]t did us as much harm as good. . . . So of course then we had to call EOD [personnel] out and waste their time and ours all because of this stupid little shithead of a robot. Every time it beached itself next to a bomb, which was at least two or three times a week, we had to do this. . . . EOD was getting sick of us, we were getting careless, and we were wasting

Figure 3. Foster-Miller's TALON is a remote-controlled reconnaissance robot that can be outfitted with a rifle, grenade launcher, or incendiary weapon. Photo courtesy of US Army.

time on stupid shit. Probably 80% of the time it was just garbage or something harmless. . . . Then one day we saw yet another IED. . . . So old shit-headed robot made an appearance. His final one. And this time, he was a force for good. We drove him straight over the pressure plate, and blew the stupid bastard to pieces. . . . All in all a good day.[7]

At first glance, there's something odd about battle-hardened warriors treating remote-controlled devices like either brave, loyal, intelligent pets or clumsy, stubborn clods—but we shouldn't be too surprised. People in many regions have anthropomorphized tools, vehicles, and machines, assigning them human traits and characteristics. For generations, Melanesian islanders have christened their canoes with humorous nicknames to recognize their distinct personalities. In India, Guatemala, and other countries, bus drivers name their vehicles, protect them with deities' images, and dress them in exuberant colors. Throughout the twentieth century, British, German, French, and Russian troops frequently talked about weapons of war—tanks, airplanes, ships—as if they were people. And in Japan, robots' roles have rapidly expanded into domains that include the intimate spaces of home—in a remarkable extension of what one cultural anthropologist has called "techno-animism."[8]

Some observers have interpreted these accounts as unsettling glimpses of a future in which men and women are as likely to empathize with artificially intelligent machines as with members of their own species. From this perspective, what makes robot funerals unnerving is the idea of an emotional slippery slope. If soldiers are bonding with clunky pieces of remote-controlled hardware, what are the prospects of humans forming emotional attachments with machines once they're more autonomous in nature, nuanced in behavior, and anthropoid in form? And then, of course, a more troubling question arises: On the battlefield, will *Homo sapiens* be capable of dehumanizing members of its own species (as it has for centuries), even as it simultaneously humanizes the robots sent to kill them?[9]

ROBO-FANATICISM

For the better part of a decade, several influential Pentagon officials have relentlessly promoted robotic technologies, promising a future in which "humans will form integrated teams with nearly fully autonomous unmanned systems, capable of carrying out operations in contested environments."[10] The *New York Times* reported in 2016: "Almost unnoticed outside defense circles, the Pentagon has put artificial intelligence at the center of its strategy to maintain the United States' position as the world's dominant military power."[11] The American government is spending staggering sums to advance these technologies: for fiscal year 2019, the US Congress was projected to provide the Defense Department with $9.6 billion to fund unmanned and robotic systems—significantly more than the annual budget of the entire National Science Foundation. (For a partial list of robotic and autonomous systems under development by the military, see table 1.)[12]

Roboticization rhetoric runs rampant among defense establishment elites from public, private, and nonprofit sectors. Arguments supporting

Table 1 Robotic and Autonomous Systems under Development by US Military Contract
Firms (Partial List)

Robotic System	Developer	Objective
ACER *Armored Combat Engineer Robot*	Mesa Robotics	Handling and removing hazardous materials, clearing routes, and decontaminating ground surfaces
BEAR *Battlefield Extraction-Assist Robot*	Vecna Robotics	Removing wounded soldiers from battlefields
Dragon Runner	Automatika-QinetiQ	Collecting intelligence, surveillance, and reconnaissance information; detecting and neutralizing explosives
Indago 3	Lockheed Martin	Conducting aerial intelligence and surveillance missions
iRobot Warrior	iRobot	Disposing of unexploded ordnance, clearing routes, and (in modified form) firing combat weapons
LS3 (BigDog) *Legged Squad Support System*	Boston Dynamics	Carrying gear over rough terrain using quadrupedal system; robotic "pack mule"
MARCbot *Multi-function Agile Remote-Controlled Robot*	Mesa Robotics	Searching for improvised explosive devices; providing surveillance support
MATILDA *Mesa Associates' Tactical Integrated Light-force Deployment Assembly*	Mesa Robotics	Conducting ground intelligence, surveillance, and reconnaissance; detecting and neutralizing explosives
MQ-1 Predator /MQ-9 Reaper	General Atomics	Conducting aerial intelligence, surveillance, and reconnaissance; launching air-to-ground missiles
MULE *Multifunction Utility-Logistics and Equipment Vehicle*	Boeing	Supporting ground combat missions in rough terrain using unmanned autonomous technology

(continued)

Table 1   (continued)

Robotic System	Developer	Objective
ORCA XLUUV *Extra-Large Unmanned* *Underwater Vehicle*	Lockheed Martin	Delivering supplies and armaments to naval vessels using autonomous guidance system
PSKT *Power-Structure* *Tool Kit*	Soar Technology	Simulation of human network dynamics and projection of future behavior
R-Gator	iRobot and John Deere	Patrolling perimeters and carrying supplies using autonomous unmanned guidance
RoboLobster	Massa Products and Northeastern University	Locating underwater mines; conducting underwater surveillance and search-and-rescue missions
SUGV *Small Unmanned* *Ground Vehicle*	iRobot	Carrying out ground intelligence, surveillance, and reconnaissance
TALON (Foster-Miller)	QinetiQ	Providing intelligence, surveillance, and reconnaissance; disarming explosives; firing combat weapons

the expansion of autonomous systems are consistent and predictable: the machines will keep our troops safe because they can perform dull, dirty, dangerous tasks; they will result in fewer civilian casualties, since robots will be able to identify enemies with greater precision than humans can; they will be cost-effective and efficient, allowing more to get done with less; and the devices will allow us to stay ahead of China, which, according to some experts, will soon surpass America's technological capabilities. The evidence supporting these assertions is questionable at best, and sometimes demonstrably false. For example, an "unmanned" aerial Predator requires at least three human controllers: a pilot, a sensor operator, and a mission intelligence coordinator—plus an entire support team of data analysts and personnel who service the drone on the ground before and after flights.[13] Yet the Pentagon's propagandists and pundits simply repeat the talking points, and over time many people take them for granted as fact.

Perhaps the most compelling rhetorical argument is autonomy's apparent inevitability. Here, Defense Department officials need only point to the fact that major automobile manufacturers and Silicon Valley firms are developing and testing self-driving cars on America's streets and highways. Several high-profile accidents in which drivers relied on their automobiles' autopilot feature may eventually delay the widespread commercial introduction of autonomous vehicles, but the momentum and the hype favor rapid technological deployment. Given the circumstances, why not just stop worrying and learn to love the robots?

. . . . .

The most outspoken advocate of a roboticized military is Robert O. Work, who was nominated by President Barack Obama in 2014 to serve as deputy defense secretary, second-in-command to the defense secretary and responsible for managing the Pentagon's day-to-day operations and its budget. Speaking at the annual Reagan National Defense Forum in 2015, Work—a barrel-chested retired Marine Corps colonel with the slight hint of a drawl—described a future in which "human-machine collaboration" would win wars using big data analytics. He used the example of Lockheed Martin's newest stealth fighter to illustrate his point: "The F-35 is not a fighter plane, it is a flying sensor computer that sucks in an enormous amount of data, correlates it, analyzes it, and displays it to the pilot on his helmet." He didn't mention the fact that each of those helmets costs taxpayers $400,000—or that an F-35 fighter has a price tag of $80 million. Operating and maintaining the F-35 isn't cheap either: it costs approximately $44,000 for each hour of service.[14]

The beginning of Work's speech was measured and technical, but by the end it was full of swagger and braggadocio. To drive home his point, he described a ground combat scenario. "I'm telling you right now," Work told the rapt audience, "ten years from now if the first person through a breach isn't a friggin' robot, shame on us." He continued: "Assisted human operations, wearable electronics, making sure that our warfighters have combat apps that help them in every single possible contingency—we can do this."

Work concluded by invoking the idea of an "iCombat world" that will be familiar to younger officers who came of age during the internet era: "If we can tap into the captains and majors and lieutenants who have grown up in this world, and we can manage that creativity together, we will kick ass!"[15]

Less than a month after his term as deputy defense secretary expired in July 2017, Work was elected to the board of directors of Raytheon—one of the top three US defense contractors and a leader in the development of military robots. Within weeks, he was also elected to the boards of two other high-tech defense contractors, HawkEye 360 and Govini, data analytics firms specializing in national security. He then started his own defense consulting company, TeamWork LLC. Work served as an adjunct professor at George Washington University and is currently a senior fellow at the Center for a New American Security, a hawkish bipartisan think tank. He exemplifies what anthropologist Janine Wedel calls "the shadow elite," people who simultaneously serve in positions of economic, academic, and governmental power to promote their agendas—in this case, robotic warfare.[16]

Work's giddy excitement about autonomous and semi-autonomous weapon systems is common among some of the Pentagon's top brass, and his breathless description of technological inevitability can be contagious: pundits, journalists, and countless Defense Department bigwigs often speak in similar terms. P. W. Singer, who appears frequently on news programs as an expert on military automation, is barely able to contain his enthusiasm for the machines. The first sentence of his best-selling book *Wired for War* is "Because robots are frakin' cool."[17] In a nationally televised interview, Singer exuberantly sang the praises of "social robots that can recognize facial expressions and then, in turn, give their own facial expressions." He added:

> You have Moore's Law going on here . . . [in that] our microchips are doubling in their computing power just about under every two years or so. . . . [W]ithin twenty-five years our systems may be as much as a billion times more powerful than today. And so this all sounds like science fiction, and yet it is real right now.[18]

Anthropologist Lucy Suchman has methodically eviscerated Singer's rhetoric, exposing its technical flaws, particularly a gratuitous linkage to

Moore's law, which "is cited endlessly to suggest the inevitability of any and all forms of technological progress." She notes that Singer's unfounded assertions are performative acts that help promote the high-tech, sci-fi "real right now" in which we supposedly live.[19]

Officers who support the further adoption of military robots tend to be more sober and relatively restrained in their assessments. US Army General Robert Cone, for example, favors the use of robots because of their purported efficiency: he estimates that an army brigade might be cut by 25 percent (from four thousand to three thousand soldiers) if support robots are deployed. US Air Force Major Jason DeSon suggests that robotic fighter pilots might be preferable to humans because they aren't subject to the physical and psychological fatigue associated with high-G maneuvers.[20] And US Army Lieutenant Colonel Phil Root, in describing an experimental program integrating drones, robotic ground vehicles, high-tech sensors, and artificial intelligence, notes that big data technologies will give soldiers a "superhuman understanding of the scene. . . . You can digest all of these tools rapidly without always monitoring many computer screens or tablets."[21] Although their tone differs from that of Work and Singer, the assumption is the same: robotic technology is unstoppable and will continue moving forward at a blistering pace.

"The debate within the military is no longer about whether to build autonomous weapons but how much independence to give them," reports the *New York Times*.[22] The rhetoric surrounding robotic and autonomous weapon systems is remarkably similar to that of Silicon Valley, where charismatic CEOs, technology gurus, and sycophantic pundits have relentlessly hyped artificial intelligence.[23] For example, in 2016, the Defense Science Board (DSB)—a group of appointed civilian scientists tasked with giving advice to the Department of Defense on technical matters—released a report titled "Summer Study on Autonomy." Significantly, the report wasn't written to weigh the pros and cons of autonomous battlefield technologies; instead, the DSB assumed that such systems will inevitably be deployed. Among other things, the report included "focused recommendations to improve the future adoption and use of autonomous systems . . . [and] example projects *intended to demonstrate the range of benefits of autonomy* for the warfighter [emphasis added]."[24] The question of whether introducing more robots and autonomous weapons into the military might have negative consequences was apparently not up for discussion.

The fanatical argument that like it or not, robots are the future is an example of the "inevitability syndrome," a means by which the proponents of a new technology attempt to sell wholesale cultural transformations while stifling debate.[25] In the case of autonomous systems, robotics boosters masked the rhetoric as a kind of cool, scientifically informed futurism. But like the Italian Futurists of the early 1900s, who "were obsessed with cars and airplanes ... emphasized youth over experience ... [and] believed that the only way to live was by pushing forward and never looking back," the Pentagon's robo-fanatics run the risk of creating "a church of speed and violence."[26] Anthropologist Andrew Bickford reminds us that the Italian Futurists sought a symbiotic relationship between warfare and technology, but they also pursued the "increased internal mechanization and anesthetization of the [soldier's] body to offset the fear of these new technologies."[27] Ultimately, many of them were killed in battle by the war machines they had enthusiastically embraced.

INTERFACES

Early in the twentieth century, military and intelligence agencies began developing robotic systems, which were mostly devices remotely operated by human controllers.[28] But microchips, portable computers, the internet, smartphones, nanotechnologies, and other developments have supercharged the pace of innovation. So too has the ready availability of colossal amounts of data from electronic sources and sensors of all kinds. The *Financial Times,* a newspaper whose journalists aren't prone to hyperbole, reports: "The advance of artificial intelligence brings with it the prospect of robot-soldiers battling alongside humans—and one day eclipsing them altogether."[29] These transformations aren't inevitable, but they may become a self-fulfilling prophecy.

All of this raises the question: What exactly is a "robot-soldier"? Is it a remote-controlled, armor-clad box on wheels, entirely reliant on explicit, continuous human commands for direction? Is it a device that can be

Figure 4. A soldier holds a remote-controlled Black Hornet miniature surveillance drone while viewing images on a display screen attached to his vest. Photo courtesy of US Army/Argie Sarantios-Perrin.

activated and left to operate semi-autonomously, with a limited degree of human oversight or intervention? Is it a droid capable of selecting targets (using, say, facial recognition software or other forms of artificial intelligence) and initiating attacks without human involvement? There are hundreds, if not thousands, of possible technological configurations lying between remote control and full autonomy.

The US military's experimental and actual robotic and autonomous systems include a vast array of artifacts that rely on either remote control or artificial intelligence: aerial drones; ground vehicles of all kinds; sleek warships and submarines; automated missiles; and robots of various shapes and sizes—bipedal androids, quadrupedal gadgets that trot like dogs or mules, insectile swarming machines, and streamlined aquatic devices resembling fish, mollusks, or crustaceans, to name a few. The Defense Advanced Research Projects Agency, or DARPA, has played a role in coordinating the development of these technologies over the past few decades, and the number of projects has increased dramatically.

The points of contact between robots and people—sometimes called the human-machine interface—can vary substantially from one case to another. In military contexts, for example, there's a qualitative difference between a MARCbot operator's interactions with his or her EOD robot and a missile operations specialist's interactions with a nearly autonomous ballistic missile. The MARCbot operator has much greater control over the robot than the missile specialist does over the missile—and these differences affect ideas about who bears responsibility for a robot's actions.

Lucy Suchman succinctly frames the issue, noting that "questions around the human-machine interface include how agencies—capacities for action—are distributed across different configurations of persons and machines."[30] She points to an emerging paradox in which soldiers' "bodies become increasingly entangled with machines, in the interest of keeping them apart from the bodies of others"—others such as suspected enemies and civilians living under military occupation, for example.[31] The interrelationship of humans and things—in other words, the entanglement of people and their artifacts—grows increasingly complex over time, and these relationships sometimes become irreversible, particularly if we become overly dependent on technological or infrastructural systems.[32] But the truly remarkable point, in military contexts, is that as the human-machine interface ties people and technologies more closely together, it physically separates human warfighters from foreign others.

The military's push toward autonomous systems is a subset of a much larger phenomenon: the growing interconnection between humans and digitally networked technologies, a process that began in the 1990s and then gained great momentum in the early twenty-first century. Archaeologist Ian Hodder argues that modern-day entanglements might be better described as forms of entrapment:

> We use terms such as "air" book, the "cloud," the "Web," all of which terms seem light and insubstantial, even though they describe technologies based on buildings full of wires, enormous use of energy, cheap labor, and toxic production and recycling processes. . . . It would be difficult to give up smartphones and big data; there is already too much invested, too much at stake. The things seem to have taken us over . . . [and] our relationship with digital things has become asymmetrical.[33]

The Defense Department's quest to automate and autonomize the battle-field is part of these larger material and cultural environments.

. . . .

The transitions projected by military planners suggest that servicemen and servicewomen are in the midst of a more or less neatly ordered three-phase evolutionary process, which begins with remote-controlled robots, in which humans are "in the loop," then proceeds to semi-autonomous and supervised autonomous systems, in which humans are "on the loop," and then concludes with the adoption of fully autonomous systems, in which humans are "out of the loop."[34] At the moment, much of the debate in military circles has to do with the degree to which automated systems should allow—or require—human intervention.

Although there has been a great deal of investment and mostly quiet optimism regarding fully autonomous systems from the Pentagon's top brass, and excitement and trepidation from the media about the prospect of a real-life Terminator, here I will take a moment to discuss the hypothetical second stage—semi-autonomous and supervised autonomous systems—by exploring the rhetoric and subsequent programs centered around what Defense Department officials refer to as "human-machine teaming"—sometimes called "centaur" warfighting.

These ideas suddenly appeared in Pentagon publications and official statements after the summer of 2015, with little warning. The timing probably wasn't accidental; it came at a time when global news outlets were focusing attention on a public backlash against lethal autonomous weapon systems. The Campaign to Ban Killer Robots was formed in April 2013 as a coalition of NGOs and civil society organizations, including the International Committee for Robot Arms Control, Amnesty International, and Human Rights Watch. In July 2015, the organization released an open letter warning of a robotic arms race and calling for a ban on the technologies. Cosigners included world-renowned physicist Stephen Hawking, Tesla founder and CEO Elon Musk, Apple cofounder Steve Wozniak, Skype cofounder Jaan Tallinn, and thousands more.[35] The fact that the Pentagon had issued "Defense Directive 3000.09: Autonomy in Weapon Systems" in 2012, declaring that "autonomous and semi-autonomous weapon systems shall be designed to allow command-ers and operators to exercise appropriate levels of human judgment," did little to assuage critics' concerns.[36]

At this point, Robert Work and his allies must have seen the writing on the wall. Fully autonomous weapon systems were quickly becoming a public relations nightmare. For the immediate future, at least, their goals had to be more modest. Work had read economist Tyler Cowan's best-selling book *Average Is Over* and was particularly struck by a section about freestyle chess—sometimes called centaur chess—a variation of the game in which skilled humans are allowed to use computers.[37] Cowan argued that, on average, human-machine "centaurs" do better than either fully human or fully computerized rivals. Work realized that this idea might also be applicable to the military. (Interestingly, chess has often served as a metaphor for war, and from its beginnings in sixth-century India, game pieces corresponded to military divisions—namely infantry, cavalry, chari-otry, and elephantry.) He began citing Cowan's book and making direct connections to the possibility of centaur warfighters.[38]

One can imagine how internal discussions around robotic systems might have changed during this period. Instead of ramming the idea of fully autonomous weapons down the throats of an increasingly vocal oppo-sition, why not push for a kinder, gentler alternative—centaurs? Turning attention away from the boundaries separating humans and machines—distinct entities often seen as competitors—might open up space for Pentagon planners and program managers to pursue human-machine "task synergies" stemming from integrated and interconnected teams.[39]

In November 2015, Work gave a high-profile speech on the importance of human-machine teaming, perhaps hoping to defuse the growing criti-cism of "killer robots," or maybe trying to forestall a formal United Nations ban on such technologies. According to one account, Work's vision of a centaur army was one in which "computers will fly the missiles, aim the lasers, jam the signals, read the sensors, and pull all the data together over a network, putting it into an intuitive interface humans can read, under-stand, and use to command the mission"—but humans would still be in the mix, "using the machine to make the human make better decisions."[40] From this point forward, the military branches accelerated their drive toward human-machine teaming.

FAITH IN MACHINES

But there was a problem. Experts loved the idea, touting it as a win-win: Paul Scharre, in his book *Army of None*, claimed that "we don't need to give up the benefits of human judgment to get the advantages of automation, we can have our cake and eat it too."[41] However, personnel on the ground expressed—and continue to express—deep misgivings about the side effects of the Pentagon's newest war machines. The difficulty, it seems, is humans' lack of trust. The engineering challenges of creating robotic weapon systems are relatively straightforward, but the social and psychological challenges of convincing humans to place their faith in the machines are bewilderingly complex.

Getting humans to trust robotic systems is more than a military concern, of course. Companies specializing in autonomous AI-based medical diagnostic systems and driverless cars are also interested in questions having to do with trust—either too much or too little. Designers are sometimes concerned about *over-trust* in automated systems: for example, automobile engineers at Nissan and Volvo have observed that many drivers tend to disengage themselves from cars with autopilot features, effectively treating automated systems as if they were fully autonomous.[42] But in high-stakes, high-pressure situations like military combat, human confidence in autonomous systems can quickly vanish.

The Pentagon's DSB outlined the problem in a 2016 report on the future of autonomous systems:

> Most commercial applications of autonomous systems are designed for operation in largely benign environments . . . such as routing packages in a fulfillment center warehouse. Design for commercial systems rarely considers the possibility of high-regret outcomes in complex, unpredictable, and contested environments. In military operations, these can include an adversary whose goal is to neutralize the use and effectiveness of such systems, either through deception, direct force, or increased potential for collateral damage or fratricide.[43]

Similarly, the Pentagon's *Defense Systems Information Analysis Center Journal* noted that although the prospects for combined human-machine teams are promising, humans will need assurances:

[T]he battlefield is fluid, dynamic, and dangerous. As a result, warfighter demands become exceedingly complex, especially since the potential costs of failure are unacceptable. The prospect of lethal autonomy adds even greater complexity to the problem ... [in that] warfighters will have no prior experience with similar systems. Developers will be forced to build trust almost from scratch.[44]

. . . . . .

Why is it that so many soldiers, airmen, sailors, and Marines mistrust robots? It might be more appropriate to ask why they *should*. In a 2015 article, US Navy Commander Greg Smith provided a candid assessment, using the example of aerial drones. After describing how drones are often intentionally separated from manned aircraft, Smith noted that operators sometimes lose communication with their drones and may inadvertently bring them perilously close to manned airplanes, which "raises the hair on the back of an aviator's neck." He concluded:

[I]n 2010, one task force commander grounded his manned aircraft at a remote operating location until he was assured that the local control tower and UAV [unmanned aerial vehicle] operators located halfway around the world would improve procedural compliance. Anecdotes like these abound.... After nearly a decade of sharing the skies with UAVs, most naval aviators no longer believe that UAVs are trying to kill them, but one should not confuse this sentiment with trusting the platform, technology, or [drone] operators.[45]

Among the earliest cases of automated military systems run amok are the "Patriot fratricides" in which semi-autonomous ballistic missiles launched by US Army personnel during the early phases of Operation Iraqi Freedom destroyed a British warplane and a US Navy fighter plane in 2003. Both pilots were killed. Investigators with the Army Research Laboratory later concluded that the events were the end result of "systemic problems resulting from decisions made years earlier by concept developers, software engineers, procedures developers, testers, trainers, and unit commanders."[46] Ghosts in the machine.

Another tragic example of a lethal "friendly fire" incident occurred in Helmand province, Afghanistan. On the evening of April 5, 2011,

Predator drone operators fired two Hellfire missiles at what appeared to be a group of Taliban fighters lying in a poppy field. When the smoke cleared, two young American soldiers were dead, victims of the drone strike. The *Los Angeles Times* reported that the decision to fire missiles was "the result of work by ground commanders, pilots and analysts at far-flung military installations [in Nevada, Indiana, California, and Afghanistan] who analyze video and data feeds and communicate by a system of voice and text messages."[47]

Lethal robotic attacks aren't limited to cases of high-tech fratricide. The victims are much more likely to be civilians that drone operators mistakenly identify as enemy fighters. For example, after a Predator drone killed twenty-three Afghan civilians in February 2010, including two toddlers, air force officials launched an inquiry into the matter. A widely publicized report summarizing the investigation found that drone operators in Creech Air Force Base, Nevada, had "not been trained to notice the subtle differences between combatants and suspicious persons who may appear to be combatants."[48] US Air Force Major General James O. Poss, who oversaw the investigation, acknowledged: "Technology can occasionally give you a false sense of security that you can see everything, that you can hear everything, that you know everything."[49] Even if the technology works flawlessly, overconfidence in automated or autonomous systems can warp human decision-making processes.

The DSB admitted as early as 2004 that robotic weapon systems don't eliminate the fog of war—in fact, they tend to make it worse: "Enemy leaders look like everyone else; enemy combatants look like everyone else; enemy vehicles look like civilian vehicles; enemy installations look like civilian installations; enemy equipment and materials look like civilian equipment and materials."[50] The number of innocent victims is appalling: according to the nonpartisan Bureau of Investigative Journalism, US drone attacks in Afghanistan, Pakistan, Somalia, and Yemen have killed as many as 1,700 civilians, including some 400 children—a conservative estimate, since there is no consensus about who counts as a "combatant." The overall death toll is estimated at 8,500–12,000 people.[51]

A number of social scientists, particularly cultural anthropologists who study the effects of US foreign policy and military actions around the world, are discovering just how disruptive, damaging, and deadly drone

Figure 5. "Unmanned" drones require support teams and up to three human operators, some of whom are stationed at Creech Air Force Base in Nevada. Photo courtesy of US Air Force/Christopher Griffin.

warfare can be. For example, Hugh Gusterson points to the dilemmas posed by remote killing, as drones redefine and reconfigure today's battlefields by shuffling notions of proximity and distance. American drone operators undergo tremendous psychological strain—and in some cases, post-traumatic stress disorder (PTSD)—as they engage in virtual warfare by day at Creech Air Force Base, before returning home in the evening to their suburban Nevada family homes.[52]

Another anthropologist, Joseba Zulaika, has conducted a detailed analysis of drone warfare from the perspectives of remote pilots, war protesters, and victims of violent attacks from above. For Zulaika, the logic of contemporary counterterrorism is grounded in magical thinking. It's a realm of sheer fantasy, of witches and monsters: the counterterrorist tends to dehumanize the adversary, imagining the Other to be a "wild animal," driven by primal impulses. In the American context, this has a long history—Zulaika reminds us that for more than a century, the US government encouraged and even rewarded "Indian-hunting operations" in the West as militia groups massacred Native Americans throughout the 1800s. He writes that "the categorizing of Indians as *barbarians* justified the burning of villages ... which prefigured the burning of Vietnamese villages in the 1960s and 1970s, much as the portrayal of Negroes as savages justified their slavery or lynching."[53] Others too have suggested that "technologies of enchantment" can serve to "manipulate desire, terror, wonder, fantasy, and vanity"—in other words, technological development in no way precludes the possibility of magical thinking.[54]

Some have called into question the very notion of precision or "surgical" strikes, including cultural geographer Derek Gregory. Although his research into "scopic regimes" is centered on aerial drones, it can just as easily be applied to ground vehicles or underwater robots that transmit images to humans. Gregory argues that high-resolution visual images from drones are transmitted exclusively from "our" point of view, and necessarily eliminate perspectives not associated with the US military. He notes that "high-resolution imagery is not a uniquely technical capacity but part of a techno-cultural system that renders 'our' space familiar even in 'their space'—which remains obdurately Other."[55] Drone warfare simultaneously stretches and compresses battlefield spaces, in both physical and psychological terms.

.   .   .   .   .

It doesn't take much analysis to understand why so many rank-and-file military personnel would mistrust robotic weapon systems. When the magazine *Business Insider* reported that the US Marine Corps was testing a remote-controlled robot called the Modular Advanced Armed Robotic System or MAARS, a Marine responded with sheer dismay in an online forum:

> This is unbelievably ridiculous. . . . This would be nothing but a burden for Marines. It basically boils down to having a blind child with a machine gun added to your squad. Not only does some asshole have to walk around behind it with a huge tan Gameboy to control it, so now you're either minus one rifleman because he can't hold a weapon while driving this thing, and his SA [situational awareness] is trash since he's looking down at a screen

while patrolling, OR you're plus one POG [person other than grunt (non-infantry)] who has to take care of a goofy-ass robot. . . . Christ, it can't even reload on its own. . . . Someone is going to have to sprint out into the open to pop a new belt into this thing.[56]

An army infantryman added to the discussion, noting how robots are a sure way for commanders to impress higher-ups:

We tested a few systems and one of them was identical to this. . . . It was absolutely terrible, our commander pushed every chance to use it because mini guns sound cool and we had a lot of top brass watching us and just about every time it failed in their faces. . . . It's very prone to falling all over the place, the crew despised the thing. They flipped it a few times, it had a loud ass engine . . . like a Bradley [tank] rolling in. Complete waste of time.[57]

So much for trust in machines.[58]

Instead of asking why so many soldiers, sailors, airmen, and Marines mistrust automated and autonomous systems, we might ask: Why do so many Pentagon leaders place an almost superstitious *trust* in those systems? And why are the military-industrial complex's staunchest robotics advocates so firmly convinced that a lack of human confidence in autonomous systems can be overcome with engineered solutions?

ENGINEERING TRUST

In a recent commentary, Courtney Soboleski, a young data scientist employed by the military contractor Booz Allen Hamilton, makes the case for mobilizing social science as a tool for overcoming soldiers' lack of trust in robotic systems. Her words reveal a worldview in which precaution and skepticism—human qualities that have served our species well over many millennia—are little more than "hurdles" and "barriers" to be overcome through persuasion and better training:

The problem with adding a machine into military teaming arrangements is not doctrinal or numeric . . . it is psychological. It is rethinking the instinctual threshold required for trust to exist between the soldier and machine. . . . The real hurdle lies in surpassing the individual psychological and sociological barriers to assumption of risk presented by algorithmic warfare. To do so requires a rewiring of military culture across several mental and emotional domains. . . . AI [artificial intelligence] trainers should partner with traditional military subject matter experts to develop the psychological feelings of safety not inherently tangible in new technology. Through this exchange, soldiers will develop the same instinctual trust natural to the human-human war-fighting paradigm with machines.[59]

Setting aside, for the moment, the questionable assertion that an "instinctual trust natural to the human-human war-fighting paradigm" exists, let's think about Soboleski's broader point: the idea that the skeptical soldier is a problem that needs to be solved. Her proposed solution has everything to do with breaking down entrenched attitudes and replacing them with "psychological feelings of safety" in order to achieve a comprehensive cultural "rewiring."

Soon, the wary warfighter will likely be subjected to new forms of training that focus on building trust between robots and humans. Already, robots are being programmed to communicate in more human ways with their users for the explicit purpose of increasing trust. As we shall see, projects are currently under way to help military robots report their deficiencies to humans in given situations, and to alter their functionality according to the machine's perceived emotional state of the user.

. . . . .

The Pentagon's trust research is a product of the military-industrial-academic complex—an interconnected web of military research agencies, private corporations, federally funded research centers, and university-affiliated science laboratories. For the sake of brevity, I will focus on the military branches' research laboratories, which play an important role in adapting experimental innovations to practical use.

At the Army Research Laboratory (ARL), military psychologists have spent more than a decade on human experiments related to trust in machines. Among the most prolific is Jessie Y. C. Chen, who joined the lab in 2003 shortly after completing her graduate training. After studying linguistics in the early 1980s at National Tsing-Hua University in Taiwan, she moved to Michigan for graduate work in communication studies. In

2000, she received a doctorate in applied human factors psychology from the University of Central Florida.[60]

Chen lives and breathes robotics—specifically "agent teaming" research, a field that examines how robots can be integrated into groups with humans.[61] Her recent experiments test how humans' lack of trust in robotic and autonomous systems can be overcome—or at least minimized. For example, in one set of tests, Chen and her colleagues deployed a small ground robot called ASM (Autonomous Squad Member) that interacted and communicated with infantrymen. The researchers varied "situation-based agent transparency"—that is, the robot's self-reported information about its plans, motivations, and predicted outcomes—and found that human trust in the robot increased when the autonomous "agent" was more transparent or honest about its intentions.[62]

ARL scientists frequently collaborate with university-based academics. For example, researchers from the University of Southern California recently joined ARL on a series of "trust calibration" experiments in which robots gave human users automatically generated explanations to increase user confidence in the machines.[63] A few years earlier, in 2012, psychologists from the University of Central Florida's Institute for Simulation and Training partnered with ARL's military psychologists on meta-analytic studies to explore basic research questions such as these: How can an abstract concept like trust be quantified? When a machine fails, "how does a human's trust level fluctuate?" And, following failure, how can trust be restored?[64] Universities bear a great deal of responsibility in encouraging and accepting funding from military and intelligence agencies, and in creating institutional structures that facilitate this kind of research. We can think of it as a kind of military-industrial-academic complex.[65]

The army isn't the only branch of the armed services researching human trust in robots. The Air Force Research Laboratory (AFRL) has an entire group dedicated to the subject: the Human Trust and Interaction Branch, part of the lab's 711th Performance Wing located at Wright-Patterson Air Force Base in Ohio. In recent years, air force leaders have expressed a commitment to autonomous technology, human-machine teaming, and other innovations that will rely on "data fusion" and even "fusion warfare"—that is, the integration of big data collected from land, sea, air, space, and cyberspace sensors.[66] In 2015, the air force began soliciting proposals for "research on how to harness the socio-emotional elements of interpersonal team/trust dynamics and inject them into human-robot teams"—which is remarkably similar to the army's efforts.[67]

Mark Draper, whose official title is "principal engineering research psychologist" at AFRL, is optimistic about the prospects of human-machine teaming: "As autonomy becomes more trusted, as it becomes more capable, then the Airmen can start off-loading more decision-making capability on the autonomy, and autonomy can exercise increasingly important levels of decision-making." He adds, "That's a migration you slowly incorporate as you unleash autonomy, as its capability dictates, and then you reel it back in when you need to, when your trust in it drops and you know that you need to become more engaged."[68]

Several air force researchers with backgrounds in industrial/organizational psychology are among those attempting to dissect the determinants of human trust. For example, four psychologists recently published the results of a project in which they examined the relationship between a person's personality profile (measured using the so-called Big Five personality traits: openness, conscientiousness, extraversion, agreeableness, neuroticism) and his or her tendency to trust. In another experiment, entitled "Trusting Robocop," two air force scientists compared male and female research subjects' levels of trust by showing them a video depicting a guard robot. The robot was armed with a taser, interacted with people, and eventually used the taser on one. Researchers designed the scenario to create uncertainty about whether the robot or the humans were to blame. By surveying research subjects, the scientists suggested that women reported higher levels of trust in "Robocop" than men.[69] Like their army counterparts, AFRL personnel have forged links with the defense industry and universities, and the laboratory has even created a "Center of Excellence" at Carnegie Mellon University, an institution well known for its robotics research.

The issue of trust in autonomous systems has even led the air force's chief scientist to suggest ideas for increasing human confidence in the machines, ranging from better android manners to robots that look more like people, under the principle that good HFE [human factors engineering] design should help support ease of interaction between humans and AS [autonomous systems]. For example, better "etiquette" often equates to better performance, causing a more seamless interaction. . . . This occurs, for example, when an AS avoids interrupting its human teammate during a high workload situation or cues the human that it is about to interrupt—activities that, surprisingly, can improve performance independent of the actual reliability of the system. To an extent, anthropomorphism can also improve human-AS interaction, since people often trust agents endowed with more human-like features . . . [but] anthropomorphism can also induce overtrust.[70]

The Naval Research Laboratory (NRL) has a dedicated group of scientists working on robots: the Laboratory for Autonomous Systems Research. Apart from designing and developing contraptions like Flimmer (an amphibious unmanned underwater-aerial drone modeled after a flying fish) and the "bio-inspired" WANDA-II (a cylindrical device with four large, lateral, fishlike fins), NRL researchers are pursuing questions related to human confidence in machines. For example, a group of engineers and computer scientists have explored how a "goal reasoning" system might enable robots to react intelligently to unexpected events, potentially increasing human trust in the machine.[71] They've also speculated that an "AI [Artificial Intelligence] Rebellion" might actually be *beneficial:* "Sci-fi narratives permeating the collective consciousness endow AI Rebellion with ample negative connotations. However, for AI agents, as for humans, attitudes of protest, objection, and rejection have many potential benefits in support of ethics, safety, self-actualization, solidarity, and social justice."[72] The idea of radical robotic revolutionaries would be laughable, if it weren't for the fact that the naval researchers suggesting this possibility are weapon scientists.

At the Marine Corps Warfighting Laboratory (MCWL), science and technology director Colonel James Jenkins had a clear vision of how robots will work alongside Marines: "These [autonomous] systems will interface with a human just like a subordinate fire team leader who goes back to their squad leader when they have something to report or need new orders," he said. He continued: "The emotional bond will be different. . . . [O]ver time, the machine is learning what I'm looking for, and it acts to me just like a lance corporal or a captain on the other end of the

Figure 6. Robotics company Boston Dynamics designed the Legged Squad Support System (LS3), shown here walking alongside a US Marine Corps patrol. Photo courtesy of US Marine Corps/Sarah Dietz.

radio, then you do start to get that bond and that trust."[73] Jenkins refers to the "irony of automation" that prevents Marines from forming bonds of trust with their robot companions: "What we found is when the bullets start flying, the Marine either becomes so absorbed in driving the robot that he loses sight of what's happening around him, or he drops the controller and becomes a rifleman."[74] Such observations are reminiscent of cognitive psychologist Lisanne Bainbridge's classic work, which suggested that for human operators, automation often creates more problems than it solves.[75]

The Marine Corps laboratory differs from the other research labs in that its researchers are focused much more intently on field testing. For example, in 2016, MCWL demonstrated and tested its Unmanned Tactical Autonomous Control and Collaboration robot (UTACC for short), a machine that resembles a medieval chandelier mounted atop a motorized wheelchair. "Imagine a squad formation where you're walking in a column or a wedge with robots to the front, overhead and flanks. What they're providing you is advanced warning of threats, locating enemies and targeting enemies," said the director of MCWL's Ground Combat Element Branch, Captain James Pineiro. He continued: "The intent is to have every robot operating in the battlespace to be a sensor, shooter, and sharer. We intend to go bigger."[76]

MCWL made headlines in late 2015, when the Marine Corps decided that the LS3 BigDog—essentially a robotic pack mule manufactured by Boston Dynamics—was too noisy to use in combat. But the leaders of the Corps haven't given up on robots: MCWL is developing a driverless platform called EMAV, or Expeditionary Modular Autonomous Vehicle. The machine, which looks like a flat-topped tank, can transport more than seven thousand pounds of cargo and has been field tested many times. Technicians can mount sensors, cameras, communication equipment, and even weapons on the machine. Jeff Tomczak, a deputy director for science and technology at MCWL, is optimistic, noting, "There's more goodness than badness with autonomy. . . . [W]e are going to continue to expand the envelope on where we can go and what we can do. We're starting to see where the cognitive burden on the squad member is starting to go down."[77]

.   .   .   .   .

The trust engineers—social scientists diligently helping the Defense Department find ways of rewiring human attitudes toward machines—are mostly involved in basic research that falls well within established disciplinary norms. No people are being harmed as they conduct their experiments, the vast majority of which are unclassified; nothing about their work suggests that they are violating professional codes of ethics. The scientists are not designing CIA torture techniques, as some American psychologists did during the post-9/11 period. They aren't embedded with combat units, wielding firearms, as did social scientists involved with the US Army's Human Terrain System, a controversial program that supported American counterinsurgency efforts in Iraq and Afghanistan. Nor are they colluding with Pentagon officials in order to curry their favor. The social and cognitive specialists profiled here are conducting mundane applied work: research on "trust calibration" that might have significant implications for both military and civilian purposes over the long term.

Even so, there's something unsettling about what they're attempting to accomplish. The trust engineers are symptomatic of a phenomenon that began during World War II and then ballooned during the Cold War: the militarization of scientific knowledge in the United States.[78] Writing more than a half-century ago, sociologist C. Wright Mills postulated that America's elite classes had accepted "the military metaphysic," a definition of reality that embraces militaristic values in all spheres of life. The military metaphysic means "the dominance of means over ends for the purpose of heightening the prestige and increasing the power of the military . . . [and the tendency for military officials] to pursue ends of their own and to turn other institutions into means for accomplishing them."[79]

Mills wrote these words in the midst of a nuclear arms race, and they are particularly germane to today's situation: as noted in the introduction, some experts now speak of China and the United States as competitors locked in a modern-day robotics arms race: *Wired* magazine grimly warns about "The AI Cold War That Threatens Us All," while some Pentagon officials warily note that China's efforts to be "the world leader in artificial intelligence by 2030 . . . might affect the United States' ability to maintain its military advantage."[80] Once rival superpowers are convinced that they're on parallel tracks, the possibilities are frightening: "The equipment in combat readiness on both sides is already devastating. . . . [O]ne 'ultimate weapon' follows another in geometric progression . . . [in] a scientific arms race, with a series of ultimate weapons, dominated by the strategy of obliteration."[81]

It's impossible to know the degree to which the trust engineers will succeed in achieving their objectives. For decades, military trainers have trained and prepared newly enlisted men and women to kill other people.[82] If, over the span of a few short years, specialists have developed simple psychological techniques to overcome the soldier's deeply ingrained aversion to destroying human life, is it possible that someday, the warfighter might also be persuaded to unquestioningly place his or her trust in robots?

Although scientific inquiry into human trust in robots is still relatively new, it appears that several researchers are optimistic that the key to solving the puzzle may be a more effective "user experience" (UX) featuring interfaces that allow humans to quickly and intuitively communicate and exchange information with robots. If researchers continue pursuing these solutions, it's possible—perhaps inevitable—that Defense Department officials will recruit specialists to achieve these goals, for UX research has become a rapidly growing field within design anthropology, human factors engineering, and social psychology. Such expertise is in short supply: there appear to be no UX researchers within the branches' research laboratories, and very few are employed by the usual Beltway defense contractors. Perhaps this is part of the reason that, in 2016, the Pentagon's top brass began pushing to find new sources of innovation and expertise by turning their attention to Silicon Valley and other high-tech outposts west of the Mississippi—the topic of the next chapter.

3 Pentagon West

Silicon Valley has attracted much attention from US military and intelligence agencies, and the interconnections linking the worlds of network technology and defense can be traced to the early 1960s, if not earlier. For more than half a century, government officials have quietly forged strategic partnerships and "synergistic" relationships in an effort to tap the region's legendary wellsprings of innovation.[1] In the twenty-first century, the Pentagon and seventeen government agencies, collectively known as the US Intelligence Community, have ramped up their efforts by attempting to "capture technological innovation" at its source.[2] Military and spy agencies have done this in several ways: by creating outposts along the West Coast; by organizing a technology advisory board that links the Pentagon to Silicon Valley firms; by coordinating summits, forums, and private meetings with influential investors and corporate executives; and by appealing directly to the hearts and minds of entrepreneurs, engineers, computer scientists, and researchers who are sometimes skeptical of government bureaucrats, especially those from the Defense Department.

Some observers describe a seemingly unbridgeable rift between the Pentagon and Silicon Valley.[3] Consider the following comparison:

It's hard to overstate just how foreign the worlds of Washington and Silicon Valley have become to each other. . . . Silicon Valley and Washington are experiencing a "policy makers are from Mars, tech leaders are from Venus" moment, with both sides unable to trust or understand each other. Even the dress codes are vexing and perplexing. In the tech industry, adults dress like college kids. Inside the Beltway, college kids dress like adults.[4]

The idea of a culture clash between the Defense Department and Big Tech has become a familiar trope in which military officers and Silicon Valley engineers appear as caricatures. Countless journalists have used it to explain why tech workers haven't always been gung ho about working on military contracts—as if those who design and create these devices and platforms are incapable of ethical commitment or collective action. But before exploring that question, let's briefly travel back in time.

.   .   .   .   .

Silicon Valley's tech industry was forged more than fifty years ago, at a time when the San Francisco Bay Area was influenced by a succession of bohemian enclaves: in the 1950s and 1960s, Beat poets, hippies, Deadheads, and communalists flocked to the region. Historian and communication studies scholar Fred Turner draws links between counterculture and cyberculture by documenting how Stewart Brand, Douglas Engelbart, and other charismatic figures articulated a future in which computers might become transcendental vehicles. In this "digital utopia," machines might give individuals the freedom to transform their very souls.[5]

In a lengthy and now famous 1972 article for *Rolling Stone* magazine, the enigmatic Brand glorified young "hackers" and "computer bums" at Stanford University's Artificial Intelligence Laboratory—and the machines they were bringing to life. "Ready or not, computers are coming to the people. That's good news, maybe the best since psychedelics," he wrote.[6] Summarizing Brand's take on the "groovy scientists," investigative journalist Yasha Levine writes that "they were revolutionizing computers, transforming them from giant mainframes operated by technicians into accessible tools that any person could afford and use at home."[7] Brand's eclectic mix of communalism and cybernetics morphed into a quirky high-tech anti-authoritarian ideology, premised on the unifying power of networked computers.

It would be a mistake to assume that computer networks were primarily tools for personal liberation. From the early 1960s forward, the Defense Department's Advanced Research Projects Agency (ARPA) played a crucial role in funding computer research that led to the ARPANET, the precursor to today's internet.[8] But there were no contradictions here—at least not for Stewart Brand. Because the agency had mostly evaded congressional scrutiny, he gushed about ARPA, describing it as "one of the rare success stories of government action. . . . [They are] able to take creative chances and protect long-term deep-goal projects."[9]

Today, not much is left of the tech industry's countercultural roots. Anthropologist Jan English-Lueck, who has studied Silicon Valley for nearly thirty years, notes that "innovators of the 1960s and 1970s who laid the foundations for personal computers and the ancestral internet were fascinated with individual augmentation and the possibility of overcoming geographic parochialism." In the 1990s, software engineers were still pursuing "the potential for 'connection' and 'community' that their devices might bring," resulting in an odd "melding of counterculture and capitalism."[10] But the few visible remnants of this mashup tend to be superficial—relaxed dress codes, unorthodox work spaces, hip buzzwords, and seemingly subversive company mottos like "Don't be evil" or "Move fast and break things." As in so many other American regions, countercultural rebellion in Silicon Valley had become corporate ideology by the end of the twentieth century.[11] The region would soon be ripe for the latest phase in the Pentagon's westward expansion.

OUTPOST

Mountain View rests comfortably between the heavily forested Santa Cruz Mountains and the southern shores of the San Francisco Bay. Through the first half of the twentieth century, it was a sleepy California town with sheep and cattle farms, fruit orchards, and picturesque downtown streets. But after a team of scientists led by William Shockley invented the semiconductor there in 1956, it grew rapidly, along with the entire Silicon

Valley of which it's now a part. Today, Mountain View is a bustling suburb with more than eighty thousand residents, just a few miles west of San Jose, the Bay Area's most populous city.

At first glance, it seems an odd place for military and intelligence agencies to set up shop. After all, Mountain View is nearly 2,500 miles from the Pentagon. Direct flights from San Francisco to Honolulu or Juneau take less time than flights to Washington, DC. But the Pentagon and Silicon Valley are not only geographically distant—there are other differences too. Many have long considered the Defense Department a bloated, stuffy, and wasteful bureaucracy, with rigidly hierarchical organizational structures and inflexible workplace norms. By contrast, Mountain View's biggest employer is Alphabet, Google's parent company, one of the world's most valuable corporations. Some describe its headquarters, the Googleplex, as an adult playground. Its twenty-six-acre campus includes more than thirty cafés, free food and drink for its employees, on-site fitness centers and swimming pools, and more than a thousand brightly painted bicycles for employees to use on the premises. A life-size iron *Tyrannosaurus rex* skeleton, lovingly called Stan by Google employees, is prominently displayed outside a main building.[12]

Yet in spite of these differences—indeed, *because* of them—Defense Secretary Ash Carter very publicly established a Pentagon outpost less than two miles away from the Googleplex. The Defense Innovation Unit Experimental, or DIUx, was created in August 2015 to quickly identify and invest in companies developing cutting-edge technologies that might be useful to the military. With DIUx, the Pentagon would build its own start-up accelerator dedicated to providing seed funding for firms specializing in artificial intelligence, robotic systems, big data analysis, cybersecurity, and biotechnology. It was a lean outfit, staffed by approximately forty military and civilian employees.[13]

As it turned out, DIUx's new home wasn't so out of place. Its headquarters was located in a building once occupied by the Army National Guard, on the grounds of the Ames Research Center, the largest of NASA's ten field research sites, and Moffett Field, once home to the California Air National Guard's 130th Rescue Squadron. Defense giants Lockheed Martin and Northrop Grumman have field offices less than two miles away, in neighboring Sunnyvale. In 2008, Google itself was encroaching

Figure 7. Hangar One is the largest of three dirigible hangars located at Moffett Field, a part of the NASA Ames Research Center currently leased by Google. Photo courtesy of NASA Ames Research Center.

on government territory: it entered into a forty-year lease agreement with NASA Ames for a new research campus. Six years later, it signed a sixty-year deal with NASA to lease Moffett Field, a one-thousand-acre site that includes three massive, historic dirigible hangars.[14] Today, Google is reportedly using the hangars to build stratospheric balloons that might someday deliver internet service to people living in rural regions—or perhaps conduct high-altitude surveillance missions for military clients.

At the same time, some of tech's biggest names were in close proximity to DIUx's office: apart from Google, there was Amazon Lab126 (the design lab that hatched the Kindle reader, Amazon Echo, and other digital devices); LinkedIn's corporate headquarters; and Microsoft's Silicon Valley campus. Apple's corporate offices were located about five miles away, in nearby Cupertino. The Pentagon's newest digs were literally at the intersection of Big Tech and Big Defense. A journalist from *MIT Technology Review* who toured the site noted that the squat brick building embraced the contradictions inherent in Pentagon West: "The corridors are old-school drab, the doors secured with combination locks. But inside, the newcomers have revamped the spaces with blackboards, whiteboards, and desks arrayed in random diagonals, to match the nonhierarchical vibe of a Valley startup."[15]

. . . . .

Ash Carter's plan was simple but ambitious: to harness the best and brightest ideas from the tech industry for Pentagon use. Carter's premise was that new commercial companies had surpassed the Defense Department's ability to create cutting-edge technologies. The native Pennsylvanian, who had spent several years at Stanford University prior to his appointment as defense secretary, was deeply impressed with the innovative spirit of the Bay Area and its millionaire magnates. "They are inventing new technology, creating prosperity, connectivity, and freedom," he said. "They feel they too are public servants, and they'd like to have somebody in Washington they can connect to."[16] Astonishingly, Carter was the first sitting defense secretary to visit Silicon Valley in more than twenty years.

The Pentagon has its own research and development agency, DARPA, but its projects tend to pursue objectives that are decades, not months, away. What the new defense secretary wanted was a nimble, streamlined office that could serve as a kind of broker, channeling tens or even hundreds of millions of dollars from the Defense Department's massive budget toward up-and-coming firms developing technologies on the verge of completion. Ideally, DIUx would serve as a kind of liaison, negotiating the needs of grizzled four-star generals, the Pentagon's civilian leaders, and hoodie-clad engineers and entrepreneurs. Within a year, DIUx opened branch offices in two other places with burgeoning tech sectors: Boston, Massachusetts, and Austin, Texas.

In the short term, Carter hoped that DIUx would build relationships with local start-ups, recruit top talent, get military reservists involved in projects, and streamline the Pentagon's notoriously cumbersome procurement processes. "The key is to contract quickly—not to make these people fill out reams of paperwork," he said. His long-term goals were even more

Figure 8. Secretary of Defense Ash Carter addresses employees of the Defense Innovation Unit Experimental, a Pentagon organization that funds tech firms. Photo courtesy of US Department of Defense/Adrian Cadiz.

ambitious: to take career military officers and assign them to work on futuristic projects in Silicon Valley for months at a time, to "expose them to new cultures and ideas they can take back to the Pentagon ... [and] invite techies to spend time at Defense."[17]

In March 2016, Carter organized the Defense Innovation Board (DIB), an elite brain trust of civilians tasked with providing advice and recommendations to the Pentagon's leadership. Carter appointed former Google CEO (and Alphabet board member) Eric Schmidt to chair the DIB, which includes current and former executives from Facebook, Google, and Instagram, among others.

Three years after Carter launched DIUx, it was renamed the Defense Innovation Unit (DIU), indicating that it was no longer experimental. This signaled the broad support the office had earned from Pentagon leaders. The Defense Department had lavished nearly $100 million on projects from forty-five companies, almost none of which were large defense contractors.[18] Despite difficulties in the early stages—and speculation that the Trump administration might not support an initiative focused on regions that tended to skew toward the Democratic Party—

DIUx was "a proven, valuable asset to the DoD," in the words of Trump's deputy defense secretary, Patrick Shanahan. "The organization itself is no longer an experiment," he noted in an August 2018 memo, adding: "DIU remains vital to fostering innovation across the Department and transforming the way DoD builds a more lethal force."[19] Defense Secretary James "Mad Dog" Mattis visited Amazon's Seattle headquarters and Google's Palo Alto office in August 2017 and had nothing but praise for the tech industry. "I'm going out to see what we can pick up in DIUx," he told reporters.[20] In early 2018, the Trump administration requested a steep increase in DIU's budget for fiscal year 2019, from $30 million to $71 million. For 2020, the administration requested $164 million, more than *doubling* the previous year's request.[21]

Q BRANCH

Although Pentagon officials portrayed DIUx as a groundbreaking organization, it was actually modeled after another firm established to serve the US Intelligence Community in a similar way. In the late 1990s, Ruth David, the CIA's deputy director for science and technology, suggested that the agency needed to move in a radically new direction to ensure that it could capitalize on innovations being developed in the private sector, with a special focus on Silicon Valley firms. In 1999, under the leadership of its director, George Tenet, the CIA established a nonprofit legal entity called Peleus to fulfill this objective, with help from former Lockheed Martin CEO Norman Augustine.[22] Soon after, the organization was renamed In-Q-Tel.

The first CEO, Gilman Louie, was an unconventional choice to head the enterprise. Louie had spent nearly twenty years as a video game developer who, among other things, created a popular series of Falcon F-16 flight simulators. At the time he agreed to join the new firm, he was chief creative officer for the toy company Hasbro. In a 2017 presentation at Stanford University, Louie claimed to have proposed that In-Q-Tel take the form of a venture capital fund. He also described how, at its core, the organization was created to solve "the big data problem":

The problem they [CIA leaders] were trying to solve was: How to get technology companies who historically have never engaged with the federal government to actually provide technologies, particularly in the IT space, that the government can leverage. Because they were really afraid of what they called at that time the prospects of a "digital Pearl Harbor".... Pearl Harbor happened with every different part of the government having a piece of information but they couldn't stitch it together to say, "Look, the attack at Pearl Harbor is imminent." The White House had a piece of information, naval intelligence had a piece of information, ambassadors had a piece of information, the State Department had a piece of information, but they couldn't put it all together.... [In] 1998, they began to realize that information was siloed across all these different intelligence agencies of which they could never stitch it together.... [F]undamentally what they were trying to solve was the big data problem. How do you stitch that together to get intelligence out of that data?[23]

Louie served as In-Q-Tel's chief executive for nearly seven years and played a crucial role in shaping the organization.

By channeling funds from intelligence agencies to nascent firms building technologies that might be useful for surveillance, intelligence gathering, data analysis, cyberwarfare, and cybersecurity, the CIA hoped to get an edge over its global rivals by using investment funds to co-opt creative engineers, hackers, scientists, and programmers. The *Washington Post* reported that "In-Q-Tel was engineered with a bundle of contradictions built in. It is independent of the CIA, yet answers wholly to it. It is a nonprofit, yet its employees can profit, sometimes handsomely, from its work. It functions in public, but its products are strictly secret."[24] In 2005, the CIA pumped approximately $37 million into In-Q-Tel. By 2014, the organization's funding had grown to nearly $94 million a year and it had made 325 investments with an astonishing range of technology firms, almost none of which were major defense contractors.[25]

If In-Q-Tel sounds like something out of a James Bond movie, that's because the organization was partly inspired by—and named after—Q Branch, a fictional research and development office of the British secret service, popularized in Ian Fleming's spy novels and in the Hollywood blockbusters based on them, going back to the early 1960s. Ostensibly, both In-Q-Tel and DIUx were created to transfer emergent private-sector technologies into the US intelligence and military agencies, respectively. A somewhat different interpretation is that these organizations were launched "to capture technological innovations . . . [and] to capture new ideas."[26] From the perspective of the CIA these arrangements have been a "win-win," but critics have described them as a boondoggle—lack of transparency, oversight, and streamlined procurement means that there is great potential for conflicts of interest. Other critics point to In-Q-Tel as a prime example of the militarization of the tech industry.

There's an important difference between DIUx and In-Q-Tel. DIUx is part of the Defense Department and is therefore financially dependent on Pentagon funds. By contrast, In-Q-Tel is, in legal and financial terms, a distinct entity. When it invests in promising companies, In-Q-Tel also becomes part owner of those firms. In monetary and technological terms, it's likely that the most profitable In-Q-Tel investment was funding for Kcyhole, a San Francisco–based company that developed software capable of weaving together satellite images and aerial photos to create three-dimensional models of Earth's surface. The program was capable of creating a virtual high-resolution map of the entire planet. In-Q-Tel provided funding in 2003, and within months, the US military was using the software to support American troops in Iraq.[27]

Official sources never revealed how much In-Q-Tel invested in Keyhole. In 2004, Google purchased the start-up for an undisclosed amount and renamed it Google Earth. The acquisition was significant. Yasha Levine writes that the Keyhole-Google deal "marked the moment the company stopped being a purely consumer-facing internet company and began integrating with the US government. . . . [From Keyhole, Google] also acquired an In-Q-Tel executive named Rob Painter, who came with deep connections to the world of intelligence and military contracting."[28] By 2006 and 2007, Google was actively seeking government contracts "evenly spread among military, intelligence, and civilian agencies," according to the *Washington Post*.[29]

Apart from Google, several other large technology firms have acquired start-ups funded by In-Q-Tel, including IBM, which purchased the data storage company Cleversafe; Cisco Systems, which absorbed a conversational AI interface start-up called MindMeld; Samsung, which snagged nanotechnology display firm QD Vision; and Amazon, which bought multiscreen video delivery company Elemental Technologies.[30] While these investments have funded relatively mundane technologies, In-Q-Tel's portfolio includes firms with futuristic projects such as Cyphy, which manufactures tethered drones that can fly reconnaissance missions for extended periods, thanks to a continuous power source; Atlas Wearables, which produces smart fitness trackers that closely monitor body movements and vital signs; Fuel3d, which sells a handheld device that instantly produces detailed three-dimensional scans of structures or other objects; and Sonitus, which has developed a wireless communication system, part of which fits inside the user's mouth.[31] If DIUx has placed its bets with robotics and AI companies, In-Q-Tel has been particularly interested in those creating surveillance technologies—geospatial satellite firms, advanced sensors, biometrics equipment, DNA analyzers, language translation devices, and cyberdefense systems.

More recently, In-Q-Tel has shifted toward firms specializing in data mining social media and other internet platforms. These include Dataminr, which streams Twitter data to spot trends and potential threats; Geofeedia, which collects geographically indexed social media messages related to breaking news events such as protests; PATHAR, a company specializing in social network analysis; and TransVoyant, a data integration firm that collates data from satellites, radar, drones, and other sensors. In-Q-Tel has also created Lab41, a Silicon Valley technology center specializing in big data analysis and machine learning.[32]

PROJECT MAVEN

Both supporters and critics of In-Q-Tel and DIUx have correctly noted that most of the companies funded by these organizations have been start-ups, including some in dire need of cash for further research and development. But the Pentagon's interest in Silicon Valley and other high-tech regions is also driven by the prospect of collaborating with the biggest internet-based companies.

To illustrate this point, consider the case of Project Maven—known more formally as the Algorithmic Warfare Cross-Functional Team. Deputy Defense Secretary Robert O. Work (see chapter 2) formally established the program in April 2017, and in a memo he described it as an effort "to accelerate DoD's integration of big data and machine learning . . . [and] to turn the enormous volume of data available to DoD into actionable intelligence and insights at speed."[33]

Project Maven was conceived as a way of dealing with the big-data deluge. A report in the *Bulletin of the Atomic Scientists* states the problem succinctly:

> Every day, US spy planes and satellites collect more raw data than the Defense Department could analyze even if its whole workforce spent their entire lives on it. . . . A single drone with these [video] sensors produces many terabytes of data. . . . Unfortunately, most of the imagery analysis involves tedious work—people look at screens to count cars, individuals, or activities. . . . [M]ost of the sensor data just disappears—it's never looked at—even though the department has been hiring analysts as fast as it can for years.[34]

The Pentagon had spent tens of billions of dollars on sensors. Creating algorithms to sort and analyze the images made good economic sense, and at a projected cost of $70 million, Project Maven must have seemed like a bargain.

The scope of the work was staggering. In their current state, artificial intelligence systems require massive data sets for "deep learning," which essentially means learning by example. During the latter half of 2017, humans working on Project Maven reportedly labeled more than 150,000 visual images to create the first sets of data with which to train the algorithms. The images—photos of vehicles, individuals, objects, events—had to account for hundreds, if not thousands, of variable conditions: different altitudes, photo angles, image resolution, lighting conditions, and more.[35]

What organization could possibly take up such a daunting task? Pentagon officials were quiet about which companies were involved, but some insiders provided oblique hints. "Project Maven's team, with the help of Defense Innovation Unit Experimental . . . managed to attract the support of the top talent in the AI field (the vast majority of which lies outside the traditional defense contracting base)," wrote an analyst with the Center for a New American Security, a think tank closely associated with Work.[36]

US Marine Corps Colonel Drew Cukor, who headed Project Maven, noted in a technology summit that his group had "a relationship with a significant data-labeling company that will provide services across our three networks—the unclassified and classified networks—to allow our workforce to label our data and prepare it for machine learning." Later in his presentation, Cukor indirectly compared the current moment to the Cold War: "We are in an AI arms race. . . . It's happening in industry [and] the big five Internet companies are pursuing this heavily. Many of you will have noted that Eric Schmidt [then CEO of Alphabet] is calling Google an AI company now, not a data company."[37]

Just eight months after the Defense Department launched Project Maven, the military was using the program's first algorithms in support of drone missions against ISIS in Iraq and Syria.

Beginning in March 2018, the technology website Gizmodo published a series of blistering exposés revealing that the Pentagon had quietly contracted Google for Project Maven work in September 2017. According to internal emails from Google executives, the initial contract was worth at least $15 million, expected to increase to as much as $250 million. Some emails detailed meetings between Google executives and Deputy Defense Secretary Jack Shanahan at the Googleplex, noting that "[our military] Customer considers Cloud AI team the core of the MAVEN program, where everything else will be built to test and deploy our ML [machine learning] models." More than ten Google employees were assigned to work on the project, and the company had partnered with several other firms, including DigitalGlobe, a geospatial imaging company, and CrowdFlower, a crowdsourcing company. According to investigative reporter Lee Fang, CrowdFlower (which has since changed its name to Figure Eight) paid crowd workers—people who complete repetitive tasks online, such as identifying photos—to label hundreds of thousands of images for algorithmic deep learning. Apparently, the crowd workers did not know what they were building or who would benefit as a result.[38]

Some of Google's internal emails implied that the company had ambitious plans going beyond what was initially suggested in the Pentagon's initial announcements. At least one suggested creating a "Google-earth-like" spy system giving users the ability to "click on a building and see everything associated with it," including people and vehicles.[39]

A Google sales executive ecstatically announced the contract via email in a weirdly Orwellian message, a mashup of Pentagon propaganda and Google advertising copy: "[Maven] will result in improved safety for citizens and nations through faster identification of evils such as violent extremist activities and human rights abuses. The scale and magic of GCP [Google Cloud Platform], the power of Google ML [machine learning], and the wisdom and strength of our people will bring about multi-order-of-magnitude improvements in safety and security for the world."[40]

However, Google officials privately worried about a potential public relations nightmare. "I think we should do a good PR on the story of DoD collaborating with GCP from a vanilla cloud technology angle (storage, network, security, etc.)," wrote Fei-Fei Li, Google Cloud's chief AI scientist, "but avoid at ALL COSTS any mention or implication of AI."[41]

Eventually, word got out.

REVOLT OF THE ENGINEERS

By February 2018, internal emails about Project Maven circulated widely among Google employees, many of whom were shocked and dismayed by what the company's leaders had done. Within months, more than four thousand Google researchers had signed a letter to CEO Sundar Pichai, demanding cancellation of the Maven contract. The letter, which included signatures from several of the company's senior engineers, began with the statement "We believe that Google should not be in the business of war." It also demanded that Google develop "a clear policy stating that neither Google nor its contractors will ever build warfare technology." Weeks later, the International Committee for Robot Arms Control (ICRAC), an organization cofounded and chaired by computer scientist Noel Sharkey, released an open letter signed by hundreds of researchers and academics, expressing solidarity with the Google employees. (Disclosure: I was among the many signatories.) By the end of the year, nearly a dozen employees had resigned in protest of the company's questionable contracts and executives' lack of transparency.[42] The employee revolt was covered widely by national and international media—but the story disappeared from the headlines after a few weeks.

Astonishingly, the employees succeeded—at least momentarily. In early June, Google Cloud CEO Diane Greene announced that the company would terminate its Project Maven work when the Pentagon contract expired, and acknowledged that the backlash had been damaging for the company. Days later, Google released a set of ethical guidelines or "AI principles," stating that the company "will not design or deploy AI" for weapon systems, for "surveillance violating internationally accepted norms," or for technologies used to contravene international law and human rights.[43] Then, in early October 2018, Google's CEO made another announcement: the firm would withdraw itself from consideration for the Joint Enterprise Defense Infrastructure, or JEDI, a lucrative Pentagon cloud-computing contract potentially worth up to $10 billion (see below).[44]

Jack Poulson, a mathematician and computer scientist who worked at Google for nearly two and a half years before quitting in protest, noted that the company's internal resistance movement was partly inspired by the so-called Group of Nine—a team of influential engineers working in Google's cloud division.[45] In early 2018, the group refused to develop a security tool called "air gap," which would have enabled Google to compete for highly profitable military contracts. Bloomberg News reported that the Group of Nine was "lionized by like-minded staff. . . . [T]he engineers' work boycott was a catalyst for larger protests," including the movement opposing Project Maven.[46]

Google's commitment to canceling its Project Maven work was too good to be entirely true. In March 2019, online news organization *The Intercept* obtained an email written by Google's vice president for global affairs, Kent Walker, which indicated that a third-party company would continue working on Project Maven using "off-the-shelf Google Cloud Platform (basic compute service, rather than Cloud AI or other Cloud Services) to support some workloads." Walker added that Google was working with "DoD to make the transition in a way that is consistent with our AI principles and contractual commitments." Several days later, reports revealed that the Defense Department had awarded the Project Maven contract to Anduril Industries, cofounded by young entrepreneur

Palmer Luckey, best known for creating the Oculus Rift virtual reality headset. The previous year, Luckey's company had piloted Lattice, a prototype surveillance system developed for US Customs and Border Protection agents. The system uses artificial intelligence to detect the presence of people attempting to cross the US border.[47]

There was a peculiar irony about the Project Maven fiasco. For years, Google had maintained an overwhelmingly positive public image because hundreds of millions of people believed that the company provided a free public service to internet users around the world. The search engine was so widely used that in the English language, Google officially became a verb. Even today, relatively few people are aware that the firm's founders relied partly on support from military and intelligence agencies to develop their algorithms.

Like many Silicon Valley companies, Google has its own origin myth, which goes something like this: in the mid-1990s, two nerdy Stanford graduate students, Larry Page and Sergey Brin, crammed together a mishmash of computers, hard drives, and other spare parts in their dorm rooms. They created a revolutionary search engine based on their PageRank algorithm and shoehorned it into Stanford's broadband networks. It became so popular that before long, the university's internet connection regularly crashed due to overwhelming demand from global users. Page and Brin quit school and founded a company with help from friends and family in 1998—and the rest is history.[48]

The problem with this celebratory narrative is that it leaves out a crucial fact: Page and Brin were receiving financial support from the Defense Department. In 1994, the two graduate students began participating in the Stanford Integrated Digital Library Project, which was jointly funded by DARPA, NASA, and the National Science Foundation (NSF) as part of a five-year "Digital Libraries Initiative" program. Stanford was awarded more than $4.5 million to create "a single, integrated, and 'universal' library. . . . [B]oth on-line versions of pre-existing works and new works and media of all kinds will be available. . . . [T]his project will provide the 'glue' that will make this worldwide collection useable as a unified entity, in a scalable and economically viable fashion."[49] Under the supervision of principal investigators Hector Garcia-Molina and Terry Winograd, Page and Brin's work "survives as one of the main components of today's Google search service," according to the NSF.[50]

Page and Brin were also funded by an intelligence community program called the Massive Digital Data Systems project (MDDS). By taking non-classified information and user data from the internet, CIA and NSA officials hoped "to make sense of what millions of human beings did inside this digital information network," notes Jeff Nesbit, who served as director of legislative and public affairs for the NSF. "That collaboration has made a comprehensive public-private mass surveillance state possible today."[51] The agency distributed MDDS funding on behalf of the CIA and NSA. The objective was to develop the ability to find "digital fingerprints" within the internet, by tracking, sorting, and linking users' online queries and activities. According to Nesbit, "their intent was to track like-minded groups of people across the internet and identify them from the digital fingerprints they left behind . . . by identifying patterns in this massive amount of new information."[52]

Stanford computer science professor Jeffrey Ullman was awarded an MDDS-funded grant. In a summary of the project's impact, Ullman—identifying Google by name—stated that the company's "core technology, which allows it to find pages far more accurately than other search engines, was partially supported" by the grant. Two intelligence community managers, Bhavani Thuraisingham of the MITRE Corporation and Rick Steinheiser of the CIA's Office of Research and Development, periodically heard Brin make presentations about his research. It's not difficult to surmise why the CIA and NSA would take interest in the Stanford research.[53] Nesbit succinctly summarizes the situation:

> Did the CIA directly fund the work of Brin and Page, and therefore create Google? No. But were Brin and Page researching precisely what the NSA, the CIA, and the intelligence community hoped for, assisted by their grants? Absolutely. . . . The CIA and NSA funded an unclassified, compartmentalized program designed from its inception to spur the development of something that looks almost exactly like Google. . . . And Google succeeded beyond their wildest dreams."[54]

The search engine was, and continues to be, the epitome of a dual-use technology.

And so it was that Google, the flagship of the most valuable corporation on the planet, was made possible with support from unwitting American taxpayers.

AFTERMATH

Although the Google researchers who resisted Project Maven represented only a modest portion of the company's seventy thousand employees, they succeeded in sparking discussion about the nature of tech-industry contracts with military and intelligence agencies—and a broader debate about the ethics of artificial intelligence.

The Google revolt resonated throughout the tech industry and inspired others to follow. For example, in February 2019, more than two hundred Microsoft employees demanded that the firm cancel a $480 million contract with the US Army. The contract will reportedly supply ground troops with more than a hundred thousand augmented-reality HoloLens headsets. The Pentagon's request for proposals outlined a need for a head-mounted display capable of giving soldiers night vision, more effective weapons targeting, and the ability to automatically recognize potential threats. The system should be designed to give soldiers "increased lethality, mobility, and situational awareness," according to the request for proposals. In an open letter to Microsoft CEO Satya Nadella, the workers expressed concern that in the hands of the military, HoloLens could be "designed to help people kill," and that the headsets would be "turning warfare into a simulated video game." The employees added that "we did not sign up to develop weapons, and we demand a say in how our work is used. . . . Intent to harm is not an acceptable use of our technology."[55] Microsoft executives refused to back away from the contract. In an interview with CNN, Nadella said that "we made a principled decision that we're not going to withhold technology from institutions that we have elected in democracies to protect the freedoms we enjoy."[56]

During the summer of 2018, approximately 450 employees from another technology giant, Amazon, signed a letter demanding that the

Figure 9. US infantrymen with the US Army's 82nd Airborne Division test a modified version of the Hololens 2 augmented-reality headset, developed by Microsoft. Photo courtesy of US Army/Courtney Bacon.

company stop selling the facial recognition software Rekognition to law enforcement agencies.[57] The employees' letter also asked that Amazon's Web Services division stop hosting Palantir, a tech company that provided data analysis software to US Immigration and Customs Enforcement when the agency was targeting unaccompanied children and their families for deportation in 2017.[58] Amazon CEO Jeff Bezos shrugged off the employees' letter. "One of the jobs of the senior leadership team is to make the right decision even when it's not popular," he said at a conference in October 2018. "If big tech companies are going to turn their back on the US Department of Defense, this country is going to be in trouble."[59] Earlier that year, Teresa Carlson, vice president of Amazon Web Services, was unambiguous about the position of the company's executives. Speaking at the Aspen Security Forum in July, she said, "We are unwaveringly in support of our law enforcement, defense, and intelligence community."[60]

As if to hammer the point home, Amazon released a slick, ninety-second promotional video in August 2018, titled simply "Amazon Web Services for the Warfighter." The production includes stunningly staged images of soldiers in command centers and on battlefields—taking enemy fire, operating laptop computers, patrolling alongside a robotic mule-like quadruped. With intense music worthy of a Hollywood action film, the narrator draws a direct connection between Amazon's Cloud and "homeland security"—the perfect marriage of Big Tech and Big Defense:

> With Cloud, the Pentagon can analyze vast quantities of data in real-time. . . . With Cloud, warfighters can access the capabilities needed to dominate the modern battlefield. . . . But most importantly, Cloud can help ensure missions are completed, homeland secured, and warfighters protected. . . . Real-time data delivers for real-time decision makers and provides real-time security.[61]

At the same time that high-tech workers were expressing reticence about getting involved in Pentagon projects, many executives peddled their companies' wares, vying for the attention of Defense Department officials. In April 2019, Microsoft announced Azure Government Secret, a cloud service for Defense Department and intelligence community clients requiring "US Secret classified workloads." Oracle's websites boasted about how its products "help military organizations improve efficiency, mission preparation, and execution," and touted the Tactical Edge Cloud as a means of bringing "mission-critical performance to the edge with a broad mix of computer cores, storage, and software all running in a ruggedized enclosure."[62]

If there was a sense of urgency about such messages, that's because company executives were angling for the grand prize: the Pentagon's $10 billion cloud-computing-platform contract, called the Joint Enterprise Defense Infrastructure (JEDI). The project is designed to modernize the Defense Department's data systems by "hosting and distributing mission-critical workloads and classified military secrets to warfighters around the globe."[63] The deal was apparently a winner-take-all contest, since the Defense Department would only award a single contract. The contest pitted rival technology companies against one another—most notably Oracle, Microsoft, and Amazon. (As noted earlier in this chapter, Google executives decided against submitting a bid following the Project Maven debacle.) JEDI was mired in controversy for months amid claims that Amazon Web Services was being favored by the Pentagon, possibly as part of a quid pro quo.[64] In the end, Microsoft scored a coup by winning the contract—one of the biggest deals ever made between the Defense Department and the tech industry—but Amazon filed a legal complaint, and the case is still tied up in the courts as this book goes to press.[65]

RED LINES

Silicon Valley technologies illustrate the often unpredictable consequences of unleashing new hardware or software. The idea that an invention can be used for either peaceful or military purposes—that is, the notion of dual-use technology—became widely accepted in American society over the course of the twentieth century (as discussed in chapter 1).[66] Much of what has been designed in Silicon Valley can be described in these terms. Historian Margaret O'Mara reminds us that throughout the Cold War era, "the Valley built small: microwaves and radar for high-frequency communication, transistors and integrated circuits. . . . Silicon Valley built elegant miniaturized machines that could power missiles and rockets, but that also held possibilities for peaceful use—in watches, calculators, appliances, and computers, large and small."[67]

These technologies continue to have dual-use applications. Google Earth can be employed for mapping and geographic research, but it can just as easily be used by Special Forces teams to target electrical power grids, bridges, or other infrastructure.[68] Microsoft first marketed HoloLens as an augmented-reality device that would be useful to gamers, artists, and architects, but it turns out that the most profitable consumers are likely to be infantry personnel. Facial recognition programs like Rekognition might be used for more secure bank or ATM transactions, but they can also be used as surveillance technologies by military, intelligence, or law enforcement agencies such as US Customs and Border Protection or US Immigration and Customs Enforcement.[69] Cloud platforms offered by Amazon, Oracle, Microsoft, Google, and others can potentially store data for science researchers, public health officials, or commercial firms. But as the Pentagon's chief management officer, John H. Gibson, bluntly told *Wired* magazine, the JEDI cloud contract "is truly about increasing the lethality of our department."[70]

For some, it might be easy to chide Google's dissident engineers, scientists, and researchers as coddled, naive Pollyannas. After all, didn't they know what they were getting into? If it's true that "most scientists understand that the knowledge they produce enters a universe in which they likely have no control over how this knowledge is used,"[71] then surely they must have understood that the devices and applications they were creating might someday be weaponized. Right?

.   .   .   .   .

As mentioned earlier, I studied mechanical engineering at a large public university in the late 1980s and early 1990s. To help pay for my schooling, I participated in the university's "cooperative engineering" initiative, a paid internship program that linked corporations with students, who gained real-world experience. The application included a yes-or-no question asking whether or not I would object to working for a company that designed or manufactured weapons. Although there were no required courses in ethics for engineers, I had enough of a moral compass to know that I wasn't interested. I checked the "no" box without reflecting much on the issue.

For several semesters and summers, I interned as a "co-op," first at a General Motors plant in Oklahoma City where workers assembled Chevrolet, Buick, Oldsmobile, and Pontiac sedans, and later at Southwest Research Institute, a nonprofit research laboratory in San Antonio that, among other things, tested automotive fuels and lubricants. Although I was dimly aware of the fact that both organizations did military contract work, I took solace in knowing that I wasn't personally involved in weapon design, testing, or manufacturing. In my mind, I had drawn a bright red line around work on weapons. Anything else was acceptable to me.

I suspect that many of the scientists and engineers who are now objecting to Silicon Valley's military work made similar ethical calculations earlier in their careers. Perhaps their decisions to work for companies like Google, Amazon, Microsoft, or Oracle had been based, at least in part, on a belief that those companies were not in the weapon business. After all, the letter written by Microsoft's protesters states, "We did not sign up to develop weapons."

The researchers may also have placed inordinate faith in their company's executives. In the case of Google, employees felt betrayed by secretive decision-making processes that led to the Project Maven contract. The business press regularly recognizes the firm as having the best corporate culture in America, not just because employees can bring pets to work and have access to organic meals prepared by professional chefs, but also because the organization has a reputation for valuing employee collaboration. Once Google's involvement in Project Maven came to light, tech workers' false consciousness began to evaporate. Earning a six-figure salary as an engineer or a programmer straight out of college makes it difficult to think of yourself as a member of the working class, especially when you're enjoying all the perks that the industry has to offer—free gourmet lunches, on-site gyms, and complimentary child care, for example. For thousands of employees, being shut out of discussions about whether the company should collaborate in AI weapon development woke up a latent sense of powerlessness.

There was also another problem: Silicon Valley's long-standing entanglements with the Pentagon. As noted by Margaret O'Mara, "Whether their employees realize it or not, today's tech giants all contain some defense industry DNA. . . . [C]ompanies need to do more to explain to their employees and their customers what they are doing and why. This involves a much fuller reckoning with the long and complicated history of Silicon Valley and the business of war."[72]

• • • • •

What does the future hold for the Pentagon's western outposts? A recent article, titled "Cultural Divide—Can the Pentagon Crack Silicon Valley?," summarized highlights from a roundtable panel convened by the journal *Defense News*, in which corporate and military elites discussed the implications of Project Maven—and strategies for overcoming resistance from concerned engineers, scientists, and programmers who are now conscious of the moral and ethical dimensions of their labor.[73] While a single event doesn't cover the full range of possible outcomes, the roundtable discussion foreshadows the ways in which both the Defense Department and tech companies are likely to deal with skeptical employees in the months and years ahead. For more than a century, social engineers have used controlling processes—methods of social and emotional manipulation—to keep workers distracted, duped, drained, or desensitized.[74] Now they're retooling their techniques for a new generation.

For many insiders, dissent in Silicon Valley is primarily a perception problem that can be overcome with proper messaging and public relations. This attitude was on full display at the *Defense News* roundtable. For example, Trae Stephens, a venture capitalist and cofounder of Anduril Industries (the company that took over Project Maven), essentially said that most tech workers are either ambivalent or undecided about military contracts. For that group, "semantics matters a lot." When Pentagon officials emphasize how a new technology will increase "lethality," engineers and scientists are likely to balk. Stephens said, "We just can't use this word. You're not going to win being like, 'Our priority is soldier lethality.'" As another example, Stephens cited the case of a smartphone app used for targeting, adopted by both the Defense Department and the Department of Homeland Security. The Pentagon calls it ATAK (pronounced "attack," for Android Tactical Assault Kit), while Homeland Security calls it TAK (pronounced "talk," for Team Awareness Kit). "Suddenly it's not a problem," said Stephens. "Everyone's happy to integrate with the 'team awareness kit.' There's this slight conflict of semantic culture. It's just kind of silly, and we should stop making unforced errors."[75]

Others postulated that by appealing to patriotism, the Pentagon is undermining its outreach to Silicon Valley. In the words of Lisa Hill, chief of operations for the San Francisco–based company Arceo, "The message of 'Come work for America to beat China or Russia' . . . is not going to resonate" in an industry with large numbers of Asian immigrants and cosmopolitan professionals. Hawk Carlisle, who heads the National Defense Industrial Association, an industry trade group, agreed, noting that the Pentagon's messages should focus less on protecting the United States and more on preserving the democratic world order.[76]

Still others suggested that tech company leaders should offer a range of options for their employees—such as the ability to opt out of military projects if they have moral or ethical objections to the work. According to Siobhan McFeeney, a vice president at a technology company called Pivotal, which at the time had begun a project for the Defense Department, such an approach can quell dissent by ensuring that "everyone gets heard" and that "[employees] still have a choice."[77]

Other ideas are circulating through the upper echelons of the defense establishment. Amy Zegart, codirector of Stanford's Center for International Security and Cooperation and senior fellow at the Hoover Institution, recently proposed a multipronged strategy to win over engineers and scientists early in their careers. She and US Air Force Lieutenant Colonel Kevin Childs argue that the Pentagon needs to appeal directly to the youthful impulse for creating large-scale change by "deploying the best young engineers against the toughest challenges, early." Zegart and Childs add that "winning hearts and minds in the tech world" must be a priority, and they suggest a "Technology Fellows Program" that would match the country's top fifty engineering students with the Pentagon's top brass in "a prestigious, one-year, high-impact stint in government service." They note that "the Pentagon needs a radically new civilian talent model" to draw young industry superstars into defense work for limited periods, without hampering their ability to return quickly to the private sector.[78] In essence, Zegart and Childs are suggesting that military elites adopt some of the same methods that Silicon Valley's corporate executives have used to attract talented engineers, researchers, and programmers.

.   .   .   .   .

The divide between the Pentagon and Silicon Valley is mostly a myth—it's never really existed, at least not in any significant way.[79] The differences are superficial and stylistic. For the better part of a century, the regional economy and culture have been shaped by what Patrick McCray calls "the iron triangle of universities, corporate interests, and the military."[80] During the Cold War, these processes intensified. The Pentagon played a major role in launching the computer industry by awarding military contracts in such fields as microwave electronics, missile and satellite production, and semiconductor research. Historian Thomas Heinrich reminds us that popular portrayals of "ingenious inventor-businessmen and venture capitalists [who] forged a dynamic, high-tech economy unencumbered by government's heavy hand" draw attention away from the crucial role of "Pentagon funding for research and development [that] helped lay the technological groundwork for a new generation of startups" at the dawn of the twenty-first century.[81] From the 1950s until the late 1990s, Silicon Valley's biggest private-sector employer was not Hewlett-Packard; neither was it Apple, Ampex, or Atari. It was the defense giant Lockheed.[82] Today the region faces a familiar pattern—though the gargantuan size and influence of today's technology firms dwarfs the computer companies of yesteryear. This is likely to have major implications in the near future. Jack Poulson, a research scientist with experience at Google and extensive networks in Silicon Valley, put it to me this way: "I believe we are witnessing the transition of major US tech companies into defense contractors and would go so far as to predict them purchasing defense contractors in the coming years—something like Amazon buying Raytheon."[83]

The real fault line isn't between the Pentagon and Silicon Valley. It's *within* Silicon Valley, where a modest contingent of politically awakened engineers and scientists have taken a stand against the weaponization of their work. When they face a full frontal attack from PR messaging, hearts-and-minds campaigns, "collaborative" discussion, more compensation and perquisites—and perhaps even the tacit threat of losing their jobs or having them outsourced—will they capitulate? At this point, it's too early to know the outcome, but the future of virtual warfare and autonomous military technologies may well rest in their hands.

4 The Dark Arts

The philosopher and historian Michel Foucault once noted that "politics is the continuation of war by other means."[1] Politics is war, virtually.

The idea that political struggle is an extension of armed conflict is well illustrated by Russian, Chinese, and—most frequently—American attempts to influence foreign elections. Of course, there's nothing new about electoral subterfuge and dirty tricks. To thwart perceived threats to American interests, US government entities orchestrated some of the most infamous, consequential, and well-documented examples of political meddling in the twentieth century and into the twenty-first. Iran in the early 1950s, Chile during the late 1960s and early 1970s, presidential elections in Russia and Bolivia in 1996 and 2002—these are just a few of the many examples of US interference.[2] More recently, such initiatives— once organized by the CIA or other government agencies—have often been farmed out to private companies and contractors.

A fundamental element of many such projects is the deployment of psychological operations, or psyops. Officially, the goal is to influence ene- mies or foreign populations in support of one's own military or political objectives. But the same techniques have sometimes been aimed at domestic audiences, to build popular support for new policies—or even to divide people against each other. Psyops are about using messages, symbols, and information to provoke strong emotional reactions that will prod people into action—or lull them into passive *inaction*. Retired US Army Major Ed Rouse notes that psyops require "learning everything about your target enemy, their beliefs, likes, dislikes, strengths, weaknesses, and vulnerabilities . . . to create in target groups behavior, emotions, and attitudes that support the attainment of national objectives."[3] Such information is called "target audience analysis" within military circles, and it reflects the recognition that cultural knowledge can become a potent force—indeed, it can even become a weapon. Propagandists have long understood this.[4]

Over the past three decades, psyops have changed significantly. In the 1950s and 1960s, a bright line separated military psyops, which often consisted of airborne leaflet drops and radio or TV broadcasts directed at foreign populations, and political consulting, which was rooted in advertising and public relations. Since the 1990s, the lines have blurred and overlapped as military and intelligence agencies have outsourced psyop campaigns to PR and strategic communication companies that have historically served corporate, rather than military, interests. Many of those firms have made a smooth transition to military work, since psyops—like public relations—apply knowledge from psychology and communication studies.

Technological developments have triggered another important change in recent years. In an algorithmic era, when immense quantities of personal data—often harvested from internet users—are available at little or no cost, propaganda campaigns and advertising have shifted from macrotargeting to microtargeting. The scattershot approach of TV and radio broadcasts aimed at particular regions, cities, or ethnic groups has given way to finely tuned individual messages and ads sent cheaply and often anonymously via social media, designed to appeal directly to a user's preferences, habits, identity, and personality type.

It's easy to get mixed up in the terminological muddle surrounding propaganda work—it's part psyops and information operations, part public relations and strategic communications, part civilian political campaigns and advertising—so it's really not worth trying to make clear distinctions. These days, there's a great deal of overlap and, not surprisingly, lots of debate about what to call these techniques. It's helpful to look

Figure 10. A US Army Black Hawk helicopter drops thousands of leaflets over an Afghan village as part of a psychological operations campaign. Photo courtesy of US Army/Richard Jones.

beyond formal definitions and terms, and to instead look at what propagandists are actually *doing*—and how target audiences are responding in America, the United Kingdom, Kenya, India, Mexico, and dozens of other countries around the globe.

. . . .

For nearly a century, observers studied propaganda and often critiqued it, but their work was generally limited to pre-internet forms of communication and mass media.[5] Lately, scholars have begun developing new, updated theories of propaganda for a world in which more people get their news from social media—Twitter feeds, Facebook tabs, Google alerts, and more—than from newspapers or television. New technologies have helped bring about "the twenty-first century's version of propaganda . . . aimed at spreading disinformation and sowing ignorance, division, doubt, and fear," thereby allowing military and intelligence organizations an opportunity to divide and conquer foreign populations—and enabling ordinary citizens and entrepreneurs to create homegrown propaganda.[6] In this virtual battleground, social media firms have laid the technical groundwork for deceptive, hostile messaging that has been largely uncontrolled and unregulated across much of the world. Silicon Valley is deeply implicated, to the extent that its firms have built this architecture, while its corporate executives have vehemently opposed government regulation.[7]

Propaganda today tends to spread laterally (from recipient to recipient), instead of vertically (from propagandist to audience). Social media retweets, "likes," and "shares" are a powerful means of distributing information and disinformation, because those who receive the messages also play a crucial role in passing them along through trusted networks—until they perhaps go viral. The portability and ubiquity of cell phones, along with easy, cheap access to social media, means that more than five billion people worldwide—two-thirds of the world's entire population—carry devices that make it possible to receive or send propaganda nearly anytime, anywhere.[8]

And yet it's not data science alone that powers propaganda today. Innovative psyop techniques also depend on the work of qualitative researchers whose methods resemble those used by cultural anthropologists who study human groups in their "natural" habitats—at home, at school, or in fields, factories, and offices. Open-ended interviews, discourse analysis, long-term fieldwork, focus groups, ethnographically inspired "day in the life of" home studies, and participant observation provide a foundation on which meaningful and more effective data analysis can be built.[9] This tends to be true regardless of whether an organization is selling yoga pants, pork rinds, conspiracy theories—or the latest brand of white supremacy.

This chapter takes a closer look at the dark arts of persuasion in the digital age by examining the inner workings of a now defunct British defense contractor, SCL Group. For nearly three decades, the enigmatic company orchestrated high-tech propaganda and psyop campaigns on a global scale, fueled by easy access to vast amounts of personal information and supplemented with cultural knowledge and qualitative data.

SCL Group isn't alone. In the United States and elsewhere, dozens of firms quietly serve military and intelligence agencies by deploying computational propaganda—politically charged, automated messages aimed at specific individuals or groups, based on their aggregated data profiles or online behaviors. Although these techniques probably don't work exactly as advertised, it's worth examining them in more depth, for a glimpse of what information warfare and mass manipulation might look like in the years ahead. It's also crucial to explore the digital infrastructures in which these forms of virtual war have flourished. After all, data is more than just enormous amounts of electronic information—it's also an industry in which companies like Facebook, Twitter, Amazon, and Google leverage information about their users to sell ads that target specific audiences.[10]

Our story begins in the United States.

FROM PR TO PSYOPS

In the months following the 2016 US presidential election, a spate of news articles reported that a political consulting firm, Cambridge Analytica, had played a pivotal role in Donald Trump's surprise victory.[11] According to these accounts, the company formulated novel algorithmic techniques to influence the American electorate during the final stages of the campaign. Cambridge Analytica and its eclectic team of young researchers—an amalgamation of social scientists, marketing specialists, and data analysts—claimed to have generated personality profiles of millions of individual voters and then used those profiles to send targeted political advertisements designed to exploit their psychological vulnerabilities.

Some journalists described Cambridge Analytica's tools as "mind-reading software," a "weaponized AI [artificial intelligence] propaganda machine" that "turned the world upside down" by saturating voters with carefully crafted TV advertisements and internet messages.[12] Then, in March 2018, amid an explosive scandal involving the company's misappropriation of personal data from tens of millions of unwitting Facebook users—and accusations that it had helped Russian hackers meddle in the 2016 American elections—Cambridge Analytica went down in flames. Days after the scandal broke, the company filed for bankruptcy and formally ended operations.

Despite the overwhelming press coverage dedicated to the Cambridge Analytica fiasco, the press often overlooked an important fact: the company was a subsidiary of SCL Group, a British defense contractor whose clients included military agencies from numerous countries, NATO, and at least one US weapons laboratory. As SCL built its reputation in the worlds of politics and psyops, the company relied on close ties with national security experts, intelligence agents, and military officials.[13]

To make sense of Cambridge Analytica, it's helpful to understand the origins of its parent company, SCL Group, and its rapid evolution into a military contract firm. It began in the late 1980s, when a flamboyant young British businessman, Nigel Oakes, reportedly became interested in the power of mass psychology to transform human behavior. Oakes, who had experience working with the advertising powerhouse Saatchi & Saatchi, founded the Behavioural Dynamics Institute (BDI) in 1989 with the help of psychologists Adrian Furnham and Barrie Gunter, who later admitted that the ad man was promising more than the social sciences could deliver.[14] Although BDI executives portrayed the organization as a global network of social scientists, it functioned more or less as a marketing firm in its early years, providing clients with a range of services, including public relations, retail product displays, and "corporate identity" campaigns. Among other things, BDI offered a "smell service" to clients, featuring customized aromas that would supposedly win over employees and customers. Oakes, in an interview with *Marketing* magazine, boasted that "we use the same techniques as Aristotle and Hitler. . . . We appeal to people on an emotional level to get them to agree on a functional level."[15] Interestingly, BDI's website described the organization's methodology as drawing "extensively from group and social psychology" and incorporating "semiotics, semantics and many elements of cultural anthropology," though no specific examples were mentioned.[16]

In the early 1990s, Oakes created a spinoff company, Strategic Communications Laboratory (SCL), to market its services to governments, military clients, and political figures. By the late 1990s, the company was undertaking overseas projects, though it's not easy to find details, since the company scarcely appeared in the media during that time. In 2000, a news report revealed that SCL worked to help improve the public image of Indonesian president Abdurrahman Wahid—but the company shut down its operations center when *Wall Street Journal* investigators blew SCL's cover.[17]

Oakes demonstrated an uncanny ability to refashion his companies in the wake of changing circumstances. During the post-9/11 period, as pro-globalization rhetoric gave way to the worldwide "war on terror," SCL refocused its efforts. For example, in July 2005, SCL very publicly rebranded itself as a psychological warfare company by taking part in the United Kingdom's largest military trade show. SCL's exhibit included a mock operations center featuring dramatic crisis scenarios—a smallpox outbreak in London, a bloody insurgency in a fictitious South Asian country—that were resolved with the help of the company's psyop techniques.[18] Oakes, a gregarious member of British elite circles and one-time beau to Lady Helen Windsor, was never bashful about feeding memorable soundbites to journalists. He once quipped, "We used to be in the business of mind-bending for political purposes, but now we are in the business of saving lives."[19]

·   ·   ·   ·

The company's strategy, and its executives' personal networks, paid off. Over the next ten years, military agencies and research labs awarded SCL many contracts. It conducted a "behavior change study" to curb violent extremism in South and Southeast Asia for Sandia National Laboratories; a training program designed to help NATO commanders counter Russian information warfare in Eastern Europe; a project for the UK Foreign and Commonwealth Office, aimed at mitigating violent jihadism in Pakistan; an assessment of the social reintegration of ex-combatants in South Sudan, commissioned by the United Nations Development Programme; surveys of the Iranian population for the US military; and a surveillance program in Yemeni tribal areas for the American defense company Archimedes, which had been contracted by the Pentagon to support counterinsurgency operations.[20]

SCL Group's turn toward the military was undoubtedly influenced by the emergence of a lucrative private psyops industry. By the early 1990s, firms such as the Rendon Group, founded by former Democratic Party campaign consultant John Rendon, were doing brisk business with the

Pentagon, the CIA, and foreign governments seeking to conduct information warfare. The Rendon Group made a name for itself by leveraging the latest communication technologies—most notably chat rooms, email messaging, blogs, and other virtual spaces—to advance military objectives. Among other things, the Pentagon hired the company to support the Office of Strategic Influence, which essentially functioned as a post-9/11 wartime propaganda agency. Even earlier, the CIA awarded the Rendon Group nearly $100 million to produce propaganda and recruit dissidents opposed to Iraqi president Saddam Hussein.[21] Veteran journalist James Bamford described Rendon's company as a private intelligence firm taking over work once reserved for CIA employees, in which "spies-for-hire have begun to replace regional desk officers, who control clandestine operations around the world; watch officers at the agency's twenty-four-hour crisis center; analysts, who sift through reams of intelligence data; and even counterintelligence officers in the field, who oversee meetings between agents and their recruited spies."[22]

The so-called war on terror brought even more opportunities. After the US-led invasions of Afghanistan in 2001 and Iraq in 2003, the Pentagon awarded lucrative contracts to new "strategic communications" companies such as the now defunct Lincoln Group—which was caught planting pro-American propaganda in Iraqi newspapers during the US occupation of that country. Older, more established defense contractors like Science Applications International Corporation and L-3 Communications also began carving out portions of the psyops market.[23]

In some cases, companies incrementally entered the world of military psyops over the course of decades, gradually slipping into the work. Take, for example, SOS International (now more commonly known as SOSi), founded in 1989 by Sosi Setian in New York. The firm began by providing translation services to local and state law enforcement agencies. Setian, an Armenian American who immigrated to the United States from Bulgaria, earned a PhD in cultural anthropology from Columbia University before she founded SOSi, which eventually secured its first federal contracts from the US Drug Enforcement Agency.[24] The company landed a major Pentagon contract to provide translators for American troops following the US occupation of Iraq, which began in 2003. By 2008, SOSi had ventured into the world of information operations and psyops, and the

Defense Department awarded the firm contracts worth hundreds of millions of dollars.[25] In this contractor's paradise, SCL was perfectly placed to capitalize on conflict.

The marriage of military work and public relations was something of a throwback to the earliest days of the PR industry. Edward Bernays, often referred to as "the father of public relations," worked for the US government's Committee on Public Information (CPI), an office created in 1917 by President Woodrow Wilson to drum up public support for American military involvement in World War I.[26] Bernays, who openly described his work as "psychological warfare," wrote several influential books after opening his own PR firm in the 1920s, including *Crystallizing Public Opinion* and *Propaganda*.[27] He recognized the dual-use nature of propaganda, noting that "the efforts comparable to those applied by the CPI to affect the attitudes of the enemy, of neutrals, and people of this country could be applied with equal facility to peacetime pursuits."[28] His writings reached wide audiences, both at home and abroad—in fact, Joseph Goebbels, who served as Nazi Germany's minister of propaganda from 1933 to 1945, was familiar with his books and had them in his private library. After learning about this, Bernays, who was Jewish, reflected on how easily ideas could be weaponized: "[Goebbels's use of my book] shocked me, but I knew any human activity can be used for social purposes or misused for antisocial ones. Obviously, the attack on the Jews of Germany was no emotional outburst of the Nazis, but a deliberate, planned campaign."[29]

During the twenty-first century, SCL (which changed its name to SCL Group in the early 2000s, reflecting its diversified portfolio of services) continued its political consulting work across the globe. By the company's own account, it was involved in more than a hundred electoral campaigns—not just in Europe, but in Southeast Asia, the Caribbean, Africa, Oceania, and South America as well.[30]

AMERICAN CARNAGE

During the early 2010s, SCL Group rebranded itself once again. Rather than defining itself as a specialist in psyops or a political consultancy, it now claimed to be a data analytics company specializing in behavior change.[31] Then, in 2014, SCL Group made an ambitious move: entering the American market. It launched Cambridge Analytica as a US-based shell company, apparently created to circumvent the Federal Election Campaign Act—a law that, among other things, bars foreign firms from political consulting in America. Cambridge Analytica's largest investors included hedge fund billionaire Robert Mercer, best known for his advocacy of far-right political causes and financial support of the ultraconservative Breitbart News. Steve Bannon, who served as CEO of Breitbart News and briefly as President Trump's chief strategist, was Cambridge Analytica's vice president for more than two years.[32]

In July 2015, Republican presidential candidate Ted Cruz's campaign hired the firm to burnish the US senator's public image. Although the cantankerous candidate ultimately failed in his bid, Cambridge Analytica CEO Alexander Nix took credit for boosting Cruz's popularity, claiming that the company's skillful use of aggregated voter data, personality profiling, and individually focused messaging made the difference.[33] Microtargeting was not new, but in the past, political consultants tended to use public records and commercially available databases to carry out the method, not algorithmically generated individual profiles. By August 2016, the Trump campaign had employed Cambridge Analytica as part of a desperate effort to challenge Hillary Clinton's formidable campaign machine. According to one account, the company deployed six PhD data scientists to pinpoint twenty million persuadable voters in swing states.[34] Cambridge Analytica was also involved in the United Kingdom's successful pro-Brexit Leave.EU campaign, apparently using similar methods.

The company's signature products reportedly employed "psychographic" techniques that incorporated the Big Five personality traits well known to social scientists: openness, conscientiousness, extroversion, agreeableness, and neuroticism (known collectively as OCEAN traits).[35] Many social psychologists have adopted this instrument over the past thirty-five years as a means of gauging an individual's personality.

Behind the scenes, Cambridge Analytica had obtained the personal data of tens of millions of Facebook users from a software developer and psychologist, Aleksandr Kogan, who had created a cell phone app that provided users with a personality quiz on social media platforms, most notably Facebook. Kogan's company, Global Science Research (GSR), lured users with the prospect of obtaining free OCEAN scores.[36] But when they agreed to the terms and conditions of the app, users also unwittingly granted GSR permission to collect their profile information—and that of all their Facebook friends. In turn, GSR shared the information with SCL Group, Cambridge Analytica's parent company. Users had no idea that this personal data had been harvested by Kogan's GSR, much less passed along to Cambridge Analytica. The data of an estimated *ninety million* Facebook users was now in the company's hands.[37]

According to some reports, these methods were reverse engineered—essentially reconstructed from research tools developed by psychologist Michal Kosinski. As early as 2013, Kosinski and his colleagues had argued that a person's private traits can be predicted with great accuracy by combing digital records of his or her behavior (so-called digital footprints): Facebook likes, Twitter retweets, and other forms of residual data.[38]

Among their most significant innovations was a Facebook app that allowed users to view their own personality profiles based on their answers to a questionnaire. In so doing, they could share their profile data with Kosinski and the other researchers. "Before long, hundreds, thousands, then millions of people had revealed their innermost convictions. Suddenly the two doctoral candidates [Kosinski and David Stillwell] owned the largest dataset combining psychometric scores with Facebook profiles ever to be collected."[39] Furthermore, the data could be reversed—that is, "not only can psychological profiles be created from your data, but your data can also be used the other way round to search for specific profiles: all anxious fathers, all angry introverts . . . all undecided Democrats. . . . [W]hat Kosinski had invented was sort of a people search engine."[40]

Cambridge Analytica's methods combined OCEAN profiles with information about personal preferences, consumption patterns, reading and viewing habits, and other kinds of data mined from a range of public and private sources. The firm's marketing materials claimed that "we collect up to 5000 data points on over 220 million Americans . . . [to] predict the behavior of like-minded people."[41]

For Cambridge Analytica, psychographics was a powerful algorithmic tool for scouring individual voters' Facebook likes, retweets, and other bits of data gleaned from social media that were then combined with commercially available personal information such as property records, shopping

Figure 11. Whistleblower Christopher Wylie, who helped expose the Cambridge Analytica–Facebook scandal, speaks at a 2018 London protest. Photo courtesy of John Lubbock/CC-BY-SA-4.0.

data, land registries, magazine subscriptions, and other information sold by data brokers such as Acxiom and Experian. Cambridge Analytica aggregated this data with electoral rolls and online data to calculate a Big Five personality profile. According to reporters, the company's data scientists performed acts of data wizardry, as "digital footprints suddenly became real people with fears, needs, interests, and residential addresses."[42]

But the firm used more than psychographics and data-crunching techniques in its work. In 2019, Christopher Wylie, who was Cambridge Analytica's director of research before becoming an outspoken whistleblower, wrote a gripping memoir detailing his work there. He didn't mince words: he referred to the company's mission as an effort to "catalyze an alt-right insurgency in America" using "a form of psychological attack."[43] Wylie, a data scientist, stressed the ways in which ethnographic and qualitative research informed the company's work. Several chapters of his book claimed that Cambridge Analytica sent foreign anthropologists and sociologists to the United States to conduct on-the-ground research on American cultures and subcultures, and Wylie himself, a Canadian, apparently conducted ethnographic home visits and focus groups. He noted:

I once met the primatologist Jane Goodall, and she said something that always stuck with me. . . . I asked her why she researched primates in the wild instead of in a controlled lab. It's simple, she said: Because they don't live in labs. And neither do humans. If we are to really understand people, we have to always remember that they live outside of data sets.[44]

By the time of the 2016 US presidential elections, Cambridge Analytica had sorted millions of voters into thirty-two different personality types for the purpose of creating targeted advertisements tailored to each of these types.[45] When Donald Trump won the majority of electoral votes, company executives—and much of the corporate media—were quick to attribute his unexpected victory to Cambridge Analytica's proprietary data analysis techniques. The future had never seemed brighter for SCL Group.

PSYOPS INTERNATIONAL

Perhaps as a result of this press coverage, right-wing, authoritarian, and populist political parties around the world began turning to Cambridge Analytica for help. The company reportedly influenced Kenya's 2017 presidential elections, which pitted incumbent Uhuru Kenyatta of the right-wing Jubilee Party against Raila Odinga of the opposition Orange Democratic Movement.[46] Although the company claimed to have limited its activities to data collection for the Jubilee Party, Mark Turnbull, a managing director at Cambridge Analytica, told undercover reporters a different story. He admitted that the firm secretly managed Kenyatta's entire campaign: "We have rebranded the entire party twice, written the manifesto, done research, analysis, messaging. I think we wrote all the speeches and we staged the whole thing—so just about every element of this candidate."[47]

Given the revelations about Cambridge Analytica's planting of fake news stories, it seems likely that the company created persuasive personalized ads based on Kenyans' social media data.[48] In essence, they were conducting a high-tech form of information warfare. Fake WhatsApp and Twitter posts exploded days before the 2017 Kenyan elections. SCL Group had employed disinformation campaigns for its military clients for twenty-five years, and it's plausible that Cambridge Analytica continued this pattern of deception.

The August elections were chaotic by any standard, with accusations of vote tampering, the inclusion of dead people as registered voters, and the murder of Chris Msando, the election commission's technology manager, days before the election.[49] When the dust settled, sixty-seven people had died in postelection violence—and Kenyatta ultimately emerged victorious. Weeks later, the Kenyan Supreme Court annulled the elections, but when new elections were scheduled for October, Odinga declared that he would boycott them.

Given Kenya's recent history of electoral fraud, it's unlikely that Cambridge Analytica had much impact on the results. Paul Goldsmith, an anthropologist who has lived in Kenya for forty years, noted that elections still tend to follow the principle of "who counts the votes"—not who influences the voters.[50]

But the significance of Cambridge Analytica's efforts extended beyond its contribution to electoral outcomes. Kenya is no technological backwater. The world's first mobile money service was launched there in 2007, allowing users to transfer cash and make payments by phone. Homegrown tech firms are creating a "Silicon Savannah" near Nairobi. Two-thirds of Kenya's forty-eight million people have internet access. Ten million use WhatsApp; six million use Facebook; two million use Twitter. As Kenyans spend more time in virtual worlds, their personal data will become even more widely available, since Kenya has no significant data protection laws. Goldsmith summarized the situation succinctly:

> Cambridge Analytica doesn't need to deliver votes so much as to create the perception that they can produce results. . . . Kenya provides an ideal entry point into [Africa]. . . . Embedding themselves with ruling elites presents a pivot for exploiting emergent commercial opportunities . . . with an eye on the region's resources and its growing numbers of persuadable youth.[51]

If data is the new oil, then countries like Kenya can be seen as opportunities for resource extraction on a grand scale. A new form of high-tech colonialism is emerging in which countries with high rates of internet connectivity, lax privacy laws, and large numbers of youth offer vast riches—that is, data—as firms harvest and commodify personal information.

By 2018, Cambridge Analytica was working on campaigns in India, Brazil, and Mexico, all of which had upcoming general elections. In

Mexico, the firm approached the ruling Institutional Revolutionary Party (PRI) with a fifty-seven-page proposal outlining a dirty campaign strategy. The plan would overhaul the PRI's poor public image while attacking the reputation of Andrés Manuel López Obrador, a former Mexico City mayor running as an opposition candidate. Cambridge Analytica's proposal stated that by "using similar techniques that were employed against Hillary Clinton in the 2016 US presidential election," the company would wage "a powerful negative campaign strategy to undermine" the unabashedly left-leaning López Obrador. PRI officials ultimately decided that they could run their own campaign—but they paid the company anyway to *not* help opposition parties.[52]

The fallout continued into early 2020, when another Cambridge Analytica whistleblower, former director of program development Brittany Kaiser, began releasing documents from internal emails and files exposing the breathtaking scope of the company's global operations.[53] The materials were related to projects in nearly seventy countries, including Ukraine, Malaysia, and Ghana. Cambridge Analytica had been able to thrive in places with weak or nonexistent internet privacy laws—including the United States.

. . . . .

Apart from Cambridge Analytica's growing global portfolio, there were clear indications that SCL Group had an interest in radically expanding its worldwide reach by appealing directly to the US military establishment. In March 2017, top executives from SCL Group met with Pentagon officials, including Hriar Cabayan, manager of the Strategic Multilayer Assessment—a program that conducts Defense Department research and cultural analysis, among other things.[54]

At about the same time, the US State Department's Global Engagement Center, dedicated to countering violent extremism in digital realms, hired SCL Group to produce counterpropaganda and to identify interventions that might disrupt ISIS's recruitment efforts in the Middle East.[55] A few months later, in August 2017, the Associated Press reported that retired US Army General Michael Flynn, who briefly served as national security advisor in the Trump administration, had signed a work agreement with

Cambridge Analytica—though it's unclear whether he actually did any work for the firm.[56] Flynn eventually pleaded guilty to lying to the FBI about his contacts with Russian operatives in late 2017, while working with President Trump's transition team. (Trump infamously pardoned Flynn in November 2020.) Given his spot in the media limelight, it's easy to forget that Flynn once headed US intelligence operations in Afghanistan, pushing for a big data approach to counterinsurgency that would, among other things, weave together data collected by social scientists, civil affairs officers, and NGO personnel (see chapter 6).[57]

The connections between Cambridge Analytica/SCL Group and the Pentagon's champions of data-driven counterinsurgency and cyberwarfare raised troubling questions once they came to light. For critics of the company, SCL Group's benign-sounding mission of behavior change rang hollow, and it appeared that Cambridge Analytica's connections to what *Rolling Stone* magazine called "spooks and right-wing generals" seemed to fit into a broader pattern of psyops, military-grade propaganda disguised as public relations, and political consulting for ultraconservative causes.[58]

CAPTURED BY COMPULSION

At this point, we might step back for a moment to ask: Did Cambridge Analytica's high-tech psyop strategy really work?

There are good reasons to view Cambridge Analytica's claims skeptically. The firm was known for its aggressive sales and marketing efforts, including a sophisticated public relations strategy and relentless self-promotion. For months, the company's main webpage featured footage of a triumphant Donald Trump interwoven with clips of CNN and Sky News reporters who breathlessly described Cambridge Analytica's decisive role in his victory. The firm obviously benefited from such media attention.

Critics charged that company executives exaggerated Cambridge Analytica's role in the US election. Some wondered whether the firm used psychographics at all. "Rather than a sinister breakthrough in political technology," wrote an investigative journalist, "the Cambridge Analytica story appears to be part of the traditional contest among consultants on a winning political campaign to get their share of the credit—and win future clients."[59]

Others questioned Cambridge Analytica's methods. For example, political scientist Eitan Hersh noted that the company's claims about predicting personality traits were impossible—"You can do better randomly guessing."[60] Engineering scientist Jamie Condliffe doubted that there was anything new about the company's techniques: "Cambridge Analytica's targeting may not be doing a great deal more than other approaches that are widely used around the internet."[61]

When I interviewed him in 2017, Michal Kosinski told me that both sides in the 2016 US presidential elections had undoubtedly used personality profiling software, and reminded me that similar tools were also used in Obama's successful 2012 presidential campaign—though the Obama team's messaging wasn't intended to deliberately stoke the fears and prejudices of target audiences. Kosinski noted that programmers can easily use off-the-shelf products and apps such as IBM Watson, Crystal, and Apply Magic Sauce to create personality profiles based on social media information and "digital footprints." In other words, Cambridge Analytica may not have been as much of an innovator as the media made it out to be.

Although we will never know for sure whether Cambridge Analytica's efforts tipped the election in Trump's favor, we might consider how much more of an effect the company could have achieved if its scientists had had more time, more detailed data, and a more refined ethnographic approach. But one thing is certain: Cambridge Analytica is a troubling example of how some specialists are engaging in efforts to manipulate voters in nominally democratic societies.[62] Data science is transforming political processes in profound ways that most people don't understand, and we ignore these changes at our peril. In a supercharged media environment where Facebook, Twitter, and WhatsApp are the primary means by which literally billions of people consume news, creating hard-hitting propaganda has never been easier. With so many people posting so much information about the intimate details of their lives on the Web, coordinated attempts at mass persuasion are likely to become more widespread in the future. The US Capitol riot of January 6, 2021, is a grim example of what can happen when persuasive messages and conspiracy theories circulate freely through virtual realms.

If politics is war by other means, then we might think of elections as global battlegrounds in which information, disinformation, and propaganda are the weapons of choice—and data is the ammunition. Methods and theories from the fields of psychology, anthropology, and political science are emerging as critical components in these projects. The expansion of the internet and smartphones into the remotest corners of the planet, and the billions of hours of screen time to which our species is exposed every day, means that there are unprecedented opportunities to conquer hearts and minds in virtual worlds, particularly where data privacy is weakly regulated, or when users are oblivious of the ways in which companies, governments, or individual actors manipulate their personal information or spread propaganda. Even in countries with high rates of internet use, many people don't know what "bots" or "trolls" are, much less how they can disinform citizens or bend media narratives.

It would be naive to think that SCL Group and Cambridge Analytica were the only companies specializing in these techniques. Political scientists generally acknowledge that the 2012 Obama campaign revolutionized the use of data analytics and social media messaging, and some of those involved would go on to create private companies leaning toward Democratic Party candidates, namely BlueLabs Analytics and Civis Analytics, the latter of which was funded partially by former Google CEO Eric Schmidt. Firms often affiliated with Republican Party candidates include TargetedVictory, Optimus, and Deep Root Analytics. If anything, it appears that Cambridge Analytica was an effort to beat these companies at their own game. But beyond the world of high-tech campaign consultancy and political persuasion, there are others doing similar work today: AggregateIQ (which, like Cambridge Analytica, was involved in the Leave.EU campaign), Data Propria (created by several former Cambridge Analytica executives), and a host of more established consultancies. These companies are thriving at a time when the Smith-Mundt Act of 1948—a US federal law prohibiting government agencies from creating and distributing domestic propaganda—is under threat.[63] Sociologist Emma Briant has analyzed these trends within a broader context, noting: "There's evidence of really quite disturbing experiments on American voters, manipulating them with fear-based messaging, targeting the most vulnerable, that seems to be continuing. This is an entire global industry that's out of control."[64]

There's a much larger issue at stake, beyond Cambridge Analytica, or SCL Group, or any of the other companies that have turned to the dark arts of persuasion in the digital age: the role of Silicon Valley firms, particularly Facebook, in paving a smooth pathway for the propagation of inflammatory, divisive messaging. Christopher Wylie knows—he saw it from the inside:

> Our identities and behavior have become commodities in the high-stakes data trade. The companies that control the flow of information are among the most powerful in the world; the algorithms they've designed in secret are shaping minds in the United States and elsewhere in ways previously unimaginable. No matter what issue you care about most—gun violence, immigration, free speech, religious freedom—you can't escape Silicon Valley. . . . My work with Cambridge Analytica exposed the dark side of tech innovation. The alt-right innovated. Russia innovated. And Facebook, that same site where you share your party invites and baby pictures, allowed those innovations to be unleashed.[65]

Wylie has a point. It's tempting to heap blame on SCL Group and Cambridge Analytica, but it's important to remember that these companies probably didn't violate any laws in the United States. In America, at least, it appears that everything the company did was legal—although SCL Group did plead guilty in the United Kingdom for violating data privacy laws. As noted in the online journal *Motherboard,* Cambridge Analytica's data-harvesting practices weren't security breaches; rather, they were "par for the course. . . . It was a feature, not a bug. Facebook still collects—and then sells—massive amounts of data on its users."[66] In other words, every Facebook post, every tweet and retweet, every Instagram caption, renders you vulnerable to forms of digital data collection that can be commodified and commercialized. The information can be used for all kinds of purposes in an unregulated market: monitoring emotional states, manipulating public opinion, or disseminating tailor-made propaganda designed to polarize people.[67]

Years after the Cambridge Analytica scandal, Facebook executives still refuse to call Cambridge Analytica's actions a data breach. As sociologist Zeynep Tufekci puts it, the company's defensive posture reveals much about the social costs of social media: "If your business is building a massive surveillance machinery, the data will eventually be used and misused. Hacked, breached, leaked, pilfered, conned, targeted, engaged, profiled, sold. There is no informed consent because it's not possible to reasonably inform or consent."[68]

Figure 12. At a 2018 congressional hearing, Facebook CEO Mark Zuckerberg acknowledged that the company hadn't done enough to keep others from using it for malicious purposes. Photo courtesy of Xinhua/Alamy Stock Photo.

Facebook CEO Mark Zuckerberg finally appeared before the US Congress in April 2018, but despite his apologies ("We didn't take a broad enough view of our responsibility, and that was a big mistake," he said)—and a few modest changes to the company's data policies—things have continued more or less as they did before. In fact, during the summer of 2020, Facebook found itself in the midst of a massive boycott, under pressure from civil rights groups that were outraged about the social media giant's apparent inability to prevent racist messages and hate speech on its platform. More than a thousand corporations—including Coca-Cola, Unilever, Honda, Clorox, Lego, and Starbucks—stopped advertising their products on Facebook. Although the boycott barely dented Facebook's revenue, and failed to bring about significant changes, some companies have continued protesting the company's inaction.[69]

Although this chapter is written as a diagnosis, rather than a prescription, it's important to listen to those who have been outspoken critics of firms like Facebook, which have created an online environment in which toxic propaganda has proliferated. Among the most lucid suggestions are those articulated by Roger McNamee, a venture capitalist and early

Facebook investor. He recommends a multipronged approach: imposing strict regulations on how internet platforms are used and commercialized; requiring social media companies to report who is sponsoring political and issues-based advertisements; mandating transparency about algorithms (McNamee says that "users deserve to know why they see what they see in their news feeds and search results"); requiring social media apps to offer users the ability to opt out; banning digital bots that impersonate humans; and creating rules that allow consumers (not corporations) to own their personal data.[70]

In world of diminishing privacy, our vulnerabilities and frailties are easily magnified. There's also mounting evidence that digital compulsions—some call them addictions—are negatively affecting human health, social relationships, and cognitive capabilities, thanks in part to the efforts of social scientists who dedicate themselves to maximizing the amount of time we spend on our smartphones and tablets. Experimental psychologists specializing in what is euphemistically called "behavior design" have largely ignored the ethical problems inherent in such work when they help companies create digital devices, apps, media platforms and other technologies that are literally irresistible to their users.[71]

If nondescript pocket-sized devices made of plastic, metal, and glass have abruptly altered patterns of human behavior, interaction, communication, and cognition in less than a decade, what will happen once wearable virtual reality interfaces like VR headsets, eyeglasses, and corneal implants are widely available? The case of SCL Group/Cambridge Analytica deserves our attention because it points to the possibility of a future in which totalitarian institutions—not just governments, but corporations, political parties, religious groups, messianic movements, NGOs, domestic terrorists, and other entities—have the tremendous and frightening capacity to mold the ideas, attitudes, and behaviors of audiences captured by their own compulsions.

5 **Juggernaut**

How exactly do scientists get drawn into military work?

There are many paths. Some are lured by the prospect of conducting applied research in their areas of expertise, without the distractions and pressures of the academic world. Others are motivated by patriotism and a desire to serve their country honorably. A few may be attracted by vanity, hoping to bring their specialized expertise to the military masses, or perhaps by romantic notions of spycraft or hidden underground laboratories. Still others are unwittingly recruited into compartmentalized projects that seem to have no direct connection to military and intelligence agencies, only to discover the truth years or even decades later.[1] And then there are countless more who see opportunities to make minute, incremental changes that might one day reach a tipping point that substantively reforms America's military establishment.

Sometimes, military work offers itself unexpectedly, triggered by odd convergences or serendipitous circumstances. This may be what happened to Adam Russell, an intelligent, affable young college student who, by the mid-1990s, had cultivated an eclectic range of interests: bodybuilding, anthropology, nutrition, chaos theory, rugby.[2] Twenty years later, he was among the most influential anthropologists in America, helping to manage multimillion-dollar contracts as a program manager at the enigmatic Defense Advanced Research Projects Agency, or DARPA—the Pentagon's premier research and development center.

Social critics have said much about the ways in which the militarization of American culture has transformed the texture of everyday life for soldiers and their families. By comparison, scant attention has been given to the topic of how individual scientists have been affected. Tracing Adam Russell's multiple careers as an athlete, an anthropologist, and ultimately a government administrator can serve as an object lesson in the militarization of American science.

THE GRADUATE

Russell didn't move to Oxford to play rugby—things just turned out that way. In 1996, at the age of twenty-five, the gregarious, handsome young American landed a prestigious Rhodes Scholarship and decided to pursue a graduate degree at one of Europe's most venerable institutions of higher learning. As an undergraduate student at Duke University, he had excelled in anthropology, completing an honors thesis with an ethnographic focus on bodybuilding and fitness gyms.[3]

For Russell, athletics was a side gig that took on more importance over time. He began playing rugby during his last two years at Duke and eventually became team captain. Later, he nostalgically recalled the social benefits of college sports: "The drinking age limit in the United States is twenty-one, so if you play rugby, it gives you access to alcohol."[4] Russell stood literally head and shoulders above his Duke classmates—at six feet, four inches tall, the 250-pound undergraduate cut an imposing figure at the private, elite university.

After arriving at Oxford, Russell tried out for the university's rugby team and made the second-string squad. But soon after, he suffered a serious stress fracture in his leg that required months of bed rest. The injury led to complications. He later recounted the physical toll: "The muscles start to atrophy as a result of being laid up, and if you try to come back too quickly you suffer this particular syndrome where the soft tissue is damaged." He added: "It was mind-numbing. The pain was as near to childbirth as I will ever be. Every day was just more parturition pain."[5]

The experience of intense suffering might have broken the spirit of weaker men, but he soldiered on through excruciating rounds of physical therapy. After multiple surgeries, and with a bit of help from the team's coaching staff, Russell recovered—and then got right back into rugby. He rejoined the Oxford team as a lock, a position often reserved for the tallest members of a squad. Through all of this, he never lost sight of his academic work.

.   .   .   .   .

Russell's doctoral dissertation was unconventional by Oxford standards. While anthropology students often conduct their research in exotic, faraway lands among peasant farmers, indigenous tribes of hunter-gatherers, or impoverished factory workers, Russell creatively combined elements of social science and sport—specifically, bodybuilding. He observed and conducted ethnographic interviews with several groups of men in southeast England who both sold and used illegal anabolic steroids for "masculine performance enhancement." His research highlighted a contradiction: although the bodybuilders had come to view themselves as entrepreneurial "local 'big men' able to remake their bodies and personalities," their actions were "reinscribing certain cultural forms and . . . Euro-American social dynamics."[6] Their deliberate and apparently subversive acts only served to perpetuate long-standing gendered hierarchies and stereotypes about working-class men.

Among other things, Russell's insightful dissertation cited journalist Susan Faludi's notion of "ornamental masculinity." He summarized the idea to a reporter: "It's essentially a way of looking at how certain objects are sold as what used to be adornments but are now the essence of masculinity, like masculine beauty products. The idea is that masculinity is a thing that's worn on the skin, whereas the supposition is that previously masculinity had been something that you are."[7]

Masculinity, pharmaceuticals, consumerism, technology, body image— these were the predominant themes that emerged from Russell's graduate work. His research was eventually summarized in a dissertation titled "Nurturing Nature: Men, Steroids, and Anthropology," and it was timely: Russell completed it at the same time that news headlines featured several high-profile sports doping scandals.[8] By the end of 2003, many reports suggested that cyclist Lance Armstrong, baseball legend Barry Bonds, and scores of other professional athletes had used anabolic steroids and other illegal performance-enhancing drugs. Russell was the among the few social scientists analyzing the topic.

As Russell immersed himself in anthropological studies, he continued honing his athletic skills with the Oxford rugby team—also known as the Dark Blues, after its indigo-hued uniforms. The climax of every season was the legendary Varsity Match.

SCRUM

Among the many thousands of rugby matches played around the world each year across the British Commonwealth, few have the cachet of the Varsity Match. It's social drama of the highest order. The annual contest pits the University of Oxford against its archrival, the University of Cambridge. The event, which takes place in the cold air of early December, is an opportunity for college students and schoolboys from elite prep schools, well-heeled businessmen from the City of London, and other alumni to rambunctiously cheer on their teams and wax nostalgic about the good old days. The contest's enduring cultural significance is remarkable, and it's something of a throwback to what some think of as a simpler, Edwardian past—although today, the game is broadcast on live television from an arena replete with jumbotrons.[9]

The Varsity Match has been held every year since 1872, with brief interruptions during the two world wars and the recent coronavirus pandemic. The competition between Oxford's Dark Blues and Cambridge's Light Blues (named after that team's teal-and-white striped jerseys) is held every year at Twickenham Stadium, capacity eighty-two thousand—a venue second in size only to Wembley Stadium. The massive structure, known affectionately as "Twickers" by rugby fans, is nestled in an affluent suburb of greater London.

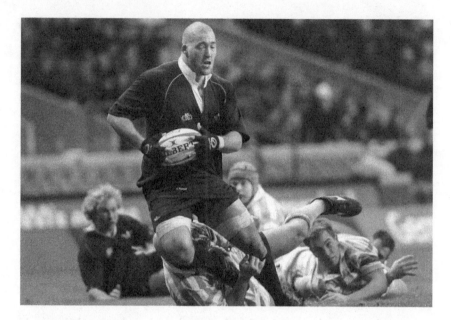

Figure 13. The rugby Varsity Match between Oxford and Cambridge takes place every year at Twickenham Stadium in London. Photo courtesy of Toby Melville/PA Images/ Alamy Stock Photo.

In the late 1990s and early 2000s, the Varsity Match was undergoing a renaissance, due in part to Twickenham's expansion. Attendance at the event, which had declined in the 1970s and early 1980s, began to increase again, thanks in part to corporate sponsorships and aggressive marketing. Russell was joining the world of rugby union at an exciting and perhaps historic moment, which in the late 1990s and early 2000s drew crowds as large as fifty or sixty thousand strong.[10]

Russell led a mostly charmed life as a Dark Blue. Though his team lost to the Light Blues in 1998, Oxford went on to win the next three Varsity Matches. Russell, who had sported a flamboyant ponytail early in his career at Oxford, eventually shaved his head during rugby season, giving him a menacing, miscreant appearance. Press photos of the big game depict Russell barreling past piles of flattened opponents. In a particularly memorable image, three Light Blues watch in helpless horror as the thundering American kicks his way out of a tackle, clutching the ball tightly with both hands.

In 2002, he almost made rugby union history. No Dark Blue had ever played four consecutive winning Varsity Matches, and Russell would have been the first ever to accomplish this feat.[11] Alas, in front of fifty thousand spectators, Oxford suffered a heartbreaking defeat that year at the hands of its opponents. Cambridge's Light Blues triumphed by a score of 15 to 13.[12]

The extent to which rugby shaped Russell's interest in the military is an open question. He was reportedly inspired by Peter Dawkins, an American college football star and Heisman Trophy winner who was a Rhodes Scholar at Oxford in the late 1950s and early 1960s.[13] Dawkins played rugby as a Dark Blue, then later became a decorated Vietnam War hero while serving in the US Army's storied 82nd Airborne Division. He was eventually promoted to brigadier general. Dawkins's lasting legacy to rugby was the celebrated "Yankee torpedo pass," a formidable projectile overarm throw undoubtedly inspired by his experience in American football.[14]

For those familiar with the sport, rugby is war, virtually. A commentator in the *Observer* once described the sport as an all-out melee, "war continued by other means," and George Orwell famously cited rugby as an example of "serious sport . . . war minus the shooting."[15] It's easy to see why. Unlike soccer, Britain's most popular pastime, rugby requires constant physical contact and determined aggression. Gashed foreheads, lacerated knees, broken teeth, and bloody noses are common, and it's not unusual for injured players to be carried off the field on stretchers or in golf carts. There's an old adage in the United Kingdom: "Football [soccer] is a gentleman's game played by hooligans, and rugby is a hooligans' game played by gentlemen."[16] The maxim says a great deal about class distinctions in British society—soccer is for the working classes, and rugby for elites. But it also points to the rough-and-tumble nature of the game that Russell cherished.

And yet, rugby's physicality involves more than just violence. For example, when executing a line-out, two teammates lift a third player into the air by gracefully hoisting him up by the haunches, so that he can catch a ball thrown from the touch-line (what in America would be called a sideline). Or consider the scrum, a formation in which opposing groups of eight or nine players are crouched down, arms locked tightly around each other's backs, shoulders, and hips in order to take possession of the ball. The mass of throbbing muscle and sinew crawls back and forth like a drunken crab, until a white leather egg pops out from below. In the words of a former player, "You have to be prepared to get beaten up for the man beside you—that requires a strong bond between teammates."[17]

Years after his last Varsity Match, an interviewer asked Russell how his experience in rugby might have influenced his work at DARPA. His response was in some ways reminiscent of comments from those who have described rugby's warlike character:[18]

> It's an inherently social sport, it really is a team-oriented sport . . . in the level of cohesion that's required, and teamwork. . . . I became really interested in the imponderables, as some people have described these things like cohesion and teamwork, even identity, commitment—these things that are clearly important, that clearly impact the real world . . . but that are really hard to measure, and remain at this point almost like magic. And we look to the best coaches who are able to summon this magic and produce performances from teams that really on paper should not have gotten there and likewise, dysfunctional dynamics where you can have the best superstars and they don't seem to perform. . . . Thus far it's remained this imponderable area of heuristics, and tradecraft, and wisdom of the ages. . . . In DoD, we fight and we work, and we frankly live or die in teams. I think that actually provides an excellent target or focus on which to go after these imponderables.[19]

As noted above, Russell's graduate research in the late 1990s and early 2000s focused on bodybuilders who used anabolic steroids for "performance enhancement." At more or less the same time that he was interviewing these men about their performance-enhancing drug habits, newspapers in the United Kingdom were alerting the public about a virtual epidemic in anabolic steroid use among British athletes—including rugby, where it was reportedly widespread and even commonplace.[20] Russell's dissertation couldn't have been more timely.

OPTIMIZATION, LLC

After receiving his doctorate, Russell returned to the United States and began conducting research for Science Applications International

Corporation or SAIC, a major defense contractor with headquarters near Washington, DC.[21] Although SAIC is perhaps best known as a weapons manufacturer that builds torpedoes, artillery guns, bomb racks, small arms, and other "lethality solutions," for many years it has also specialized in a range of services broadly defined as mission support.[22]

Russell and two other SAIC researchers, Bartlett Bulkley and Christine Grafton, prepared a report on "human performance"—that is, the ability of men or women in the armed services to accomplish tasks effectively.[23] In the military context, human performance had historically been linked to physical fitness, but by the late 1990s the term encompassed a wider range of factors, including psychological fitness and cognitive performance. At this time, several researchers were seeking to identify ways in which soldiers, airmen, and sailors might achieve enhanced performance through dietary, pharmacological, or other means.[24] SAIC's client for the project was the Defense Department's Office of Net Assessment (ONA), sometimes referred to as the Pentagon's internal think tank.[25] President Richard Nixon created the office in 1973 to examine long-term trends shaping America's military capabilities and those of its potential adversaries, and the ONA has been highly influential since its inception.

Human performance enhancement is an interdisciplinary field that draws from sports medicine, nutritional science, kinesiology, and the cognitive sciences. Andrew Herr, a microbiologist who also has a background in security studies, was selected to participate in the US Army's Training and Doctrine Command's "Mad Scientists" initiative, which hosts conferences and workshops featuring experts from academia and industry. Herr also founded Helicase, a company that specializes in enhancing the performance of sports teams. "A lot of the work being done in the military draws from research done in sports," said Herr. "But I think a lot of human performance research has been funded by the military. Everybody is using the same research, and it's conducted on athletes."[26] Some of the same neuroscientists who train professional teams in the National Football League also train US Special Operations forces in techniques such as "inner-game training," the ability to slip into and out of optimal states of consciousness.[27] Given these links—and his long-standing interest in human performance and the limits of the human body—it was a logical leap for Russell to enter this field. Within the world of military contracting, it happened to be a growth industry.

At SAIC, Russell and his fellow researchers introduced several new ideas into military discussions of human performance.[28] Perhaps most importantly, they made a distinction between enhancement and optimization. For the SAIC team, *enhancement* referred to improving a single aspect of performance, for example manual dexterity. *Optimization,* by contrast, meant sharpening a person's overall performance at a specific task through a tailored combination of enhancements. In their report to the ONA, Russell and his colleagues constructed three "archetypes": the "Versatile Warrior," the "Pencil Warrior," and the "Techno Warrior," corresponding to Special Forces, submarine crews, and aviation crews, respectively. The SAIC researchers argued that for optimal performance, each type of warrior needed a specific combination of thirteen potential enhancements, ranging from strength and endurance to intelligence and empathy.[29] Their report, published in May 2005, was widely cited in the field of military medicine and led a three-day Defense Department health conference a year later, with nearly a hundred participants.[30] This and other conferences and symposia may have given Russell an opportunity to expand his professional networks with representatives from military contract firms, Pentagon officials, and university-based researchers.

The SAIC project had an obvious link to Russell's graduate work, to the extent that it examined human "performance enhancement," a topic explicitly mentioned throughout his Oxford dissertation. However, there were significant differences. Apart from the obvious fact that Russell conducted his doctoral research among male bodybuilders in southeast England—not American servicemen and servicewomen—there was another striking difference. Russell's writing had undergone a metamorphosis. His Oxford dissertation was highly esoteric, not unlike those of many other fin-de-siècle anthropology graduate students influenced by post-structuralism and postmodernism. For example, Russell conjured up the then fashionable (at least among academic social scientists) image of the cyborg, as he referred to men on steroids as "caught in the interstices among a post-modern imperative towards self-invention with (or submission to) biotechnology, the call of hegemonic masculinity, and the criminalization of certain drugs that call into question the otherwise self-evident distinction between natural bodies and 'enhanced' machines."[31] By contrast, in his new role as a researcher for a major defense conglomerate, his writing was clean, crisp, unencumbered by theory, packaged for quick consumption by military audiences.

Perhaps more importantly, at SAIC Russell worked closely with Bartlett Bulkley, a brilliant young woman who had just completed a master's degree in security studies from Georgetown University's School of Foreign Service. She later earned a doctorate in neuroscience and cognitive science at the University of Maryland.[32] Bulkley was the daughter of Dr. Bernadine Healy, a well-known cardiologist who in 1991 became the first woman to head the US National Institutes of Health.[33] Bartlett Bulkley was undoubtedly influenced by her mother's intellectual and professional achievements, and her ability to navigate her way smoothly between the worlds of government, industry, and the academy might be attributed in part to Dr. Healy's extraordinary example.[34]

Russell became a trusted colleague to Bulkley over the years as their research interests overlapped. His work continued to emphasize human physical performance, while hers examined the cognitive performance of humans facing stressful conditions in militarized settings. Eventually, the two were married.[35]

.   .   .   .   .

Around 2006, Russell and Bulkley made a career shift—they began working for Scitor Corporation, a defense contractor once described as "the most secretive and least-known of the companies that collect and analyze signals intelligence for the Pentagon."[36] Since its founding in 1979, the company, which had extensive experience in covert operations (or "black ops"), had done work for the CIA, the US Army, and the US-NATO command in Afghanistan.[37] Scitor also reportedly undertook eighty-seven defense contracts between 2000 and 2015, worth nearly $200 million and focused on "biomodification" and "performance enhancement."[38]

By 2007, Russell and Bulkley were helping Scitor prepare a report for the Pentagon, summarizing technological and medical developments that might soon lead to breakthroughs in performance optimization. In the report, they described innovations such as drugs for overcoming combatant fatigue, genetic techniques for accelerating muscle growth or cell strength, improvements in human-machine interfaces, and predictive models for assigning individuals to specific combat roles.[39]

The two researchers participated in numerous workshops and conferences with titles such as "Readiness and Performance: Optimizing the 21st Century Warfighter" and "Human Performance Modification."[40] One conference, coordinated by the MITRE Corporation on behalf of the Pentagon's Office of Defense Research and Engineering, focused on the potential military applications of "brain plasticity" (specifically the creation of "new neural pathways, and thus new cognitive capabilities") and the "brain-computer interface" (including electronic or magnetic "direct implants into the brain").[41]

Somehow, through all of this, the indefatigable Russell managed to find the time to keep up his rugby—he made his test debut as a member of the US national team at the 2007 Rugby World Cup Qualifiers.

AGENCY MAN

Russell's career took another significant turn in 2010, when he accepted a position as a program manager at the Intelligence Advanced Research Projects Agency, or IARPA—a research and development office created by the US Office of the Director of National Intelligence in 2007. Modeled after DARPA, IARPA was described by officials as a "high-risk, high-payoff research and development arm" focused on futuristic, paradigm-shattering technological advances. Among the agency's first efforts was a program seeking to explore the possibility of reverse engineering "algorithms of the brain."[42]

Russell helped manage a program called Tools for Recognizing Useful Signals of Trustworthiness, or TRUST. (In the words of a DARPA program manager, "We have wacky acronyms. It's our thing." IARPA emulates the wackiness.)[43] The program's stated objective was "to learn whether one's own neural, psychological, physiological and behavioral signals can reflect and predict a partner's trustworthiness."[44] Although he was venturing away from his anthropological roots, Russell managed to navigate his way through the intelligence community's narrowly defined version of social science, which tends to favor quantitative, not qualitative, methods and analysis.

To promote the TRUST program, IARPA launched its first public contest, the INSTINCT Challenge (Investigating Novel Statistical Techniques to Identify Neurophysiological Correlates of Trustworthiness). The agency was probably inspired by DARPA, which in the early 2000s coordinated a series of "Grand Challenges"—highly publicized robotics competitions open to corporate, nonprofit, university, and individual researchers. To entice participants, DARPA awarded cash prizes to the winners. IARPA's debut in the world of competitive events was piloted in a program managed by Russell—though it was somewhat more subdued. The INSTINCT Challenge was a crowdsourcing competition rather than a robot race across the desert—but it received a great deal of attention nonetheless. The winning researchers were two engineers from defense giant BAE Systems, who came up with a hybrid solution integrating mathematics and neuroscience. By developing statistical techniques that integrated a person's heart rate, reaction time, and other variables, the scientists were allegedly able to improve predictions by 15 percent over "baseline." The researchers also developed a clever acronym, which received as much media coverage as their scientific work. In a tribute to the *Star Wars* franchise, they named their program JEDI MIND, for "Joint Estimation of Deception Intent via Multisource Integration of Neuropsychological Discriminators."[45]

Russell also coordinated an IARPA program called Strengthening Human Adaptive Reasoning and Problem-Solving (SHARP), an initiative seeking "evidence based interventions" for optimizing humans' ability to logically solve problems. The program provided at least $12 million in funding to compare how a wide range of techniques—such as meditation and mindfulness, electrical brain stimulation, memory games, "brain training" regimens, exercise, and more—might improve reasoning.[46] In 2014, IARPA awarded the SHARP contract to an artificial intelligence and robotics firm, Charles River Analytics, for a proposal entitled Multifaceted Intervention for Robust, ARP-Focused Customized Learning and Enhancement—or MIRACLE for short. The effort brought together researchers from Georgia Tech, Harvard, and the University of New Mexico.[47] Additional contracts were awarded to the University of Illinois's Beckman Institute for Advanced Science and Technology and Honeywell's aerospace division, which partnered with researchers from Oxford, Harvard, and Northeastern University.[48]

Yet another IARPA program managed by Russell, which ventured much more directly into the world of gaming, was UAREHERE (Using Alternate Reality Environments to Help Enrich Research Efforts), ostensibly an effort to scoop up data from online alternate reality games, which often take the form of multimedia narratives that participants play out in the real world. As an example, IARPA mentioned the 2010 game *Conspiracy for Good,* sponsored by telecom giant Nokia.[49] In *Conspiracy,* players were pitted against a fictional corporation seeking to repress citizens through widespread surveillance and harassment. During the final days of the game, the plot moved into the streets of London for live enactments and game play. (Ironically, Nokia had been criticized just months earlier for providing the Iranian government with technologies for monitoring protesters' communications.)[50] To help promote UAREHERE and solicit ideas, Russell moderated a panel at ARGFest 2013, an annual conference of alternate-reality-game aficionados and producers. On the panel were computer scientists from defense contractors BBN Technologies (a subsidiary of Raytheon) and SRI International.[51]

It seems that UAREHERE never officially made it past the exploratory stage, but the initiative raises questions about how multimedia and online gaming might create opportunities for new forms of surveillance in the digital era—a possibility that may already be occurring in defense intelligence agencies.[52] IARPA's announcement included the following research questions:

> What protections can be put in place to maintain the privacy, safety, and anonymity of subjects? How have previous AREs/ARGs [alternate reality experiences/alternate reality games] addressed these issues? Responses should consider issues regarding the collection of data via personal identifiers that may be sensitive (e.g. user names, phone numbers, emails, IP addresses, etc.), other data that may potentially be sensitive, and data security and protections.[53]

While such statements imply that the intelligence community in general and IARPA in particular are seeking better ways of protecting personal data—a goal that would obviously be important for protecting the identities of CIA agents, for example—it's easy to imagine how an initiative like this might also enable new forms of digital surveillance. Dual-use technologies can protect people or harm them, depending on the circumstances. IARPA, after all, is not in the business of funding basic scientific research across a wide range of domains. The agency has a narrow mandate to support work that, over the long term, might provide new technologies and techniques to America's spy agencies.

In 2012, one of Russell's programs attempted to bring quasi-anthropological sensibilities to IARPA. The program was cleverly titled EMIC—short for Emic Training to Improve Cross-Cultural Prediction. IARPA released a "Request for Information," a preliminary public announcement to generate interest and ideas, which cited the renowned cultural anthropologist Clifford Geertz:

> Whereas Geertz was pessimistic in 1974 about the possibility of ever truly perceiving what someone else perceives (saying that all that could be done was to "scratch surfaces . . ."), in the 35+ years since his address to the American Academy of Arts and Sciences, we have seen the advent of new technologies and new research that may help us move past scratching surfaces in trying to perceive the world from the "native's point of view." Examples include improvements in computing, massive data collection and aggregation, novel methods for data visualization, new graphic user interfaces, rich multi-sensory and immersive environments, as well as significant advances in the behavioral sciences, cultural psychology, neuroscience, and psychophysiology.[54]

Some might envision Geertz rolling in his grave at the suggestion that big data analytics and graphic user interfaces might accelerate cultural interpretation, as if greater bandwidth might lead to supercharged semiotics. But although he was skeptical about grand theories, Geertz never dismissed the notion that the discipline was a science—quite the opposite. In his most famous book, *The Interpretation of Cultures,* he metaphorically described culture itself in computational terms. He wrote, "Culture is best seen not as complexes of concrete behavior patterns—customs, usages, traditions, habit clusters—as has, by and large, been the case up to now, but as a set of control mechanisms—plans, recipes, rules, instructions (what computer engineers call 'programs')—for the governing of behavior."[55]

IARPA convened an invitation-only workshop during the summer of 2012 to more fully explore EMIC, which was attended by researchers and representatives from several companies, including Creative Technologies Incorporated, a Hollywood production company specializing in immersive simulation tools for the Pentagon.[56] In the end, EMIC appeared to be less about understanding and empathizing with "the native's point of view" and more about creating virtual training tools such as avatars and video games for learning about culture. Although IARPA never formally launched EMIC as a program of record, the agency funded numerous projects over the following years that attempted to use virtual technologies to simulate emic perspectives.[57]

DARPA'S ANTHROPOLOGIST

In 2015, Russell was offered a position with DARPA, the Defense Department agency that had served as a model for other organizations. Several years later, in 2019, his wife (now Bartlett Russell) also joined DARPA as a program manager.

On the surface, Russell's success in securing a DARPA position looked like a coup. The agency had once funded anthropologists and other social scientists to conduct counterinsurgency work in Southeast Asia during the Vietnam War era, but those days were long past. From the 1970s forward, it had steered almost entirely toward the "hard" sciences, such as biology, chemistry, and physics.[58]

Tony Tether, who served as DARPA's director from 2001 to 2009, exemplifies the agency's institutional disdain for the social sciences. Tether had little interest in anthropologists, sociologists, or psychologists unless they could produce data that could be plugged into a computer program.[59] Montgomery McFate, a cultural anthropologist who developed the US Army's Human Terrain System program, which embedded social scientists with combat brigades in Afghanistan and Iraq, described Tether as "very anti-social science." Even programs purportedly designed to predict

Figure 14. DARPA has launched various initiatives, including its Insight program, to help analyze large datasets using machine learning and prediction algorithms. Photo courtesy of DARPA.

armed conflict were viewed with skepticism. According to McFate, Tether was "not exactly supportive" of social science programs like DARPA's Pre-Conflict Anticipation and Shaping initiative, even though it was managed by an electrical engineer, Robert Popp.[60]

But by 2013, DARPA had begun to take interest in a particular kind of social science—the kind capable of making sense of big data. DARPA director Arita Prabhakar, testifying before a US House subcommittee, stressed how the widespread deployment of sensor technologies necessitated "efficient processing of streamed data."[61] She assured members of the subcommittee that DARPA intended to confront the persistent threat of weapons of mass destruction by launching new programs in "big data intelligence analytics."[62] Prabhakar's predecessor at DARPA, Regina Dugan, had already pushed the agency in this direction by funding Nexus7, a controversial and mostly classified counterinsurgency program that analyzed enormous amounts of data, ostensibly to predict insurgent attacks (see chapter 6).[63]

Russell had probably spent enough time in the Beltway to have acquired an intuitive sense of the agency's new priorities. If anthropology was still not quite fashionable at the "department of mad scientists," then the social sciences might be in need of a makeover.[64] DARPA project managers are essentially temporary workers—typically hired for three to five years before they're replaced by others, in order to periodically inject the agency with fresh blood and new ideas.[65] Russell had to prove his worth quickly if he wanted to stay at DARPA for more than a couple of years.

He had his work cut out for him. The agency had long been dominated by engineers, physicists, chemists, biologists, and other natural scientists, and many of them probably doubted the scientific rigor of the behavioral sciences. To make matters worse, a widely publicized "reproducibility crisis" was sweeping across America's largest and most influential social science—psychology.[66] The results of many, if not most, psychological experiments could not be consistently replicated—a devastating blow for those who had made exorbitant claims about the discipline's status as an objective science.[67]

Russell came up with a shrewd idea: to beat the nerds at their own game. Why not tackle them at the knees, rugby style, by using DARPA to help give a harder edge to the "soft" sciences? Within his first few months at the agency, Russell found a way to combine the Pentagon's growing obsession with using big data to predict conflict with an emphasis on solving the problem of replicability. If he succeeded, he might be able to open a pathway for psychologists, cognitive scientists, and others seeking to tap DARPA funding.

●   ●   ●   ●   ●   ●

It took less than a year for Russell to launch his debut program, modestly called Next Generation Social Science or NGS2. The initiative focused on the ways in which researchers might use huge datasets to conduct social science. DARPA's press release on NGS2 announced that the program would support the development of large-scale studies of human behavior by "harnessing virtual or alternate reality and massively distributed platforms" such as crowdsourcing for data collection. The agency touted the program as an effort to confront the reproducibility crisis.[68]

It's ironic that Russell, an anthropologist, would take up social science's existential crisis with such zeal. While some psychologists may have felt threatened by problems of replicability, many cultural anthropologists had recognized the futility of a rigid social science long before. For example, nearly half a century ago, Margaret Mead observed that in a nonexperimental field like anthropology, repeatability is a moot point. She wrote: "Cultures are swallowed up, remote, isolated human populations interbreed, rare languages vanish when the last two old women who speak them die, archaeological remains are destroyed by road-building and dam construction. The data can never be re-collected." Mead was blunt about the limitations of her discipline: "The explicit demand of the natural sciences that an experiment be replicable is simply impossible in anthropology. The nearest approach we can make to it is to preserve observations in as complete a form as possible."[69]

Officials at DARPA might have had a more immediate objective in launching NGS2: to uncover the mechanisms by which "collective identities" take shape, particularly in virtual domains. In an official description of the program, DARPA noted that NGS2 was aimed at examining "how a group of individuals becomes a unified whole, and how under certain circumstances that community breaks down into a chaotic mix of disconnected individuals."[70] Such questions were particularly salient at a time when ISIS had demonstrated an uncanny ability to radicalize young people using the internet and social media.

DARPA tended to award NGS2 funds to interdisciplinary teams consisting of psychologists, computer programmers, mathematicians, and cognitive scientists, particularly those developing computational modeling and simulation programs. For example, researchers from UC Berkeley were awarded nearly $4.8 million for a proposal called "Culture-on-a-Chip Computing: Crowdsourced Simulations of Culture, Group Formation, and Collective Identity."[71] Another team was awarded more than $5 million for a project entitled "The Statistical Mechanics of Crowds: Predictive Modeling in the Social Sciences," which relied partly on analysis of "public mood and emotion" as expressed by millions of Twitter users.[72]

Still another group, from Virginia Tech's Discovery Analytics Center and its Biocomplexity Institute, was awarded nearly $3 million for a proposal entitled "Montage: Capturing Collective Identity through

Multidisciplinary Modeling and Experimentation." In addition to creating games designed to gauge the ways in which individuals align themselves with group objectives, the project seeks to mine social media (specifically, from Twitter and Reddit) "to examine increased scales of collective identity effects—in particular, forming a collective identity for or against a cause or purpose."[73] It's not difficult to understand why DARPA would be interested in such projects—with military funding, some of the Virginia Tech researchers developed a framework that could supposedly be used to predict violent crowd behavior, based on data collected from Argentina, Brazil, Colombia, Paraguay, and Venezuela. They published the results of their research in an article, unambiguously titled "When Do Crowds Turn Violent? Uncovering Triggers from Media."[74]

Russell wasted no time in laying the groundwork for a follow-up. In September 2016, just a few months after NGS2 was announced, DARPA made a preliminary announcement intended to spark interest and ideas, called Forensic Social Science Supercollider, or FS3 for short. Like the famous particle accelerators that have become essential for testing the foundations of physics, it was pitched to the public as a system that would help social scientists test the accuracy of inferences about human social behavior, "with precision and certainty almost never available in the real world."[75]

FS3 overlapped to a degree with Russell's next DARPA program, Ground Truth. Like NGS2 and FS3, Ground Truth focused largely on modeling and simulation. However, the goal of Ground Truth was to create "objective testbeds for calibrating social science methods" used in simulations, "for testing the power and limitations of various social science modeling methods." It's likely that the DARPA program was meant to address claims that social scientists weren't serious enough about calibrating their research instruments or scientifically validating their results. DARPA's statements about Ground Truth were explicit about the ways in which the program's social science modeling and simulation projects might support military missions, including counterinsurgency operations.[76]

Russell managed yet another program, SCORE (Systematizing Confidence in Open Research and Evidence), in mid-2018. Like other DARPA initiatives managed by Russell, it was focused on addressing criticisms about the perceived unreliability of social science. According to the agency, SCORE was designed to explore algorithms that might assign a "confidence score to social and behavioral research"—a kind of credit score for social science work. By calibrating claims about social science literature, Pentagon personnel might be able to more effectively use reliable research for "enhancing deterrence, enabling stability, and reducing extremism." DARPA was clearly concerned about unreliable behavioral science research: "Taken in the context of growing numbers of journals, articles, and preprints, this current state of affairs could result in an SBS [social and behavioral science] consumer mistakenly over-relying on weak SBS research or dismissing strong SBS research entirely." Russell's newest program had admirers—including *Wired* magazine, which referred to SCORE as DARPA's "real, live, bullshit detector"—and the agency eventually awarded a joint contract worth $7.6 million to the nonprofit Center for Open Science, the University of Pennsylvania, and Syracuse University.[77]

• • • • • •

Even though many of these programs were geared toward salvaging psychology's bruised reputation, Russell succeeded in managing several initiatives that were more closely aligned with his own areas of expertise.

For example, in 2019, DARPA announced a program focused on human performance—with an artificial intelligence twist. TAILOR, or Teaching AI to Leverage Overlooked Residuals, sought to explore ways in which "third wave AI methods" might be used to optimize the performance of individuals and teams. According to the DARPA program solicitation, the Defense Department often uses universal recommendations for individuals, based on group averages. "The resulting interventions (e.g. diet, physical training regimen, brain stimulation) are at best suboptimal and at worst deleterious for each person" in a group.[78]

The agency announcement cited the Special Operations Command's Close Combat Lethality Task Force to illustrate the need for optimizing warfighter performance. The magazine *Breaking Defense* noted that the Task Force, brainchild of Defense Secretary James "Mad Dog" Mattis, "is dedicated to the premise that close combat soldiers are the ultimate athletes. . . . Thus the Task Force is dedicated to replicating an NFL sports science regime . . . [and] enhanc[ing] the ability of infantrymen to excel in the deadly skills of close combat."[79] Human performance optimization, in short, is about creating more efficient warfighters. Given the new, high-profile effort to maximize the physical, psychological, and cognitive capabilities of America's servicemen and servicewomen, Russell's experience as an athlete and an anthropologist gave him the credibility to help manage DARPA programming in this area.

Russell also tried adding some anthropology to the agency's portfolio before leaving DARPA in 2020.[80] In early 2018, the agency announced a new initiative called Understanding Group Biases (UGB) under his management, which might be seen as an effort to inject an explicitly cultural perspective into the agency's programs. DARPA's public announcement began with a definition of "cultural models"—cognitive frameworks that "impose structure on the world by classifying objective phenomena that might otherwise be incoherent, inconsistent, or inexplicable into subjective cultural categories."[81] The subtext seemed to be that culture can help the Defense Department and the armed services make sense of a tumultuous, confusing, chaotic world.

Citing the work of Clifford Geertz, the DARPA program description referred to these models as "webs of significance."[82] It also implied that Geertz's idea of "thick" description—that is, highly contextualized information about a specific culture—might be reconciled with big data's imperatives. The DARPA document lays bare the processes by which ethnographic perspectives might be hammered into instruments to be used by military consumers:

> [A]nthropologists have traditionally tried to capture these cultural models using largely qualitative methods. . . . Ethnography is an approach that often relies on interviews, longitudinal engagement, and participant observation to try to capture "the native's point of view." However, ethnography suffers from significant limitations. This largely qualitative, often in situ study of humans—which results in "thick data"—is often resource-intensive . . . [and] limited in scope, scale, and speed. . . . In the context of these limitations, ethnography's "thick data" stand in contrast to current "big data" approaches, which leverage the explosion of digital text and other media and are increasingly common in computational social science and network science. . . . DARPA hypothesizes that there may be new opportunities for overcoming this current trade-off between qualitative, "thick" data and quantitative, "big" data . . . in part by leveraging big data via media sources and cultural texts.[83]

The UGB program didn't lead to any immediate revolution in the way most social scientists understand biases, but it did result in at least two DARPA contracts. The agency awarded one of these to Minneapolis-based company Smart Information Flow Technologies, for developing MARGARET, or Multidimensional Algorithm Generated Anthropological Recording and Ethnographic Tool.[84] The principal investigator, Sonja Schmer-Galunder, has a master's degree in anthropology from Lund University in Sweden and is involved with SocialSim, a long-running DARPA program focused on social simulation software. For MARGARET, Schmer-Galunder and her colleagues partnered with a Stanford computer scientist specializing in mining massive online datasets.[85]

DARPA awarded another UGB contract to two computer scientists, Yu-Ru Lin and Rebecca Hwa, and educational psychologist Wen-Ting Chung, all from the University of Pittsburgh. Their grant, worth nearly $1 million, funded a project called "TRIBAL: A Tripartite Model for Group Bias Analytics," which seeks to "reveal biases of different groups or cultures by analyzing social media data with cutting-edge methods of natural language processing and machine learning." The "cutting-edge methods" relied on "social theories on how groups' cultural mindset [sic] are shaped across three theoretically grounded facets including value, emotion, and context."[86]

Such proposals reveal the extreme reductionism that is part and parcel of the military metaphysic. Researchers reduce ambiguous and elusive social constructs to simple variables that can be quantified and ultimately fed into computer models that can supposedly illuminate "biases of different groups or cultures."[87] If we're to believe the programmers, computational wizardry can pack Geertzian thick description tightly into algorithms that, over time, will be able to diagnose bias, foresee political unrest, and perhaps even predict armed conflict—all for the protection of the free world. As we'll see in the next chapter, such projects are already well under way.

6 Precogs, Inc.

Imagine a computer program that tells its users which neighborhoods in a faraway city—Kabul, Aleppo, Sanaa, Mogadishu, or Tel Aviv—are most dangerous. The software predicts whether these neighborhoods are prone to riots, gun violence, sniper attacks, or suicide bombings, and it even foresees when such events are likely to occur. With all the speed and imagery of a video game, it also identifies the names of probable participants in the violence, as well as their addresses, fingerprints, and photo IDs, along with names of their relatives, friends, and close associates.

Such a program might appear to be beyond the realm of possibility, but the Pentagon has spent many millions of dollars in a quest to find this technological holy grail.

Consider, for example, the case of a group of computer scientists and mathematicians that became obsessed with the idea of creating a "social radar" capable of detecting political instability at home and abroad. About a decade ago, this group, which had close ties to the Defense Department, was convinced that if such a device could aggregate enough real-time data from radio, television, newspapers, websites, cell phones, social media, and other sources, they might be able to accurately foresee conflicts ranging from protests to ethnic violence to insurgency and war. By collecting

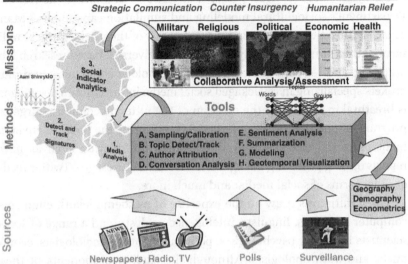

Figure 15. "Social radar" was a predictive modeling concept popularized by the US Air Force's chief scientist, and this PowerPoint slide highlights its components. Photo courtesy of US Air Force/Mark Maybury.

and synthesizing vast amounts of political, economic, sociocultural, personal, and biometric data from around the world, those developing the technology hoped to detect "changing trends in population perceptions . . . [and] to forecast who will cluster with whom in a network, where, and when in what kinds of relationships."[1] A prominent architect of the social radar concept noted that the technology should be designed "to see into the hearts and minds of people."[2] Others suggested that in order to be effective, social radar would need "a dashboard of socio-cultural indicators created from online news, blogs, and social media data processed at scale, as well as decision support tools."[3]

The pursuit of social radar was a modest part of a much more ambitious effort involving multiple Pentagon offices, including the Defense Advanced Research Projects Agency (DARPA), the Office of Naval Research (ONR), the Combating Terrorism Technical Support Office

(CTTSO), the Army Research Laboratory (ARL), and the Office of the Secretary of Defense's Human Social Culture Behavior Modeling Program (HSCB), the latter of which was created in 2008 to improve the Defense Department's sociocultural modeling and simulation capabilities.[4] Many other organizations have been involved: a few of the world's largest military contract firms (and many small ones); university-based research laboratories; and telecom giants, internet technology companies, and data brokers specializing in repackaged social media information. The end goal is breathtaking in scope: the creation of the ultimate counterinsurgency program, a tool capable of continuously monitoring the political environment for social unrest—using open-source information such as news reports or blog posts; big data gathered from text messages, Twitter feeds, or other forms of social media; and much more.

These initiatives draw on the expertise of mathematicians, engineers, computer scientists, linguists, intelligence analysts, and a range of social scientists including psychologists, political scientists, sociologists, economists, and anthropologists. Although the leading proponents of these programs tend to have backgrounds in engineering, math, and computer programming, they fully recognize the need to work with "subject matter experts" from the social sciences.[5]

To make sense of all this, it's helpful to learn technical terms from fields as diverse as business, applied mathematics, and military studies—terms such as *sociometrics, activity-based intelligence, agent-based modeling,* and *human domain,* to name a few. It's also helpful to understand different models used to analyze data—Bayesian statistical models, agent-based models, epidemiological models, and others.[6]

The programs appeal to multiple constituencies within the Defense Department. For example, the idea of social radar has been touted by battle-hardened intelligence officer Lieutenant General Michael Flynn, former director of the Defense Intelligence Agency, who briefly served as National Security Advisor in the Trump administration (see chapter 4)—but also by psychologist and retired US Navy Captain Dylan Schmorrow, who has dedicated much of his career to research in "augmented cognition."[7] The programs align neatly with new and old Pentagon trends, including a preference for high-tech computational approaches, a renewed interest in military applications of cultural knowledge, the rise of counterinsurgency theory and practice, the development of "network-centric warfare," an obsession with quantitative analysis, and long-standing interests in cybernetics and human-machine interfaces.

These sociocultural modeling programs provide insight into an institution with tremendous size and global influence. The Defense Department is the largest employer in America, with approximately 1.3 million servicemembers, 1.1 million reservists, and more than 700,000 civilian employees worldwide. These numbers don't account for additional defense contractors working at military bases in dozens of countries. The Pentagon has an annual budget of more than $700 billion, and its activities affect billions of people around the globe.

Sociocultural modeling and simulation programs also illustrate how the virtual lives of *Homo sapiens*—our online musings, blogs, posts, likes, tweets, and email messages—are being rapidly integrated into economic and military databases whether we are aware of it or not. It's not only Facebook and Amazon that follow our digital footprints—so, too, do military and intelligence agencies and their subcontractors. Although these agencies have a long history of secretly intercepting private communications—by steaming letters open, wiretapping telephones, and bugging rooms with hidden cameras or microphones, for example—data mining is dramatically different in terms of scale and scope.

These programs also have important implications for the social sciences. It's likely that military and intelligence agencies will aggressively recruit social scientists of all kinds—students and professionals, practitioners and academics—for modeling and forecasting work in the near future.[8]

WEAPONIZING CULTURE

Researchers developed predictive modeling programs during a period marked by anxieties about military and intelligence officials' inability to grasp cultural knowledge in the post-9/11 period. A significant effect was the Pentagon's renewed interest in cultural and ethnographic data. This manifested itself in many ways, including initiatives designed to embed social scientists with combat brigades, culture "smart cards" and other heuristic devices, and new funding sources for social science research tailored to military consumption.[9] In 2006, the Office of the Secretary of Defense set into motion a series of directives that eventually led to the creation of the HSCB program.[10] The objective was "to develop a science base and associated technologies for modeling human, social and cultural behavior . . . [and] to enable DoD and the US Government to understand and effectively operate in the human terrain during non-conventional warfare and other missions."[11]

Other Pentagon agencies and research centers—not only those mentioned above but also the Air Force Office of Scientific Research, the Army Training and Doctrine Command, the Defense Intelligence Agency, and many more—began to fund similar initiatives at about the same time. The emphasis on quantification, predictive modeling, and computational systems stretches back more than fifty years, as the Pentagon relied on the efforts of the RAND Corporation and, later, its own Office of Net Assessment to create high-tech forecasting tools.[12] Contemporary predictive modeling programs are the most recent manifestations of these long-term projects.

By 2010, all branches of the armed forces (except the Coast Guard) and the Defense Department's research centers had begun experimenting with sociocultural modeling for training military personnel, analyzing intelligence, and predicting future conflict scenarios. Since then, billions of dollars have been distributed to defense corporations, university-based academics, and federally funded research centers for sociocultural modeling. Though some funding has been used for basic research, much of it has been directed toward product development: software packages, video games, databases, visualization tools, virtual training platforms, and other technologies useful for the combatant commands (such as CENTCOM and SOUTHCOM), troops on the ground, or other Pentagon "customers." Political events have sparked the growth of new predictive modeling projects in recent years, most notably the Arab Spring, the rise of ISIS, China's growing global influence and technological development, and Russia's reemergence as a global superpower.[13]

Despite the fact that HSCB was phased out in 2013 in accordance with its original plan, today the Defense Department's predictive modeling programs appear to be larger than ever. Over the past decade, the Pentagon has supported an enormous number of projects, ranging from basic academic research to technology development and acquisition contracts subject to competitive bidding.

Several professional anthropologists were involved in planning during the early stages, according to a summary of a July 2008 HSCB workshop convened at the National Defense University in Washington, DC.[14] The potential value of social scientific approaches was recognized at several points throughout the workshop. For example, the final report discussed "thick ethnography" and ways in which thick description might be incorporated into behavioral modeling: "The involvement of more social scientists requires that social scientists become re-educated. . . . [C]ultural anthropologists should not be discounted. Rather, actual working workshops in which ethnographers partner with modelers to build a few prototypes are needed." A different part of the report noted that "far more [social scientists], particularly anthropologists, should be part of the endeavor."[15]

By 2010, the director of the Defense Department's nascent HSCB program recognized that the Pentagon had a significant gap in the area of "sociology/anthropology for irregular warfare and support ops."[16] The message was clear: the Pentagon needed sociocultural knowledge to fight terrorists, non-state actors, and other potential threats to American interests.

PROTEST = PATHOLOGY

To get a better sense of how industry has been shaped by Defense Department imperatives, it's helpful to focus on a company that has responded frequently to the Pentagon's call for sociocultural modeling and forecasting. Aptima is a defense contractor based in the Boston suburb of Woburn, Massachusetts, and its motto, "Human-Centered Engineering," is appropriate given the academic qualifications of its 120 employees: many, if not most, have graduate degrees in psychology, computer science, linguistics, or engineering.[17]

Shortly after its founding, Aptima secured Pentagon contracts for research on team decision-making processes, but by 2006 many of its employees were specializing in sociocultural modeling. Consequently, Aptima was well positioned to respond to the Defense Department's "cultural turn," and it received multiple contracts in this area. For a partial list of predictive modeling projects secured by Aptima and other defense contractors, see table 2.

Among the earliest Aptima contracts was SCIPR, a software program that reportedly determined cultural identities and predicted popular responses to hypothetical US military actions. According to a project summary, "SCIPR draws on cultural anthropology to understand how cultural identities are defined and how they may change over time in response to events."[18]

Aptima researchers designed other projects for processing large amounts of information to predict future events. For example, STAR (Semantic Temporal Association Retrieval) combined "methods for digesting masses of textual data" with "temporal analysis techniques for making predictions." Researchers created another program, called MIST (Models of Information and Sentiment Transmission), to take open-source data and use automated language processors to gauge public sentiment and to "extract entities and high-level concepts" to find "memes, or units of cultural information about the attitudes and opinions" of people in different societies, especially the Middle East, as "recent uprisings in the Arab world have highlighted the importance of early warning capabilities to detect areas of potential instability." Similarly, FACETS (Forecasting Activity through Cultural, Epidemiological, and Temporal Semantics) would "forecast likely opinion changes of individuals and groups [in repsonse] to certain events. . . . [It] will be rooted in theories of social identity and influence to better shape the sociocultural landscape of a given population."[19]

Perhaps Aptima's most publicized project was E-MEME (Epidemiological Modeling of the Evolution of MEssages), a web-based software package that used epidemiological models to track the movements of "infectious" ideas through Twitter, blogs, and other electronic media, "helping model and forecast how sentiment can spread over time and place to influence susceptible populations." Robert McCormack, the

Table 2 US Department of Defense Predictive Modeling and Simulation Programs
(Partial List)

Program Acronym and Name	Developer	Description
AARDVARK *Adaptive Agents for Real-time Data-driven Visualization and Analysis for Relevant Knowledge*	Aptima	Agent-based visualizations for operational planning and effects assessment
ASPEN *Agent-based System Produced Emergent Networks*	Charles River Analytics	Social media analysis and influence operations support tool
CADSIM *COA Analysis by Integration of Decision and Social Influence Modeling*	Perceptronics Solutions	Modeling and simulation for military COA (courses of action); potential "futures"
CAMPHOR *Cultural Agent Model to Predict inHabitant Opinion Reactions*	Aptima	Simulation of "cultural dynamics" to gauge effects of Special Operations Forces on public opinion
C-CAT *Cross-Cultural Awareness Tool*	361 Interactive	Modeling behavioral cognitive competence of military personnel in cross-cultural settings
DignityTRAC	NSI, Inc.	Framework for analyzing "dignity as a key variable associated with people's strong emotional and behavioral responses to events"
E-MEME *Epidemiological Modeling of the Evolution of Messages*	Aptima	Tracking and modeling flows of social media and messages using epidemiological modeling
ERIS *Ethnic Conflict, Repression, and Social Strife*	NSI, Inc.	Simulation of population dynamics, including social conflict
Face2Face	V-Com 3D	Three-dimensional simulated scenarios for recognition of "insider threats," cultural competency, etc.
Gleaner	SoarTech	Conflict modeling and forecasting for commander-level decision-makers

(continued)

Table 2 (continued)

Program Acronym and Name	Developer	Description
GUARDS *Goal-Driven Users and Agents for Recognition Discovery and Synthesis of Knowledge*	Edaptive Computing	Analysis of large-scale datasets for intelligence analysis
MAMBA *Modeling and Algorithmic Methods for Behavior Anticipation*	Edaptive Computing	"Predictive analytics" tool for military commanders
OCCAM *Organizational and Cultural Criteria for Adversary Modeling*	Charles River Analytics	Modeling and simulation guide for "assessing, analyzing, and forecasting human behavior"
PRISM *Planning, Research, Intelligence Scalable Modeling System*	BAE Systems	Modeling software that "supports analysis of the topography, planning, and anticipation of the effects of US actions"
PSKT *Power-Structure Tool Kit*	Soar Technology	Simulation of human network dynamics and projection of future behavior
RAMBO *Real-Time Analysis of Motivations and Behaviors for Operations*	Aptima	Tool for visual analytics; "an intelligent dashboard to help visualize multisource information"
RiftLand	George Mason University, Office of Naval Research	Agent-based model incorporating cultural data for modeling responses to disasters and crises
RIPPLE *Reactive Information Propagation Planning for Lifelike Exercises*	Concurrent Technologies Corporation	Analyzing and integrating geospatial data for military planning
SAVANT *Susceptibility and Vulnerability Analysis Tool*	Charles River Analytics	Assessing, analyzing, and forecasting human behavior

(continued)

Table 2   (continued)

Program Acronym and Name	Developer	Description
SCARE *Spatio-Cultural Abductive Reasoning Engine*	Lab for Computational Cultural Dynamics (University of Maryland)	Predicting attacks, location of "high-value targets" using geospatial and cultural data
SCIPR *Simulation of Cultural Identities for Prediction of Reactions*	Aptima	Simulation tool enabling users to ask "what-if questions in order to gauge the effects of alternative courses of action on identities and beliefs"
SentiBility	SentiMetrix	Predicting future stability of countries and governments, based on news and social media
SIMPL	Strategic Analysis Enterprises	Forecasting program to "parse and geo-locate dynamic events data at the sub-national level"
V-CAT *Virtual Cultural Awareness Trainer*	Alelo	Virtual culture and language training, and role-playing software
V-SAFT *Virtual Strategic Analysis and Forecasting Tool*	Lustick Consulting	Virtual sociocultural models, forecasting
VIBES *Visualization of Belief Systems*	Alion Science	Forecasting, prediction of "effects of new strategies and tactics on a society [and] awareness of the level of risk"
W-ICEWS *Worldwide Integrated Crisis Early Warning System*	Lockheed-Martin	Monitoring, assessing, and forecasting international crises

project's principal investigator, drew an explicit analogy between protests and uprisings on the one hand and contagious diseases and epidemics on the other:

> We witnessed the profound power of ideas to replicate in what began as anti-government sentiment in Tunisia, then moved like a virus, reaching and influencing new groups in Egypt, Syria, and Libya. . . . Public health has used epidemiology for years to identify the origin and spread of illness through populations. If we can better understand the flow of ideas through electronic channels to sway the perceptions of groups, we may be better prepared to develop appropriate strategies, such as supporting democratic movements or perhaps dissuading suicide bombers.[20]

It's not clear why Aptima's researchers used such a model, which assumes that ideas, sentiments, and dissent (even dissent against illegitimate governments) are comparable to contagion. Why assume that ideas are like viruses or bacterial infections? What is an appropriate "vaccine"? The analogy seems questionable at best. An Aptima press release elaborated:

> Aptima's LaVA platform for text analytics scours large sets of Internet data sources and documents to characterize and quantify . . . "protests" and "elections." Epidemiological models might capture the dynamics of the growing voice of opposition, as it occurs hourly, daily, and weekly, mapping where the sentiment is diffusing, and its potential to influence predisposed populations elsewhere. Such models may help forecast both where and when violent protests and potential uprisings are most likely to spark.[21]

An intriguing aspect of E-MEME was Aptima's partnership with a small Virginia-based company, Circinus LLC, on the project. Circinus specializes in intelligence analysis, and its executive staff members have extensive experience in either special operations or intelligence. For example, Circinus's cofounder Carson Edmondson conducted psychological operations during the US occupation of Iraq. The company's contracts included the provision of intelligence support to American forces, ranging from "targeting officers" to "human intelligence analysts" to "combined information data network exchange operators."[22]

Circinus's website claimed that it was providing expertise to Aptima, but questions remain about the nature of the partnership. Given the fact that E-MEME was designed for "shaping or changing perceptions," is it possible that Circinus deployed its psyops and Special Ops expertise for the project?[23]

Equally intriguing was the involvement of Circinus and Aptima (and the pharmaceutical company Abbott Laboratories, among others) in INSIGHT, a $12.7 million project funded by the US Intelligence Advanced Research Projects Agency (IARPA), aimed at helping intelligence personnel "reason through complex, ambiguous and often novel problems common to the Intelligence Community."[24] INSIGHT was characterized as an "integrative system for enhancing fluid intelligence through human cognitive activity, fitness, high-definition transcranial direct-current brain stimulation, and nutritional intervention," and its researchers boldly claimed that their goal was to "build a better brain."[25]

Dozens of other companies are also involved in modeling and forecasting, including Soar Technologies, Charles River Analytics, Perceptronics, Lustick Consulting, 361 Interactive, and more. Though these firms aren't widely known to the public, they are at the forefront of a rapidly multiplying field. This is ironic, given the lack of evidence that predictive modeling programs work as advertised. Despite thousands of contracts awarded to defense firms over the past decade, Pentagon officials and US intelligence agencies have been surprised by many unanticipated events, including the Arab Spring and the rapid rise of the self-styled Islamic State of Iraq and Syria.

Given these facts, it's reasonable to assume that a crucial, if unstated, function of these programs is to grease the wheels of the military-industrial machine. New surveillance technologies and sensors have inundated the Pentagon and the US Intelligence Community with data, and there's no easy way to analyze it all. Defense companies are more than willing to help—for a price. Contractors adopt a tried-and-true strategy: keep busy, sound smart, get paid. Repeat as necessary. Under these conditions, as Kerry Fosher (an anthropologist working in the national security sector) writes, culture becomes a commodity:

> National security organizations are good at acquiring things: weapons, supplies, classes and data. Budget cycles and line items are set up for buying. Program offices are arranged to make it happen. . . . [C]ulture is described as a *thing*. It is described as data or as a skill that can be acquired by hiring consultants. . . . [T]his discourse leads many people in the security sector to conclude that culture is something that can be bought or contracted out.[26]

Over the long run, those most affected by modeling and forecasting programs may well be US taxpayers who are stuck with the tab.

.   .   .   .   .

Like Aptima, some companies and university research centers have successfully recruited anthropologists, psychologists, and other social scientists to help develop and refine their models. For example, in 2013, Carnegie Mellon University's Center for Computational Analysis of Social and Organizational Systems undertook a project aimed at "extracting sociocultural networks of the Sudan" by combing through forty thousand articles published in an English-language Sudanese newspaper.[27] The researchers, who were mostly sociologists, worked with an anthropological team led by Richard Lobban of Rhode Island College. The team "examined the tribal affiliation networks that we [Carnegie Mellon researchers] had extracted from the text data and marked the changes that they considered necessary in order to correct for false negatives and positives in the data."[28] The Carnegie Mellon researchers are also developing "rapid ethnographic retrieval (RER)" technologies, including an "RER thesaurus" (with the help of anthropologist Jeffrey C. Johnson of East Carolina University), which is reportedly based on the Human Relations Area Files and "associated terms and concepts that subject matter experts have identified as being crucial for answering questions about the culture of groups and societies."[29]

Sometimes anthropologists have worked directly for predictive modeling companies. For example, shortly after Robert Popp founded National Security Innovations (NSI) in 2007, he hired anthropologist Lawrence Kuznar (Indiana University–Purdue University Fort Wayne) as chief cultural sciences officer. NSI describes itself as a "human behavior analysis" company and has landed multiple contracts since its creation, many of which have been awarded by Pentagon agencies or defense contractors such as BAE Systems, BBN/Raytheon, and Science Applications International Corporation.

The extent to which Kuznar has been involved in NSI's projects isn't clear. If anything, it seems that he has been circumspect about these programs. Among Kuznar's papers is a cross-cultural comparison of prediction. In the concluding section, he paraphrases Bronisław Malinowski:

"Prediction, in the form of divination, is nearly universal in human societies, and often appears to provide a degree of psychological assurance used to deal with uncertainty and randomness, rather than provide any scientifically defensible predictions about the empirical world." He continues: "When beliefs in predictions become dogmatic and not adjustable in light of new data, the benefits of prediction are lost and whole societies can be destroyed due to a collectively held fantasy."[30]

Others have also expressed skepticism about computer programmers' claims regarding the accuracy of predictive models. Some Defense Department anthropologists have attempted to stem the tide of sociocultural modeling and simulation efforts. According to one (speaking on condition of anonymity), "it would be much worse if there was nobody pushing back . . . [by] refusing to sponsor or transition [modeling and simulation] projects." And according to Kerry Fosher,

> we do not have the basic science that would allow us to render complex cross-cultural practices into computer algorithms, nor does the nature of knowledge about culture allow it to be parsed for storage in databases. Yet, we continue to fund these projects as though such scientific realities were irrelevant. Projects are described as though it is just a matter of getting the programming right and then we will have the ability to store information about culture, to analyze it, to predict behavior.[31]

In 2011, as Pentagon researchers and contractors were rapidly developing similar programs, anthropologist Robert Albro noted: "I am not saying that computational social science is voodoo science. I'm saying that voodoo science is all too frequently being generated from the work of computational social science. . . . [The technology] does not answer our questions for us. It does not solve that dilemma of what decision I need to make."[32] Hugh Gusterson raised an even more troubling critique. "Are we going to detain someone if a computer predicts that he will become an insurgent?" he asked. "The real danger of models is their seductiveness. They can be so realistic and powerful that it is easy to forget they are just a model, and then start to rely on them more and more."[33]

These observations raise a larger point about the ways in which expert discourses on terrorism and the figure of "the terrorist" are permeated by magical thinking, taboos, and fear of witchcraft. For example, when counterterrorism experts and computer scientists with security clearances develop behavioral modeling software and data-driven programs designed to predict terrorist attacks, their initial premise is that they should never see, listen to, or get close to their subjects—much less understand them as *people*—lest they be infected by the terrorist's ideological contagion. Another example of the counterterrorist's mystical fantasy world is the idea that big data, predictive analytics, and machine learning absolve the counterterrorism expert of knowing anything of substance about the basic cultural contexts in which the insurgent or militant thinks, or believes, or acts.[34]

.   .   .   .   .   .

The Pentagon's sociocultural modeling, simulation, and forecasting programs have grown at an extraordinary pace. Much of this work relies on processing big data—that is, massive quantities of digital information easily shared across communication networks—with new data analytics tools. According to Hal Varian, chief economist at Google, "between the dawn of civilization and 2003, we only created five exabytes of information; now we're creating that amount every two days."[35] The so-called data revolution is largely due to recent innovations, including

> the plethora of digital devices encountered in homes, workplaces and public spaces; mobile, distributed and cloud computing; social media; and the internet of things (internetworked sensors and devices). These new technical media and platforms are leading to ever more aspects of everyday life—work, consumption, travel, communication, leisure—and the worlds we inhabit [being] captured as data and mediated through data-driven technologies.[36]

It's in this context that computational social science has arisen, and that predictive modeling has evolved. The application of these technologies to law enforcement evokes the possibility of real-life "Precognitives" or "Precogs." In Philip K. Dick's science fiction story "The Minority Report," the Precogs were clairvoyant mutants with the ability to foresee crimes before they occurred.

Despite the fundamental flaws built into the Defense Department's high-tech counterinsurgency programs, not all social scientists have been critical of the potential misuses of such projects. In fact, some have embraced them.

PRE-CRIME

Among those directly involved in the development of predictive modeling programs is archaeologist Jeffrey Brantingham, who has played a leading role in the use of computational social science to anticipate criminal activity. His entrepreneurial approach may be a bellwether of applied anthropology in the twenty-first century.

Several years ago, Brantingham cofounded a company called PredPol (short for "predictive policing"), located in Santa Cruz, just outside of Silicon Valley. He currently sits on the company's board of directors and serves as its chief of research and design. Over a decade ago, Brantingham began collaborating with mathematician Andrea Bertozzi to develop algorithms for predicting when and where crimes are likely to occur. In 2006, the National Science Foundation awarded them a grant to develop technology for forecasting crime hot spots in Los Angeles, using historical police data.[37]

The Defense Department was also interested. In 2006, the Pentagon began awarding grants to Brantingham and Bertozzi for similar projects. Soon the researchers were comparing California gang violence to Iraqi insurgent attacks, and by 2010 the Defense Department had awarded them more than $1 million to study "dynamic models of insurgent activity" and "information fusion of human activity and social networks."[38] Later, Brantingham and Bertozzi were awarded grants from the Army Research Office, the National Geospatial Intelligence Agency, and the Air Force Office of Scientific Research for related projects.[39]

Brantingham has made occasional references to the ways in which anthropology informs his predictive models. His analogies are sometimes dubious:

> Criminal offenders are essentially hunter-gatherers; they forage for opportunities to commit crimes. . . . The behaviors that a hunter-gatherer uses to choose a wildebeest versus a gazelle are the same calculations a criminal uses to choose a Honda versus a Lexus. . . . An insurgent who wants to place an IED (improvised explosive device) in a particular location will make the same kind of calculations that a car thief will use in choosing which car to steal.[40]

Let's take a look at this assertion in more detail. Brantingham claims that thieves prefer cheap Hondas over luxurious Lexuses because stealing them requires less energy expenditure, and therefore provides greater reward, in relation to expended effort or energy—in much the same way that foragers hypothetically prefer wildebeests over antelopes. Though most cultural anthropologists (and wildlife biologists) would probably be skeptical of this idea, the editors of *Crime Science Journal* were impressed enough to publish an article summarizing Brantingham's work.[41]

A more critical view would question the validity of Brantingham's analogy. Ethnographic accounts of hunting practices—for example, among the Hadza people of Tanzania—indicate that foragers aren't rational-choice robots. Their hunting expeditions are deeply embedded within patterns of cooperative work, reciprocal food-sharing, and ideas about masculinity, among other things.[42] The motivations of car thieves are equally complex and shaped by cultural dynamics, but Brantingham's model doesn't account for such nuances. It's another example of how flawed assumptions and poorly conceived models can lead to questionable results.

Although the extent to which the military has used Brantingham's work is not clear, PredPol's products have been used by dozens of police departments across America and elsewhere. The company markets its software as a way to improve efficiency. This is appealing in many parts of the United States as police departments face budgetary cutbacks and layoffs. PredPol advertises its products as having "a proven track record of crime reduction," and its website lists cities that recorded lower crime rates after adopting the software.[43] However, PredPol reportedly requires its clients to refer the company to other law enforcement agencies and provide officers to appear in endorsements.[44]

There are many concerns about the application of such technologies. Because PredPol's algorithms are based on historical crime data, its predictions are likely to become self-fulfilling prophecies, resulting in increased surveillance of poor neighborhoods. In the words of Hamid Khan, an outspoken critic of police surveillance programs, "there's a clear bias that is inherent because it can only predict the information that is being uploaded. . . . [I]t's garbage in, garbage out."[45] In other words,

Figure 16. Citizens take to the streets of Ferguson, Missouri, in August 2014 to protest the killing of Michael Brown, an African American teenager shot by a white police officer. Photo courtesy of Jamelle Bouie/CC-BY-2.0.

predictive policing software is prone to algorithmic bias (which we'll explore in more detail in chapter 7). Significantly, a number of statisticians and criminologists doubt PredPol's claims about its ability to reduce crime.[46]

PredPol and similar technologies coincide with a broader militarization of American society. At the same time that police are being outfitted with military-grade equipment—assault rifles and armored personnel carriers, for example—many are now adopting technologies developed with tax-payer-funded Pentagon research and repackaged for domestic use by private firms. This is profoundly changing the ways in which police departments patrol and pacify America's cities. According to Kade Crockford of the American Civil Liberties Union of Massachusetts, there is a trend toward "para-militarizing our police, turning all of them into robocops who take directions from computers as to how they go about their day.... Policing shouldn't be influenced by corporate interests that profit from big data and that have an obvious interest in promoting these new technologies."[47] The Black Lives Matter movement and thousands of protests that have occurred throughout America in recent years have demonstrated, among other things, how militarized policing makes it more likely for local law enforcement agencies to escalate conflict and aggravate racial tensions.

·   ·   ·   ·   ·

Some scientists view predictive modeling as a way of avoiding conflict and war. They argue that if military leaders can anticipate the next global hot spot, then steps can be taken to mitigate future conflict. For example, Barry Silverman, a University of Pennsylvania engineering professor, argues: "War is the worst-case scenario. The goal is to resolve things long before that."[48]

Silverman has spent more than a decade developing behavior-modeling software designed to uncover terrorists' motivations and their networks. The programs integrate models and theories from the social sciences and combine them with empirical data culled from medical and social science research. Simulations represent "physical stressors such as ambient temperature, hunger, and drug use; resources such as time, money, and skills; attitudes such as moral outlook, religious feelings, and political affiliations; and personality dispositions such as response to time pressure, workload, and anxiety."[49] Among Silverman's best-known programs is NonKin Village, a training game that uses cultural data to create interactive avatars designed to help players experience foreign cultures and sensitize them to local customs.[50] The software appeals to some people because, like online education, it offers the prospect of cheaply and efficiently delivering cultural "content" to large numbers of learners. Such products betray a rigid yet seductive engineering ethos that fits comfortably with certain social science theories (structural functionalism, rational choice theory, game theory, and social network theory, for example). When a village or a country—or even the entire world—can be taken apart and reassembled into tidy mechanical structures, social engineering appears as a real possibility, not just an illusion. In the words of Gary Ackerman, a terrorism expert with a doctoral degree in war studies, these are tools to "build a world in a bottle."[51]

Figure 17. Predictive modeling and simulation programs, such as MetaVR's Virtual Afghanistan Village, have become an important tool for training US and NATO forces. Photo courtesy of W. Garth Smith/MetaVR Inc.

What happens when a virtual program is recruited for real-world battlefields? When Silverman was launching NonKin Village, he was approached by an unnamed US government agency that asked him to create a model of a real village in Afghanistan—and its inhabitants—using data collected on the ground. Silverman (who declined to state the agency's name) said, "This was not for training. It was for intel collection and analysis."[52] This apparently did not dissuade Silverman—he received initial funding from the agency, and was reportedly awaiting a second grant to complete the model. "I think the goal in the long run would be just to crank out village after village," he said.[53]

At about the same time the undisclosed agency was soliciting Silverman, DARPA was undertaking an ambitious predictive modeling project for use in Afghanistan. It came to be known as Nexus7. But before examining that program, let's consider the rise of big data in the service of national security.

COMPUTATIONAL COUNTERINSURGENCY

The Worldwide Integrated Crisis Early Warning System (W-ICEWS) may be the biggest sociocultural modeling initiative of all. It began in 2006 as ICEWS, a DARPA project involving hundreds of scientists from private and public organizations. (The name cleverly references the Pentagon's Ballistic Missile Early Warning System developed during the Cold War—a chain of twelve massive radars designed to detect incoming Soviet missiles.) From the early stages, defense giant Lockheed Martin took a leading role in coordinating the project. Like other predictive modeling programs, ICEWS was originally designed to foretell international crises, ethnic violence, rebellions, and insurgencies.[54] However, unlike most other programs, ICEWS was developed for Defense Department planners—particularly those in the combatant commands—once it made the transition to a "program of record." It was also unusual in terms of cost: by early 2011, DARPA had spent nearly $40 million on the program. In 2012, the Office of Naval Research awarded Lockheed Martin an additional $8.5 million to continue the project as W-ICEWS.[55] According to Pentagon insiders, it was extraordinarily accurate—though apparently not accurate enough to predict the Egyptian uprising that led to the toppling of Hosni Mubarak, or the emergence of ISIS in the Middle East, or Russia's invasion of Crimea.[56]

An unusual feature of W-ICEWS is its reliance on multiple models: "agent-based" (in which experts are consulted to create computerized versions of real-world decision-makers and political players), "macro-structural" (in which demographic, economic, and other data are collated), and "event data" (in which news reports are combed and fed into language processors).[57] It's also unusual because it uses social science theories to analyze the data.[58]

Lockheed Martin's website designers chose a revealing set of photos to illustrate the program: two of the three images feature young women holding protest placards. The photos appear to have been taken in American or European cities. The third image is a long-range shot of an Arab Spring–style protest, with hundreds of people visible in the frame. The subtext communicates an unambiguous message: W-ICEWS can predict protests whether at home or abroad. The website has little substantive information about the program other than a brief summary. It describes W-ICEWS's four components, named as if they were proprietary Apple products: iData, a database holding approximately thirty million news stories from six thousand global publications; iTrace, which uses open-source documents to monitor worldwide political activity; iCast, a software program that "provides six-month rolling forecasts for destabilizing Events of Interest (EOI) for 167 countries"; and iSent, a means of "tracking regional sentiment by exploiting social media as an intelligence source."[59]

As mentioned earlier, the data scientists and counterterrorism experts who are creating these kinds of programs appear to be making a remarkable assumption: that massive amounts of digital information hold within them the key to predicting the future—*if* the right algorithms can be developed. The problem is that there's no real evidence that the accumulation of more and more data can help us understand the underlying motivations or actions of human beings. To get an idea about what potential insurgents or militants in Egypt or Afghanistan or Yemen are thinking, or what they might do, you really need to talk with them—and get to know them as fellow humans, with hopes, fears, and aspirations just like anyone else. When you take a hard look at the Pentagon's predictive modeling projects, beyond the slick websites and PowerPoint slides, they reveal themselves as bizarre forms of magic cloaked in the mantle of science—high-tech numerology, digital sorcery for twenty-first-century war planners.[60]

·   ·   ·   ·   ·

If W-ICEWS was the most visible predictive modeling tool created for the military, then Nexus7 was among the most secretive. DARPA director Regina Dugan forcefully promoted the program and eventually convinced US military intelligence officers in Afghanistan to use it. Nexus7 was "a war-zone surveillance effort [that] ties together everything from spy radars to fruit prices in order to glean clues about Afghan instability." It gathered "hundreds of existing data sources from multiple agencies" to create "population-centric, cultural intelligence."[61]

Since its creation, Nexus7 went virtually unnoticed by the public. According to one report, DARPA contracted three companies to implement Nexus7: Potomac Fusion, Data Tactics Corporation, and Caerus

Figure 18. The National Security Agency built the $1.5 billion Utah Data Center to process massive amounts of information it gathers from surveillance activities. Photo courtesy of Electronic Frontier Foundation/CC Zero.

Associates.[62] Government documents indicate that the Pentagon awarded related contracts to other companies, including Science Engineering Technology Associates, Terremark Federal Group (a subsidiary of Verizon Telecommunications), and Virginia-based Giant Oak.[63]

Nexus7's genealogy is linked to the National Security Agency (NSA). After the 9/11 attacks, the NSA began collecting phone records from millions of Americans and then initiated a program to process data on suspected terrorists collected from internet companies. US military and intelligence agencies spent $16 billion to organize the staggering amount of data, yet the NSA struggled to manage it.

The NSA began applying its techniques to a program called Real Time Regional Gateway (RTRG), which was implemented in Iraq in 2006.[64] RTRG gathered and analyzed information that included "phone conversations, military events, road-traffic patterns, public opinion—even the price of potatoes."[65] This was combined with data from drones equipped with high-resolution cameras capable of scanning expansive tracts of land.

NSA director Keith Alexander was hell-bent on getting "everything: every Iraqi text message, phone call and e-mail that could be vacuumed up by the agency's powerful computers."[66]

Veteran *Washington Post* journalist and editor Bob Woodward described RTRG as revolutionary: now "there was a way to capture all [Iraqi mobile phone and email] data, store it, and make it instantly available to intelligence analysts and operators, allowing the US to react quickly in response to the enemy. . . . [RTRG] gave the NSA an incredible exploitation capability—reading other people's mail, listening to their conversations, and sorting their data."[67]

Some military officials claimed that RTRG anticipated insurgent attacks with astonishing accuracy—attacks could reportedly be predicted 60–70 percent of the time. However, the criteria used to gauge this accuracy, and whether independent researchers ever evaluated RTRG, are unknown.[68] But one thing appears to be certain: predictive models were eventually used by the Joint Special Operations Command (JSOC) and its "kill teams" in order to gather real-time intelligence. "We want to be everywhere, know everything, and we want to know what happens next," announced JSOC commander Lieutenant General Joseph Votel.[69]

By late 2010, DARPA began underwriting RTRG, and the program underwent a transformation. While RTRG was primarily designed to collect data feeds and to use those information streams to track and target insurgent cells, DARPA's offshoot brought additional elements that introduced the use of sociocultural data to predict insurgent attacks. The new program was named Nexus7. Open-source software such as Hadoop helped DARPA manage big data across thousands of computers.[70] Although little information about Nexus7 is publicly available, we can assemble a partial picture of the program from reports and Pentagon documents.

Nexus7 was unusual in that it was deployed for military operations in Afghanistan from the beginning. DARPA has historically functioned as an agency supporting basic research for technologies that might get used years later. With Nexus7, DARPA played a much more assertive wartime role. Pentagon documents described Nexus7 as a rather ordinary package of data extraction and predictive modeling software, but it apparently functioned as a full-blown spy program for trawling massive amounts of intelligence data to find pockets of instability in Afghanistan, and to determine which villages or neighborhoods supported the Kabul government or the Taliban. At least for a time, a small team of Nexus7 analysts worked with military intelligence officers in Kabul while others crunched numbers in Virginia.[71] Many officers weren't convinced of Nexus7's usefulness, but the program had powerful advocates, including generals David Petraeus and James "Hoss" Cartwright (then vice chairman of the Joint Chiefs of Staff), who said, "One of the strengths DARPA brings to operations is an ability to meld huge pools of data in new ways and use it to map terrain in great detail, track patterns of life, and improve our understanding of the warfighting environment."[72]

Nexus7 was also championed by David Kilcullen, a well-known counterinsurgency theorist who served as a close advisor to General Petraeus in Iraq from 2007 to 2008 and to the International Security Assistance Force (ISAF) in Afghanistan from 2009 to 2010. He founded Caerus Associates, one of the companies that was awarded Nexus7 contracts. Kilcullen, who has a PhD from the School of Politics of the University of New South Wales, wrote a doctoral dissertation on insurgency in West Java and East Timor based on multidisciplinary fieldwork methods, including anthropological techniques and analysis. He used similar approaches in his military work. In the book *Counterinsurgency*, Kilcullen developed the idea of creating quantifiable metrics to measure progress in Afghanistan, such as the percentage of reported IEDs found, voluntary reports from Afghan informants, transportation prices, progress of NGO (non-governmental organization) development projects, tax collection records, and the prices of exotic vegetables.[73] Kilcullen argued that such metrics, when pooled together, might give military planners a powerful tool for accomplishing missions.

Another influential Nexus7 advocate—perhaps *architect* is a more appropriate term—was computer scientist Alex Pentland, director of the Massachusetts Institute of Technology's (MIT) Media Lab and its Human Dynamics Laboratory, which are supported by more than a hundred public and private institutions, ranging from Google to DARPA. Pentland developed "reality mining," a data collection and analysis method that aggregates "digital traces" and then uses them to construct models designed to predict human behavior and social networks. Applied to

Afghanistan, reality mining meant scooping up as much intelligence in as many ways as possible, whether from traditional sources such as police and military records, soldiers' accounts, and informants, or from newer technologies such as mobile phones, remote sensors, and biometric databases. "From these massive databases, Nexus7 enables analysts to use cluster and dynamic network analysis to get a sense of the daily rhythm and movement of the insurgency in and through the everyday activity of the Afghan population."[74] Pentland's best-known work focuses on "human signals," which include a person's "mannerisms, quirks, and affectations that are alive in conversations and human-machine interactions, and which exceed what is thought to be formal language exchange."[75]

Pentland has noted that "the sort of person you are is largely determined by your social context. . . . [P]eople are so enmeshed in the surrounding social fabric that it determines the sorts of things that they think are normal, and what behaviors they will learn from each other."[76] To this end, Pentland suggests collecting "environmental data" that can be measured electronically—mobile phone communications, online purchases, internet searches, and geospatial location—to map social relationships based on human-machine interaction and patterns. He calls this a "God's-eye view" of human action, and it became an integral part of Nexus7's architecture. By 2011 Pentland was giving presentations on "Computational COIN [counterinsurgency]" as a means of predicting human behavior.[77] Such an approach "marks a real move toward conducting human terrain intelligence 'at a distance' within strategic centers of calculation in Washington, DC and Virginia. . . . Nexus7 also is a movement in this direction of 'intelligence at a distance' . . . to track the aggregate movement of the *entire* Afghan society in its activity."[78]

Though media reports have not mentioned the program since 2013, there is evidence that it continued into the following year. Arati Prabhakar, who was DARPA director at the time, publicly said little about Nexus7, but in February 2014 she confirmed that it still existed and stated that it had been a valuable tool for the Pentagon.[79] Government procurement records indicate that as late as June 2014, Potomac Fusion had been awarded a $4.5 million contract for work related to Nexus7. Furthermore, Defense Department documents reveal that tens of millions of dollars were committed to Nexus7 through fiscal year 2014.[80] The documents also indicate that elements of Nexus 7 had likely been integrated into other DARPA programs, notably XDATA, National Defense, MEMEX, and Quantitative Methods for Rapid Response (QMRR).[81] According to DARPA, QMRR builds upon Nexus7's capabilities: it "develops and applies big data analysis . . . to track the development of ISIL [ISIS] force structure, funding, and logistics . . . [and its] ideology."[82]

· · · · ·

"It's algorithms, not anthropology, that are the real social science scandal in late-modern war," writes geographer Oliver Belcher in a critical analysis of militarized social science in Afghanistan.[83] Significant advances are being made in the field of machine learning, and the rapid development and deployment of the Pentagon's sociocultural modeling and forecasting programs is worrisome for many reasons. The Defense Department's budget for big data programs ballooned from approximately $250 million in 2012 to more than $2.5 *billion* in 2021—more than a tenfold increase in funding.[84]

As DARPA and Silicon Valley rush headlong toward the technological dream of artificial intelligence, we should take pause, for these same centers of power are also rushing toward greater surveillance and predictive capacity, in the name of national security.[85] We should remember that DARPA and its contractors brought into being stealth bombers, GPS, and the internet. Perhaps computational counterinsurgency is a step toward robotic warfare realized by means of algorithmically armed automatons. Before we hastily conclude that such scenarios are strictly the stuff of dystopian Hollywood films, we should listen to the voices of many scientists and tech luminaries—including the late renowned physicist Stephen Hawking, Tesla CEO Elon Musk, Apple cofounder Steve Wozniak, and others—who have warned of the existential dangers posed by artificial intelligence. It's not too late to take action, but time may be running out.[86]

7 Postdata

Two energetic currents have coursed through American society for the better part of a century: militarization and techno-optimism. Militarization is a wide-ranging process in which a society's cultural norms, policies, dominant ideologies, and institutions are oriented toward military power and shaped by war. It's difficult to pinpoint a precise date for the militarization of the United States, but many scholars suggest that the process accelerated in the wake of World War II, particularly after Congress passed the National Security Act of 1947—a law that radically restructured and overhauled the country's military and intelligence agencies. From that point forward, Americans found themselves locked into a permanent state of war readiness.[1]

Techno-optimism fits comfortably alongside militarization in America today. It's the idea that scientific and technical innovations will eventually resolve complex social, economic, and environmental problems. Those who place the most faith in technology's ability to redeem our world often deify entrepreneurial inventors and celebrity scientists. In the United States, techno-optimism and militarization are often intertwined with American exceptionalism, a deeply rooted belief that the country is fundamentally different from and superior to others—and inherently virtuous.[2]

147

The internet itself can be understood as an embodiment of the link between militarization and techno-optimism, a node connecting these cultural currents. When scientists at the Pentagon's Advanced Research Projects Agency (ARPA) developed the precursor to today's internet in the 1960s, they did so with the goal of harnessing science and technology to build a communication system capable of maintaining control over US military forces—and its nuclear arsenal—in the event of an enemy attack.[3] As noted earlier, this history has been largely erased from public consciousness. But despite this social amnesia, it's important to remember that the internet cannot be completely disentangled from America's military-industrial complex, in part because the Pentagon created it. This fact can help us understand why big data—including big data harvested from social media—is so easily weaponized.

As the internet and mobile technologies have become part of everyday life for billions of people around the world, many military and intelligence agencies and firms are capitalizing on gargantuan amounts of information that users produce. In an algorithmic era, the militarization of data is perhaps unavoidable, unless measures are taken to retake control of personal information—and unless engineers and scientists speak out.[4] For this to happen, there will need to be a much greater awareness of the politics of algorithms, the politics of data, and the politics of technology itself.

Of course, that would be a massive undertaking, since in America, so many of us have been indoctrinated to think of technologies as neutral. Or to think of them as boring. Or worse yet, to not think about them at all.

·   ·   ·   ·

One day in the early 1980s, my parents, both elementary schoolteachers, brought home a new toy for their four children. It was unlike anything we'd ever seen before. According to the salesman, our cream-colored Commodore VIC-20 was one of the first sold in our town, a predominantly Mexican-American border community.

Even though the personal computer was much cheaper than either Radio Shack's TRS-80, IBM's PC, or the legendary Apple II, I'm sure it took my parents many months to save up enough money to buy the VIC-20. They've always had good instincts, and must have sensed that the little beige box could be an educational tool, not just a video game.[5] In hindsight, it's funny that neither of them had any interest whatsoever in using the machine, and I don't remember them ever sitting down at the keyboard, not even for a minute.

My parents insisted that we use an antique portable Sylvania TV as a computer monitor—even though the black-and-white set's knobs were stripped so smooth that we needed pliers to change the channels. Maybe that was their way of making sure that we used the VIC-20 to learn BASIC, a computer programming language, rather than to play video games. Or maybe they just didn't want to give up our family's other TV—a state-of-the-art, faux walnut, twenty-one-inch Magnavox color console, perched precariously on a matching pedestal.

During the sweltering south Texas summers, when we weren't biking around the neighborhood, firing slingshots at birds, or trapping lizards in bottles, my brothers, sister, and I slowly worked our way through the VIC-20's instruction manual. The little spiral-bound book had a couple of video game programs added as an appendix, with names like "Killer Comet" and "Tank vs. UFO." We took turns laboriously typing each line of code, pecking away at the chocolate-colored keyboard, and then carefully saved our work on the Datasette (Commodore's souped-up cassette recorder, which served as a data storage device) each evening before dinner.

Eventually, we finished typing hundreds of lines of code, and to our astonishment, after lots of debugging, the video games worked! Sometimes, when we were at home alone—which happened quite often in the latchkey hours before Mom and Dad returned from work—we surreptitiously connected the VIC-20 to the color Magnavox, cranked up the volume, and played a few rounds of "Tank vs. UFO." We were at war, virtually, with space aliens—until the family's wood-paneled Chevy station wagon rumbled up the driveway.

We didn't realize it at the time, but as my brothers, sister, and I were reading, typing, and retyping, we were learning the basics of BASIC: oddly capitalized terms like GOTO, CHR$, RND(X), DEF, and RUN revealed themselves as an exotic language bestowing us with magical powers. The strings of letters, numbers, and symbols gave us the ability to hack the battered old television, which was now our own vacuum-tube-powered electric laboratory for creating pixelated images, flashing lights, and bizarre, otherworldly synthetic sounds.

Some of the weird phrases in that language were built from familiar prepositions, conjunctions, and occasionally adverbs. They seemed so mundane, innocuous, even innocent: IF-THEN (a "conditional," used to determine different courses of action) and FOR-NEXT (a "loop," sequences that are repeated a specified number of times). Little did we know that these bits of computer code, these pieces of syntax, were the building blocks of algorithms. We were too enthralled with technology— and far too naive—to understand algorithms as cultural products, subject to the same distortions, biases, and historical baggage as the societies that created them. Garbage in, garbage out.

ALGORITHMS HAVE POLITICS

Having studied engineering for several years, I think it's likely that quite a few engineers and computer programmers don't reflect too much on the idea that algorithms have politics.[6] You can't really blame them. The problem is systemic, and in some ways it reflects a kind of technological naivete, not unlike what I experienced during the years of my early adolescence—or during my training as an engineer.

It's also characteristic of a blindness that has long permeated much of American society, an unwillingness to see how hardware, software, and data—tools, technical programs, and information—are not purely neutral. They contain within them tangled, often erroneous or biased, sets of ideas and values—imprinted assumptions about the world and how it works, preconceived notions about groups of people, about what they think and how they behave. They can also have profoundly dehumanizing effects.

Over the past few years, some shocking cases have come to light. Among the most notorious examples is the clear racial bias embedded in facial recognition technologies increasingly used by federal, state, and local law enforcement agencies. The first reports surfaced in 2018, when MIT and Stanford University researchers discovered that algorithms in these pro- grams misidentified darker-skinned faces far more often than lighter- skinned faces. Joy Buolamwini, one of the MIT researchers, found that commercially available software was correct 99 percent of the time when identifying white men, but *less than half* as accurate when identifying darker-skinned women. Among the main reasons suggested by the study: AI datasets that were overwhelmingly white and male.[7]

A sweeping 2019 study conducted by the US National Institute of Standards and Technology (NIST), the federal agency tasked with ensuring minimum standards for everything from weights and measures to government IDs, revealed alarming discrepancies in how facial recognition software identified people from minority groups, compared to nonminorities. The NIST study, which analyzed nearly two hundred facial recognition algorithms—more than half of those used at the time—exposed deep flaws, including significantly higher rates of false positive matches for African Americans compared to their lighter-skinned counterparts. According to *MIT Technology Review*, the NIST results indicated that "one-to-many matching systems had the worst false positive rates for African-American women, which puts this population at the highest risk for being falsely accused of a crime."[8]

The case of algorithmic bias in facial recognition technology points to the connections between algorithms, data, culture, and history. You see, it turns out that it's not just algorithms that are biased. Data can also be biased—or stripped from its cultural and historical contexts. It's not that data itself is bad, or that big data is somehow worse than small data. Data, and the algorithms that process it, become problematic when people assume that the numbers or the formulas themselves represent objective truth. In the words of Buolamwini, "data reflects our history, and our history has been very biased to date."[9]

Buolamwini is right. In fact, not only is data reflective of our society's legacy of slavery, segregation, discrimination, and cultural bias, but the tech industry itself, which has been built on data harvesting and the production of algorithms, embodies many of the same biases.[10] As the US military and intelligence agencies embrace big data solutions, artificial intelligence, predictive modeling, and autonomous systems, it's important to step back and think carefully about what these biased distortions and deficiencies might mean for the future.

Let's consider, for a moment, what might happen if forms of algorithmic and virtual warfare become more acceptable for use in real-world situations. Imagine a scenario, for example, in which military and intelligence officials are convinced that a predictive modeling program can foretell a terrorist threat with 90 percent accuracy. What then is to prevent military operatives or CIA agents from using drones to "take out" a home in which a young man is theoretically assembling an improvised explosive device, a car that is statistically likely to be carrying explosives, or a woman who—with a 95 percent confidence level—is a potential suicide bomber?

Given the kinds of biases that are inadvertently programmed into datasets and algorithms, it's inevitable that errors will be a routine part of the process. If, within the United States, algorithms and data have biases that negatively affect women, ethnic minorities, and poor people, how much greater will these biases be when military commanders unleash the algorithms—written into code by the same programmers employed by the same companies—in cities and communities in Africa, Latin America, Asia, or the Middle East?

Apart from the problem of biased algorithms, there's the larger problem of prediction itself. In his book *The Black Swan*, Nassim Nicholas Taleb puts it bluntly: "We just can't predict." He convincingly argues that "in spite of the empirical record we continue to project into the future as if we were good at it, using tools and methods that exclude rare events. . . . [W]e are suckers for those who help us navigate uncertainty" even when they use "phony mathematics."[11] Or, as legendary New York Yankees catcher and sometime philosopher Yogi Berra once said, "It's tough to make predictions—especially about the future."

.   .   .   .   .

From the Vietnam War era to the present, US military and intelligence agencies have a history of relying on computer-generated data and automated processes to make crucial decisions. This has often had the effect of appearing to absolve humans of individual responsibility for killing.[12] New forms of virtual warfare—including robotic systems, automated psyop initiatives, and predictive modeling programs—will prolong this pattern. Despite the fact that many computer scientists and mathematicians have acknowledged the limitations of big data—for example, it's frequently stripped of context and, as we have seen, it often reflects significant biases—its boosters have successfully persuaded many Pentagon planners (and purchasing agents) of its infallibility.[13]

Part of the problem is that techno-optimism has trapped within it a peculiar kind of methodological fetish—an obsessive preference for quantitative data, rather than qualitative data. It's here that ethnographic approaches and cultural knowledge can make a difference—particularly as a critical means of reframing fundamental questions of conflict and cooperation, war and peace.

As noted earlier, at some point in the early twenty-first century, *data* became synonymous with *quantitative data*—numbers—in the minds of many Americans (see chapter 1). It's too bad, because numbers only tell part of the story. When it comes to data, we don't need more *quantity*, we need more *quality*—that is, qualitative data, especially ethnography, a powerful tool for cultural description and analysis.[14] Some of the most important insights about how to avoid war, reduce violence, or circumvent conflict come from ethnographic observations and other forms of qualitative work.

Few disciplines are as well-positioned to make valuable contributions to the study of war and peace than anthropology, since its practitioners have long been interested in questions of human survival in times of ecological, political, or technological change. It's tempting to think that anthropologists might be able to help the military "contribute to better killing" by creating more refined algorithms, or by slavishly serving as "subject matter experts."[15] But when social science is applied in this way, broader questions beyond the frame provided by military and intelligence agencies are never asked. Flawed assumptions go unchallenged and bad situations can get much worse. In societies where citizens cherish common values like human equality, religious tolerance, and empathy for others, a far more responsible role for the social scientist is that of the social *critic*, particularly when democracy and science itself are under attack from authoritarian figures, demagogues, and conspiracy theorists.

What follows is a discussion of the work of three people who provide an escape from the trap of virtual war—not by recommending that we return to low-tech forms of warfare or old-school counterinsurgency, but by pursuing preventative measures that may reduce the likelihood of escalating conflicts. What's striking about these approaches is that they don't rely on predictive analytics, big data, or even quantitative analysis. Instead, they're rooted in ethnography.

HELLFIRE

Earlier in this book, I discussed how military planners are pushing hard to introduce various forms of autonomous and remote-controlled weapon systems. There's no better example of this than the widespread use of drones by American military and intelligence forces in the so-called war on terror. While one can easily envision social scientists supporting the war effort by serving as on-the-ground intelligence personnel to aid in the identification of targets, or as cultural analysts providing information on Afghan or Yemeni customs for use by drone crews, there are other possibilities—namely, to critique the effects of such forms of virtual war by giving voice to its victims, while exposing the root causes of extremism.

Akbar Ahmed's work is a good example. His analysis of the effects of aerial drones and the war on terror—seen from the point of view of tribal peoples in the Middle East and Central Asia—is a searing indictment of the ways in which high technology can aggravate conflict. Ahmed's research team studied forty groups on the margins of global society, ranging from Somalis in the Horn of Africa to Bedouin tribes in the Middle East. In his book *The Thistle and the Drone,* Ahmed provides ample evidence of how the US-led war on terror was manipulated by many national governments, which he refers to as "the center," to wage war against tribal peoples living in rural areas, or "the periphery." Consequently, the post-9/11 period is characterized not so much by struggles between Muslims and Christians—as suggested by Samuel Huntington in his "clash of civilizations" thesis—but between struggles within predominantly Islamic nation-states. Ahmed notes:

> The war on terror has been conceptualized as a triangle formed by three points—the United States, the modern state within which the tribes live, and al Qaeda. . . . [T]he third point, however, is actually not al Qaeda. . . . It is the tribal societies that have directly or indirectly provided a base for al Qaeda and other groups advocating violence. Many of these peripheral groups had been clamoring, or even fighting, for their rights from central

Figure 19. US military and intelligence personnel have used drones armed with Hellfire missiles extensively in Afghanistan, Pakistan, Yemen, and other countries. Photo courtesy of US Air Force/Larry E. Reid, Jr.

governments for decades. A small number of al Qaeda operatives, in Afghanistan and elsewhere, found these tribes to be receptive hosts.[16]

The main organizing principle of tribal society is the segmentary lineage system, consisting of "pyramid-like structures of clans and subclans. ... [T]he operative level is the subsection, consisting of several extended families, which is part of a larger section, which, in turn, is part of an even larger clan."[17] Tribes tend to be highly egalitarian (with decentralized leadership structures) and to define territorial rights in terms of kinship. Most also have strict codes of honor.

Ahmed begins by examining the collapse of what he calls the "Waziristan model" of tribal society, named for the federally administered tribal areas of northwest Pakistan. A series of tragic interconnected events have chipped away the foundations of tribal life among Pukhtun people in Waziristan over the past four decades—beginning with the Soviet invasion of Afghanistan in 1979 and the subsequent US arming of the Afghan mujahideen in the 1980s; continuing with Pakistani president Pervez

Musharraf's military invasion of the province in 2004; and ending with the relentless, ongoing US drone strikes that escalated during the presidency of Barack Obama and then continued through the presidency of Donald Trump.[18]

Out of the chaos, disaffected Taliban from various tribes formed a radical coalition, the Tehrik-e-Taliban Pakistan (TTP) in late 2007. The group systematically destroyed the authority of Pukhtun tribal elders and the code of honor, *pukhtunwali*, then sought to replace it with its own vaguely defined notion of an Islamic state. At the same time, TTP leaders created their own warped version of *pukhtunwali* that emphasized disproportionate revenge and violence against civilians. TTP members beheaded elders, sent suicide bombers to gatherings of tribal leaders opposed to the Taliban, and began attacking mosques as a way of challenging the authority of traditional religious leaders. The Pakistani military's response further ripped apart Waziri Pakhtun society, while the US drone war added fuel to the fire by killing hundreds of civilians.

Ahmed's analysis reveals that contrary to popular belief, twenty-first-century terrorism is not rooted in Islam; it stems from the troubled relationship between central governments and tribal peoples living in the periphery. As he argues in *The Thistle and the Drone*, it is

> the result of the failure of the modern state to deal effectively and peacefully with the periphery. The center is marked by poor governance, corruption, and incompetence. It is applying short-term callous tactics to exterminate "terrorists." But the center has no long-term strategy to maintain its own integrity while including the periphery in the nation with its identity and rights respected.[19]

Instead of helping to reduce violence, US intervention in countries such as Pakistan, Yemen, Somalia, Afghanistan, Iraq, and others has further poisoned the relationship between those countries' national governments and the tribal periphery. "Central governments around the world still cannot provide a satisfactory explanation for the violence or are merely manipulating the United States into supporting their efforts against the periphery," he notes.[20] Government officials claim to be attacking religious extremists—but they use this as a pretext for continuing to destroy tribes living within their borders. The US-led war on terror has become a global assault on Islamic tribal societies that continues today, with devastating effects on civilians—the primary victims of drone warfare.

To find peace, argues Ahmed, central governments must grant tribal societies meaningful political and economic autonomy, and the right to preserve their cultural heritage and languages. Tragically, global economic integration—that is, corporate capitalism—has tended to do the opposite. As central governments have opened the doors to foreign investors seeking natural resources, they have recklessly allowed settlers and profiteers to colonize the peripheral lands of tribal peoples in Xinjiang, Mindanao, Baluchistan, and many other regions across the world. Ahmed's work suggests that virtual warfare will do nothing to eliminate the root causes of resentment and the tacit (if not explicit) support for extremism among those peoples. In fact, it will only make the problem worse.[21]

THE DEVOTED

Earlier in this book, I outlined how a growing number of military contractors and university researchers have been trying to develop programs capable of predicting violent hot spots by gathering and analyzing big data, particularly data gathered from smartphones, computers, and other communication devices. Many of these initiatives have incorporated methods and theories from the social sciences, and psychologists, sociologists, and anthropologists have sometimes been involved in these efforts either as subject matter experts or as quantitative methodologists. There's little evidence that these programs work in the real world, even after government agencies have spent hundreds of millions of dollars searching for a cybernetic crystal ball capable of foretelling the future.

Scott Atran's work demonstrates how ethnography can contribute to a more sophisticated understanding of social conflict and violence. He has criticized the wasteful use of taxpayer dollars on pseudoscientific counterinsurgency and counterterrorism programs, particularly those carried out on virtual battlegrounds. "Millions are spent, and mostly wasted, on speculative gaming, counter-narratives, and modeling this or that, but nary a penny on scientific attention to what is actually happening on the ground," he notes.[22] Such a critique is similar to that of other anthropologists who have observed that contemporary counterterrorism experts, despite their current obsession with big data analytics, predictive software, and statistical methodology, live as much in the world of fantasy as in that of science.

Atran has spent much of his career conducting research on cognition and classification. More recently, he has focused on human motivation—for example, what inspired people to take up arms and join ISIS (the Islamic State of Iraq and Syria). Atran rhetorically asked, "What propels people from 100 countries to come to this place to blow themselves up? There's something in human beings that this appeals to; otherwise it wouldn't work."[23]

Such perspectives call into question fundamental assumptions made by experts and policymakers. For example, Atran has argued that suicide bombers in the Middle East are not psychopaths, nor are they typically impoverished or uneducated—in fact, they "generally are not lacking in legitimate life opportunities relative to their general population." After conducting interviews with people espousing political violence against civilians in a number of countries, including Indonesia, Pakistan, Iraq, Israel, and Palestine, he has concluded that those branded as "radical Islamists" by Western politicians "are much closer in spirit and action to Europe's post-Renaissance Counter-Reformation . . . [their] clearest historical model [being] in the Holy Inquisition," not in any previous Islamic movements. According to Atran, "the idea that religion must struggle to assert control over politics is radically new to Islam."[24]

Atran and his colleagues have developed a theoretical model called the "devoted actor framework," which is grounded in psychological anthropology. It hypothesizes that people who are willing to make extraordinary sacrifices for a cause are often driven by sacred values that are embodied in networks of "imagined kin." Furthermore, the devoted actor's self-identity becomes subsumed into that of the collective group.[25]

Yet, for Atran, the key variable is not so much religion; what matters most is the promise of glory, esteem, and friendship. Extremists may carry out acts of violence and self-sacrifice "for friends—campmates, schoolmates, workmates, soccer buddies, bodybuilding buddies, paint-ball partners—action pals who share a cause."[26] In other words, the motivation may be comparable to what drives young American men to join the military: "Maybe they die for dreams of jihad—of justice and glory—and devotion to a family-like group of friends and mentors who act and care for one another, of 'imagined kin,' like the Marines."[27] The devoted actor framework might also apply to certain messianic cults, particularly those in which the members are willing to commit collective suicide in the name of a greater cause.

The idea that those who join groups like ISIS may be doing so more for camaraderie and glory than for religious conviction undermines conventional assumptions about so-called jihadi terrorism. For example, policymakers, the media, and some military planners typically frame violence perpetrated by Muslims—the 9/11 attacks, ISIS beheadings of Western journalists, and so on—as a manifestation of an epic "clash of civilizations." According to this idea, the twenty-first century will be a period inevitably marked by deepening tension and conflict between world religions. But Atran's research directly contradicts this claim. His point is all the more compelling because ISIS recruits often know very little about Islam. In fact, many appear to be either relatively recent converts or young Muslims who weren't raised to be devoutly religious. For Atran, both "homegrown terrorists" and ISIS recruits are motivated by a lack of opportunity—and a lack of hope.

Some aspects of Atran's work are controversial. His research was partially funded by grants from the Minerva Initiative, a US Department of Defense program that was created in 2008 for the explicit purpose of funding social science research in narrowly targeted areas. Some suggest that Pentagon funding might be creating a warped version of social science that strips away any serious analysis of American military intervention and imperialism. A critic, David Price, noted: "Minerva doesn't appear to be funding projects designed to tell Defense why the United States shouldn't invade and occupy other countries; its programs are more concerned with the nuts and bolts of counterinsurgency, and answering specific questions related to the occupation and streamlining the problems of empire."[28] Some might also ask why it took Atran so long to comment on the violent extremism of white nationalists, the "alt-right," and neo-Nazis.[29]

Despite these concerns, Atran's research may be changing the way some policymakers understand insurgency, violence, and war, by forcing them to think of people not just as collections of data points, but as real, flesh-and-blood human beings with emotions, ambitions, strengths, and vulnerabilities. Unlike proponents of virtual warfare, he emphasizes the need to incorporate substantive historical and cultural contexts when analyzing the motives for violence. To his credit, Atran has made a concerted effort to publicize his work by writing commentaries for the general public, appearing frequently on TV news programs, and speaking before US congressional committees about his ideas. His perspectives could potentially lead to creative ideas for reducing violence and de-escalating armed conflict.

TOLERANCE

As we saw in chapter 4, when it comes to psychological warfare, and organized efforts to turn citizens against one another, social science can be potentially useful as a tool for influencing or manipulating others. But it can also be an effective means of pushing back against processes of political polarization—a problem affecting many countries around the world, including the United States. When authoritarian leaders declare war on their own domestic political opponents, using social media and other forms of digital communication as their propaganda weapons of choice, socially responsible scientists need to counter these efforts, not support them.

Technology firms have played a significant, if passive, role in helping to foster extremism on a global scale. More than a decade ago, critics accused Google, Facebook, and Twitter of not doing enough to prevent violent extremists from using their platforms to spread propaganda and recruit new members. Many tech companies—for instance, Facebook—have often been reluctant to interfere with their users' online posts, claiming that doing so would violate their right to free speech and expression. But with pressure mounting after the August 2017 "Unite the Right" rally, in which white supremacists and neo-Nazis marched through the streets of Charlottesville, Virginia, social media companies began making token efforts to self-regulate their platforms by monitoring and removing hateful and divisive messages. They have been largely ineffective—so ineffective, in fact, that as late as 2019, the US House Judiciary Committee summoned Facebook and Google executives to address concerns about white nationalists' use of their platforms.

But there's a larger question to be addressed: How is it that nationalist movements, anti-immigrant rhetoric, and the politics of fear have become such powerful forces in so many countries, including our own? Here, fine-grained ethnographic perspectives are needed for a better understanding of these significant historical shifts.

For example, in a careful analysis of the factors contributing to Donald Trump's 2016 electoral victory and the passage of Brexit in the United Kingdom, Hugh Gusterson argues that the dominant media narrative explained the US elections as the result of surging support from blue-collar voters who felt abandoned by the Democratic Party. While he acknowledges the significance of these voters, particularly in midwestern states that had previously been won by Democratic candidates, Gusterson argues that the story is far more complex. He notes that

> instead of representing Trump as the champion of US workers, the media would have been just as accurate in portraying him as the candidate of wealthier Americans: after all, he won the majority of votes among those earning over $50,000 a year. . . . [T]he blue-collar trope makes the billionaire in the red baseball cap a man of the people.[30]

For Gusterson, working-class Americans are but one segment of a much bigger coalition, including suburban voters, evangelical Christians, and many other groups. The petty bourgeoisie are particularly important—small-business owners who, like their pro-Brexit UK counterparts, "are deeply alienated from distant bureaucracies (Brussels, London, and Washington) and ever-expanding regulatory regimes, and they are particularly disposed to believe that their tax dollars go to undeserving welfare cases. They tend to be intensely patriotic, resentful of the educated cosmopolitans above them, and intensely fearful of slipping into the working class below them."[31]

There is another layer to Gusterson's analysis, which is critically important for understanding the rise of nationalist populism and right-wing extremism. This layer is perhaps less obvious to academics and the media, for they're often trapped within it. A new elite class—located in revitalized, trendy urban centers or picturesque college towns—has emerged. Thus,

Figure 20. Armed rioters, mobilized on social media, stormed the Capitol Building as the US Congress met to certify presidential election results on January 6, 2021. Photo courtesy of Tyler Merbler/CC-BY-2.0.

even as the white working class is engulfed by a claustrophobic sense of being trapped in decaying local communities, a vibrantly fluid transnational and cosmopolitan urban lifeworld has evolved, buoyed by the expanding economies of international finance, information technology, biomedicine, and social media. These expanding economic sectors, and the universities that feed them with knowledge workers, are the locus of a glamorous, socially liberal culture of transnational cosmopolitanism, conspicuous consumption, metrosexual broadmindedness, and affirmative action. . . . The disdain that such elites feel for the white working class is perfectly captured in Hillary Clinton's leaked characterization [of that population] (to a group of affluent donors) as a "basket of deplorables" who are "racist, sexist, homophobic, xenophobic, Islamophobic—you name it."[32]

Universities are often part of the problem: while they may pay lip service to the principles of diversity and tolerance, "they can, perversely, function as engines of a liberal illiberalism that is complicit in creating new social schisms."[33] Gusterson warns that increasingly polarized politics might spin out of control by creating a feedback loop in which "university-educated cosmopolitans" and "nationalist populists" drive each other into a downward spiral of mutual scorn—a truly prescient point that foreshadowed the US Capitol riot of January 6, 2021. One can easily imagine a cycle of such events being propelled by nonstop news feeds, inflammatory social media messages, and targeted online advertisements in the years to come.

Gusterson concludes by calling for a more sophisticated approach to political analysis and action, based on ethnography among those whose values are diametrically opposed to those held by many social scientists: "If we are to contribute to the analysis of current menacing trends, and to help find a way to reverse them, we need rich, deep, nuanced encounters with the conservative Other, encounters that will require all the skills of reflexivity, relativism, and humane critique that our discipline can summon."[34]

LIGHTING THE MATCH

These examples demonstrate just how important qualitative, ethnographic data is for a deeper, more substantive understanding of war—not to fight more effectively on the battlefield, but to avoid armed conflict altogether. Part of the problem with virtual warfare—whether in the form of autonomous and automated weapon systems, computational counterinsurgency, or high-tech psyop initiatives—is that unlike in conventional war, people and other living things are often transformed into faraway objects, data points, mere abstractions. Modern warfare makes it extraordinarily difficult for most Americans to fully comprehend its human costs. Virtual warfare makes it virtually impossible.

Before data-driven war becomes normalized, it's important that those able to understand the potential effects of the new militarized technologies provide policymakers and the general public with broad contextual views of the issues at hand. Otherwise, we might find ourselves dealing with catastrophic events created by technical experts unable or unwilling to comprehend the full impact of their work. Gillian Tett's reflections on the origins of the global financial crisis are equally applicable to those confronting the prospect of automated warfare and autonomous weapons:

Why did nobody know what was going on? What was going on in the geeky little silo, what was going on in that conference . . . just seemed to be technical and complex, geeky and boring. And if something is labelled as boring in modern society, it's the surest possible way to hide it in plain sight, immediately. Because the reality is that things that are labelled boring and geeky are very hard to get on the front page. . . . How was it that anybody ever let this system spin out of control? . . . A small group of technical experts [are] engaged in technologically complex activity that has the ability to affect us all, and yet which almost nobody else understands.[35]

Today we are all subject to processes of social control run amok: the symbolic transformation of human lives into mere statistics or datasets; distancing mechanisms that conceal the ripple effects of destructive government or corporate policies; economic and social theories that assume that some lives are more expendable than others; coercive, lethal, and addictive technologies that become normalized tools of social control, political apathy, and disinformation; and a host of institutions ranging from university laboratories to NGOs to think tanks providing a veneer of legitimacy to ossified political structures and a heavily militarized society.[36]

The twenty-first century is likely to be one in which leaders of powerful institutions will continue seeking technical and sociocultural experts to help them accomplish their goals, whether for purposes of warfare, commerce, surveillance, or social control. If recent history is any guide, these would-be controllers will "crave anthropological knowledge. . . . [T]hey need our *spirits*—our ability to symbolically and humanly process the human environments these machines dominate. . . . The war machines can track and control the movement of human bodies, but they cannot understand the webs of cultural meaning of those they physically dominate."[37] At a time when applied social science work is more attractive than ever, particularly in a militarized tech industry, it's important for all of us to think critically about how we fit into larger systems of political, economic, and military power, and how we can confront and challenge those institutions.

There's good reason to be optimistic about the future. As noted previously, a relatively small but growing group of engineers, researchers, and scientists are pushing back against tech executives' willingness to meet the

Figure 21. Demonstrators in New York protest Amazon's collaboration with US Immigration and Customs Enforcement as part of the #NoTechForICE movement. Photo courtesy of Lev Radin/Pacific Press/Alamy Live News.

Defense Department's virtual warfare needs (see chapter 3). By now there are several important examples: Google researchers resisting Project Maven (a contract in which the company used artificial intelligence to analyze drone footage); Amazon workers' protests against the use of the company's facial recognition technology by US Immigration and Customs Enforcement and other federal law enforcement agencies; and Microsoft employees' opposition to the firm's contract to provide augmented-reality headsets to the US Army. Such efforts will undoubtedly encounter difficult barriers—for example, it would be easy for corporate executives to off-shore controversial military projects to subcontractors in India, Israel, or other locations. And of course, there will always be tech firms, such as Palantir Technologies and Anduril Industries, whose workers have *not* opposed the idea of working for military and intelligence agencies, and whose executives eagerly pursue Pentagon contracts.

But despite these obstacles, the commitment and tenacity of the tech resistance movement has, in a short period of time, led to a blossoming of organizations that are beginning to disrupt Silicon Valley's status quo. Some of the most interesting new experiments include Tech Inquiry, dedicated to exposing the links between tech firms and the US Defense Department; EPIC (the Electronic Privacy Information Center), which in recent years filed Freedom of Information Act requests exposing US government contracts with Palantir and other tech firms; Foxglove, a UK nonprofit that is fighting biased algorithms, digital surveillance, and other tech abuses; the Own Your Data Foundation, organized to promote individual users' data rights and data ownership; the Tech Workers' Coalition, founded to protect technology workers' labor rights; Mijente, which launched the #NoTechforICE campaign to protest the involvement of tech firms in the deportation of undocumented immigrants; NeverAgain.tech, formed to counter the creation of a government database that would have registered individuals on the basis of race, religion, and national origin; and the Worker Agency, an advocacy organization that specializes in helping grassroots campaigns in support of "gig workers" and "digital employees"—among others. Equally inspiring and important are the efforts of organizations like Black Girls Code, Latina Girls Code, Hack the Hood, Techqueria, and others that are helping African Americans and Latinos/Latinas enter the tech industry, and providing guidance and support once they're there. These are just a few of the many new efforts aimed at transforming our technological future.

Resistance to power can indeed change history, but most of the time, you've got to be in it for the long haul. Instead of assuming that autonomous weapons, biased and militarized data, and predictive policing programs are inescapable and will be with us forever, we need to think strategically about how to confront and control them. Passive acceptance of these potentially dangerous technologies is a threat to our democracy, and even to the long-term viability of human society. It's crucially important to imagine alternative possibilities and to start building them now.

Those who claim that virtual war is inevitable fundamentally misunderstand the process of social change. Movements always take time—not months, but years, decades, sometimes even centuries. The late Howard

Zinn, best known for his book *A People's History of the United States,* put it this way:

> You do things again and again, and nothing happens. You have to do things, do things, do things: you have to light that match, light that match, light that match, not knowing how often it's going to sputter and go out and at what point it's going to take hold. . . . Things take a long time. It requires patience, but not a passive patience—the patience of activism. . . . We should be encouraged by historical examples of social change, by how surprising changes take place suddenly, when you least expect it, not because of a miracle from on high, but because people have labored patiently for a long time.[38]

Historical examples abound: abolitionists worked for decades to end the "peculiar institution" of slavery; India's independence movement stretched out over the course of nearly a century; women's suffrage in many countries (including the United States) occurred only after generations of activists filed court cases, pressured politicians, and protested; the end of South African apartheid didn't happen overnight; the American civil rights movement took many years to come to fruition, and recent events have shown that it's still a work in progress.

Those of us who care must continue laboring patiently and cultivating awareness. Small efforts can have disproportionately large effects over time: a campus teach-in, an op-ed piece in the local newspaper, a classroom lecture, a simple conversation with a neighbor or even a stranger. More often than not, change happens as the end result of simple day-to-day actions such as these—which, over time, have a transformative impact.

Now is the time to practice the patience of activism—and to keep lighting the match.

Acknowledgments

My interest in militarization and its consequences began in 2007, in the midst of controversies surrounding the US Army's Human Terrain System program. At that time, I had the good fortune of being invited to join a group that was deeply concerned about the ways in which military and intelligence agencies were recruiting social scientists. I've learned a great deal from all of them: Catherine Besteman, Andrew Bickford, Gregory Feldman, Hugh Gusterson, Gustaaf Houtman, Jean Jackson, Kanhong Lin, Catherine Lutz, Katherine McCaffrey, David Price, and David Vine. I'm especially thankful for detailed comments on the manuscript from Andrew Bickford, Hugh Gusterson, and David Price, and for the support of Gustaaf Houtman, who edits the journal *Anthropology Today*. Parts of my book began as brief articles written for that publication.

I've benefited from the insights of others who have written about military and intelligence agencies, including Robert Albro, Joe Bryan, Derek Gregory, Barbara Rose Johnston, David Miller, Gina Pérez, Robert Rubinstein, and Jeffrey Sluka. Kerry Fosher has played a critical role in helping me appreciate the range of roles played by social scientists within military institutions. I'm grateful to her for taking the time to provide detailed comments on the manuscript. I thank Vito Laterza for comments on a key chapter, and Michal Kosinski for his insights into the political uses of big data. Several investigative journalists, particularly Sharon Weinberger and Jesse Witt, shared their knowledge about military and intelligence programs. Jack Poulson of Tech Inquiry was extraordinarily helpful and informative, and pointed me to reports detailing Big Tech contracts with US military, intelligence, and law enforcement agencies.

While writing this book, I served as a councilor on the board of the American Ethnological Society (AES). It was a rewarding and enriching experience, and I learned a great deal about the craft of ethnographic writing from very talented board members, including Niko Besnier, Chelsey Carter, Marc Edelman, Danielle Good, Ken Guest, Michael Hathaway, Naveeda Khan, Christopher Krupa, Christopher Loperena, Caitrin Lynch, Kate McCaffrey, Carole McGranahan, Shanti Parikh, Stacey Pigg, Carolyn Rouse, Shalini Shankar, Jacqueline Solway, and Gina Athena Ulysse.

San José State University has been my academic home for twenty years, and many people there have been supportive. The anthropology office staff—Agnes Borja, Shannon Gallagher, and Kristen Constanza—managed the day-to-day operations of the department with true dedication, and their work provided me the time I needed to write early chapter drafts. I prepared several sections of the book during a sabbatical semester, during which time Jan English-Lueck graciously took over my duties as department chair. She also provided thoughtful comments on a draft of the manuscript. Others in the department, including A. J. Faas, John Marlovits, Jay Ou, Charlotte Sunseri, and William Reckmeyer, have shared ideas and sources. Melissa Cefkin, who for a time was a visiting scholar in my department, read the manuscript and made insightful comments on automation, autonomy, and the social sciences. This project was supported by release time from San José State University's College of Social Sciences, and I appreciate opportunities that have been provided by Walt Jacobs, Ron Rogers, Cami Johnson, Garrick Percival, and Shishir Mathur. The university's Office of Research provided release time and internal grants that helped me complete portions of the book.

While she was an editor at the University of Chicago Press several years ago, Priya Nelson took time to meet with me and talk about my publication plans, and offered advice and resources during the earliest stages of this project. I appreciate her support and interest.

At the University of California Press, Kate Marshall has been an extraordinarily energetic and thoughtful editor, and both she and assistant editor Enrique Ochoa-Kaup helped me develop an appropriate tone. They guided the manuscript quickly through peer and editorial reviews, and gave responsive support and practical advice at every stage. Project editor Julie Van Pelt and copyeditor Richard Earles expertly facilitated the production process. I'm also grateful to Teresa Iafolla, Katryce Lassle, and Ramón Smith for their support and advice. Two anonymous peer reviewers selected by UC Press's editorial team made helpful comments that improved the manuscript. Many thanks to Lia Tjandra for designing the book cover.

I assembled the final portions of this book during the spring, summer, and autumn of 2020—a dark and disorienting period. My wife and young sons helped keep things in perspective when I drifted too far out into the world of written words. So too did my parents, brothers, and sister, who have all been bedrocks of support over many years. Many others kept me grounded during the uncertainties of pandemic time, including Kike Arnal, Anna Basallaje, Ricardo Castro, Salvador Contreras, Sean Feree, Eduardo Flores, Yasmín Flores, Erik Harms, Richard Hernández, Christina Koci, Ramón Lozano, Anthony Pape, Adam Rodríguez, and Paul Spitzmueller. Friends in and from Oaxaca were also a vital source of inspiration.

Finally, Laura Nader's pioneering work on controlling processes and Cold War anthropology has helped me understand how unthinkably perilous scenarios can unfold slowly and incrementally—and then become normalized over the course of decades. Her ideas have influenced and inspired generations of students, and her example has always motivated me to do better. I offer my sincere gratitude for her friendship, guidance, and sound advice, time and time again.

APPENDIX   Sub-rosa Research

When I began researching programs coordinated by US military and intelligence agencies and defense contractors more than a decade ago, I was immediately faced with methodological hurdles. Graduate studies in anthropology had prepared me well for participant-observation among peasant farmers, but not for research into obscure agencies and programs. Here I will review some of the methods I used as my work expanded beyond conventional anthropological settings, into the world of secretive organizations and projects.[1] For this book, I gathered materials from and about many such public and private organizations, including DARPA, SCL Group/Cambridge Analytica, military research laboratories, and defense contractors of all sizes.

Writing more than twenty years ago, Hugh Gusterson posed a provocative and prescient question: "How does an anthropologist study such institutions as weapons laboratories and corporations? In most cases participant-observation will be highly problematic, if not impossible. . . . [P]articipant-observation is a research technique that does not travel well up the social structure."[2] This dilemma affects many social scientists undertaking research on government projects, proprietary software programs, and other initiatives not open to public scrutiny.

When participant-observation isn't feasible, what techniques can one use to shed light upon secretive programs, particularly those involving military and intelligence agencies and their contractors? What methods are available to those seeking to understand the inner workings of projects organized by the US

Department of Defense, MI6, Mossad, or defense corporations such as Lockheed Martin, Raytheon, or Palantir?

Laura Nader anticipated these dilemmas more than fifty years ago, when she asked, "How can you study organizations that won't let you in the door?" She recognized that participant-observation was typically not possible when studying government agencies or elite institutions. The problem is clearly one of power and politics, and it requires an innovative set of techniques for "studying up, down, and sideways."[3]

Nader suggested three ethnographic possibilities that might substitute for participant-observation: (1) documentary analysis, including analyses of public relations material and internal memos; (2) interviews, especially face-to-face interviews; and (3) "self-analysis," defined as "an awareness on the part of the [anthropologist] of how he or she as a social scientist is perceived, run around, enculturated, and described in the veiled and not-so-veiled encounters with . . . members of organizations."[4]

.   .   .   .   .

I found that Nader's first suggestion, documentary analysis, was the most important in the early stages of my work, for the simple reason that I had a very difficult time convincing people within military or intelligence agencies to talk with me about their programs, and participant-observation was not a viable option because I had no security clearance.

I began by searching library databases, where I stumbled upon a parallel research universe, one in which a small number of PhD anthropologists were planning and promoting social science for military consumption in the pages of military journals. For example, *Military Review*—edited and published by the US Army Combined Arms Center at Fort Leavenworth, Kansas—gave insight into military worldviews and lots of information about cutting-edge initiatives. For another example, the online *Small Wars Journal* contains multiple blogs and hundreds of discussion groups that provide a great deal of information about counterinsurgency and autonomous weapons.

Later, I began looking through military field manuals, many of which are now posted online at the Federation of American Scientists' website, a rich resource.[5] I also combed through Pentagon budget reports, which the Defense Department's comptroller provides to the US Congress every year. The most useful were documents associated with "RDT&E," or Research, Development, Test, and Evaluation. I eventually found pages from these budget documents listing such things as Nexus7 (see chapter 6) and MAP-HT, a computerized ethnographic mapping tool.[6] Other potentially useful government documents included parts of the Congressional Record—for example, funding bills. In summary, unclassified official documents can provide small pieces that help reveal the main features of much bigger puzzles.

A more colorful, and cryptic, group of openly available Defense Department documents consisted of PowerPoint presentations posted online. Venn diagrams, complex acronyms, color-coded maps, and byzantine charts with microscopic text were typical of these materials, all worthy of serious linguistic analysis. Although they're often difficult to decipher, they provide a great deal of information about nascent programs.

Yet another group of documents emerged, which I eventually came to recognize as public relations material. For example, I found during one of my previous projects, a critical analysis of the US Army's Human Terrain System (HTS), that the latter's official website provided a glimpse into how the program presented itself to the world: as a life-saving humanitarian enterprise that improved the lives of Iraqis and Afghans.[7] In reality, HTS deployed embedded social scientists who collected data for army brigade commanders. Dozens of newspaper articles sympathetic to HTS—and the involvement of a Washington Beltway PR expert—made it obvious that the program was undergoing what might be called product placement. Within a matter of months, HTS was featured favorably in *Time* magazine, the *New York Times*, the *Wall Street Journal*, *Elle* magazine, and dozens of other venues.

Another example of PR material came from a short-lived blog created by a one-time professor of anthropology at Christopher Newport University. His accounts (and photos) of military deployment were self-aggrandizing snippets of life in a human terrain team—until his website suddenly vanished, shortly after I wrote a critical description of his blog. This leads me to mention a very helpful resource for anthropologists trying to access websites that have mysteriously dropped down the memory hole: the Internet Archive "Wayback Machine," which maintains a partial record of previously posted webpages by taking periodic "snapshots" and storing them away in perpetuity.[8]

. . . . .

Classified and leaked documents can also provide a wealth of information. Among the most creative methods for doing sub-rosa research is to request files from the CIA, the FBI, the National Security Agency, and the US Departments of State, Defense, and Homeland Security by using the Freedom of Information Act (FOIA)—a potentially rich resource for social scientists. David Price has outlined specific areas in which FOIA can be particularly effective:

> The FOIA can be used by anthropologists conducting research in areas of the world where American military and intelligence agencies have clashed with foreign indigenous groups. The FOIA can also help anthropologists gain access to previously

unreleased diplomatic documents relating to regions where they've done foreign fieldwork. . . . In short, any researcher investigating groups or individuals who have had contact with US government agencies can benefit from using the FOIA to access records held by all branches of federal government.[9]

However, there are limitations. Price notes that the CIA and FBI often "take years to comply with even the simplest FOIA requests." Furthermore, "documents are being destroyed faster than they can be released under the FOIA."[10] Even so, organizations like the National Security Archive—a nonprofit research center based in Washington, DC, that holds more than a hundred thousand declassified government records—offer plenty of opportunities for social scientists.

Leaked documents are another potentially fruitful source of information about the inner workings of secretive organizations. WikiLeaks is the best-known archive for leaked documents, but there are others that provide vast collections. Public Intelligence is one such archive; it includes confidential documents such as manuals distributed by Facebook to US law enforcement agencies, detailing retrievable user information (for example, messages and IP addresses). Another important collection of materials is the Snowden Surveillance Archive, a joint effort of the organization Canadian Journalists for Free Expression and the University of Toronto. It includes all the documents leaked by former National Security Agency contractor Edward Snowden that have been published in the news media.[11]

Finally, unpublicized reports filed by insiders can be another vital source of information. After I gave a talk at an anthropology conference more than a decade ago, an acquaintance I hadn't seen in many years approached me, greeted me, and revealed himself as a former HTS employee. Later that evening, after several drinks, he gave me copies of several reports detailing his activities, and asked that I not quote or use any part of them. I never have.

This highlights one of the challenges facing social scientists doing this sort of work. One may build rapport with insiders, and collect large amounts of data, only to find that to publish or disseminate the material would violate the trust of the informant and perhaps even get him or her in trouble. Sub-rosa research often raises thorny ethical and legal dilemmas.

· · · · · ·

On several occasions, employees and former employees of military programs have contacted me anonymously (most using pseudonyms), wanting to talk about their experiences. If this happens to you, it's best to be patient. To begin with, if you receive an unsolicited email or phone call from an anonymous person claiming to be employed by a secretive organization, be skeptical. There's a good chance that the person is not whom he or she claims to be. And even if the person is being honest, he or she may have an ax to grind, either with you or with their organization. I've found that the best approach is nonchalance. I usually wait a day or two before returning such emails or phone calls, because replying too quickly—and sounding desperate for information—might give the informant the upper hand. Over time, all of these people eventually identified themselves by name (usually within a few weeks), and I was able to confirm that each was indeed the person he or she claimed to be. Although most, understandably, didn't want their names publicized, they nonetheless provided valuable information and, sometimes, criticisms of their respective programs or program managers.

When I researched HTS, those whom I interviewed typically remained supportive of the concept—that is, they sincerely believed that cultural knowledge could lead to less conflict between troops on the ground and those living under US military occupation. However, they were usually upset about incompetent leadership, on-the-job harassment, or the predominant role of muscular, aggressive special forces types. Over time, I was able to conduct face-to-face interviews with several former HTS employees, and these were much more rewarding than phone interviews or email exchanges.

When conducting this kind of work, rapport building is often challenging. Participating in some military and intelligence programs is often difficult, sometimes traumatic—and keeping confidential, secret, or top-secret information under wraps becomes a normal way of life for many people. It's also the case that some organizations may foster abusive work environments (as often happens in secretive corporate and academic settings), since there is relatively little public scrutiny over work conditions. In some ways, the situation is similar to what medical anthropologist Merrill Singer has described as the challenges of studying "hidden populations."[12]

Sometimes, those who participate in military or intelligence programs become whistleblowers. On the topic of HTS, the most insightful self-analysis has come from an anthropologist who was briefly employed there before resigning. In John Allison's self-reflective account of the training process, which often took the form of indoctrination, he writes that

> the military had a conscious agenda for reframing the civilians' [i.e., social scientists'] consciousness. . . . Part of the cognitive restructuring was overt, as in the classes that made it clear that the HTT [human terrain team] member will be "embedded" in the military structure, just as are news reporters; "harnessed" would be an apter description. Repeatedly, the Stockholm Syndrome was brought up to make clear the shaping function of the classes. . . . I began to see that I was enclosed by those I opposed; and my options were limited. . . . If I accepted their assumptions about "reality," I would have had to agree with their conclusions about patriotic responsibilities; the call to action, The Mission, The Chain of Command, the [cheap] value of [Afghan] lives.[13]

Such insight from a former participant (and then outspoken critic) of the US Army program goes a long way in helping us understand its coercive nature.

.   .   .   .   .

What, if anything, makes this different from investigative journalism? I raise this question because in my experience, peer reviewers occasionally deride research on military and intelligence programs as journalistic, gratuitous, or polemical. It's as if some academics are unable to accept scientific work that confronts contemporary issues in a direct way that is intelligible to a broad public audience.

There are several points of departure. To begin with, because most of this work involves documentary analysis, it can benefit from the social scientific search for meaning. For example, what are the deeper meanings—not only the text, but the subtexts—of military documents in which highly abstracted forms symbolize people? What does it mean that military planners are so easily able to transform a war zone into a grid of color-coded tribal maps, flow charts, Venn diagrams, and bar graphs, ready to be neatly inserted into PowerPoint presentations? How can such phenomena help us understand the process of distancing and even dehumanizing others?

Second, unlike most investigative journalists, the social scientist often uses theoretical concepts or hypotheses to make sense of certain phenomena. Yet another point of difference is that social scientists typically don't analyze military and intelligence organizations from a structural perspective. In other words, social scientists are well prepared to analyze the rise of virtual warfare not exclusively as a military phenomenon, but as a set of practices that is intimately connected to hundreds of corporations that benefit from it—including a growing number of Silicon Valley technology firms.

Research on secretive military and intelligence programs may have the effect of upsetting those who would prefer that social scientists concern themselves exclusively with trivial questions couched in the language of high theory. But it's worth remembering the words of American sociologist C. Wright Mills, who observed:

> In many academic circles today anyone who tries to write in a widely intelligible way is liable to be condemned as a 'mere literary man' or, worse still, 'a mere journalist.' . . . It may be that it is the result of an academic closing of the ranks on the part of the mediocre, who understandably wish to exclude those who win the attention of intelligent people, academic and otherwise.[14]

By using a wide, eclectic range of methods, we have the potential to make military and intelligence agencies and their subcontractors more open to public scrutiny. We shouldn't let the opportunity slip away.

Notes

CHAPTER 1. WAR VIRTUALLY

1. Data-driven warfare is part of a much larger effort that (rhetorically, at least) seeks to protect the warfighter: "The politics of military protection in the US today dictate and drive a massive research and development regime designed to prevent US soldiers from suffering any casualties or injury—at least in theory. In an era of increasingly lethal weapons, we are somehow to believe that our soldiers will not suffer trauma or die in combat" (see Bickford 2020, 33).

2. Researchers have written about many different aspects of virtual war in recent years, but there is no consensus about its definition (see, for example, Ignatieff 2001; Der Derian 2009; Whitehead and Finnstrom 2013; Allen 2017). There are, of course, many others who have examined more specific topics such as cyberwarfare, drone warfare, and automated weapon systems (see, for example, Latiff 2017; Del Monte 2018). Here I have deliberately chosen the term *virtual war* because it's broad enough to encompass a wide range of military projects and institutions that integrate automation, algorithms, and the analysis of large datasets.

3. The term *big data* is difficult to define. Following anthropologist Justin Lane's research, I will use it to describe "massive amounts of electronic data that are indexable and searchable by means of computational systems . . . [and] stored on servers and analyzed by algorithms" (see Lane 2016, 75). Another anthropologist, Rebecca Lemov, reminds us that big data is actually small, to the

extent that it's made up of aggregated information about the intimate details of individual people's everyday lives. She notes that "much of this newly created stuff is *made of and out of* personal data, the almost literal mining of subjectivity" (Lemov 2016). For a thought-provoking collection of essays on big data from a range of anthropological perspectives, see Boellstorff and Maurer 2015.

4. For example, see the special series of reports entitled "The AI Arms Race," published by the *Financial Times*. See also Lee 2018.

5. Quoted in Rohde 2009.

6. See, for example, Galtung 1967; Jorgensen and Wolf 1970.

7. Latiff 2017; Del Monte 2018; Kanaan 2020. For an examination of how societies can drift to war, see Nader 1986.

8. Cockburn 2016, 17–31.

9. Valentine 1990.

10. Many consumers have been seduced by the convenience of voice assistants like Amazon's Alexa, but critics have noted that such technologies also function as surveillance devices. For an overview, see Hao 2019a.

11. For an outstanding collection of articles on how algorithms are changing daily life, see Besteman and Gusterson 2019.

12. Ingram 2017.

13. Tau 2021.

14. Scahill and Greenwald 2014; see also Taibbi 2018.

15. Taylor 2015.

16. Weisgerber 2017.

17. Hugh Gusterson used the memorable phrase "culture in a box" in the documentary film *Human Terrain* (see Der Derian, Udris, and Udris 2010). Among the most thorough anthropological analyses of the military's use of cultural knowledge for training and education is Brown 2008 (see also Davis 2010).

18. In 2015, the typically understated magazine *The Economist* ran a cover story entitled "Planet of the Phones," which described the devices as ubiquitous, addictive, and transformative, noting that smartphones "have become the fastest-selling gadgets in history." See *Economist* 2015.

19. Molla 2020.

20. Zarkadakis 2015, 250–51.

21. ISIS was known by several names, including ISIL (Islamic State of Iraq and the Levant) and Daesh (its Arabic acronym).

22. Warrick 2015.

23. Atwan 2019. See also Koerner 2016; Ward 2018.

24. Cook and Vale 2018.

25. For example, in 2014, Attorney General Eric Holder announced the creation of a Justice Department task force to combat "homegrown" terrorists within the United States, citing the 2013 Boston Marathon bombings and other

incidents. Holder noted that "we face an escalating danger from self-radicalized individuals within our own borders." See Phelps 2014.

26. For a clear articulation of Petraeus's approach, see Kilcullen 2009. For a sharp critique, see Gentile 2013.

27. See Flynn, Pottinger, and Batchelor 2010. A colleague with contacts in the US Intelligence Community told me that some within the IC were annoyed by the report, since, at the time it was published, they were busily creating the very kinds of social science–based programs that Flynn and his coauthors proposed. When a high-level officer publishes such a report, it results in a swarm of what my colleague calls "the contracting vultures" (that is, defense contractors) seeking to pick off "money dropping from the sky."

28. Flynn quoted in Tucker 2016.

29. Kroenig 2020; see also Clinton 2011.

30. By 2019, numerous publications addressed the "weaponization" of social media, the "military-internet complex," and cyberwarfare more generally. See, for example, Mazarr et al. 2019; Singer and Brooking 2019; Harris 2015.

31. Correll 2019.

32. Price 2016, xiv.

33. Ibid., xvi.

34. Singer and Sang-Hun 2020.

35. Nicas and Wakabayashi 2020.

36. Prasso 2020. See also Khalid 2020; Amnesty International 2020.

37. Biddle 2020; see also Schubarth 2020. In 2020, Palantir moved its headquarters from Palo Alto, California (where many Silicon Valley firms are located), to Denver, Colorado—presumably to conduct operations in a more lightly regulated political environment.

38. Quoted in Prasso 2020.

39. Mozur, Zhong, and Krolik 2020.

40. Cockerell 2019; Cain 2021.

41. Quoted in Nebehay 2018.

42. Wang 2019; see also Human Rights Watch 2018.

43. Jacob L. Moreno and Helen Jennings (a psychiatrist and psychologist, respectively) developed modern social network analysis. Anthropologist W. Lloyd Warner used a similar approach, which he created independently of Moreno and Jennings (Freeman 2004). Social anthropologist John Barnes developed yet another version of the method during the late 1940s and early 1950s; he is credited with coining the term *social network* in his 1954 study of a Norwegian fishing village. See Barnes 1954.

44. McCurry 2020.

45. Zastrow 2020; Kim 2020. Although South Korean laws are very explicit about the fact that such data is only to be used for public health purposes, the government has been reluctant to destroy contact-tracing data from the last

epidemic outbreak in 2015, MERS (Middle East Respiratory Syndrome), even though there have been very few cases over the past four years.

46. Ferguson 2017.

47. Schrader 2019; Ferguson 2017. A Pentagon initiative known as the 1033 Program has allowed US police departments to acquire excess military weaponry, combat gear, and other equipment at very little cost. The program, which involves transferring surplus or outdated military equipment to local law enforcement agencies, was created in 1997 as part of the Clinton administration's effort to fight the so-called war on drugs. Police departments essentially receive the items at no cost, other than shipping fees.

48. Srinivasan 2019.

49. Tett 2018.

50. Ferryman quoted in Tett 2018.

51. Mauss 1990 [1925], 30. There is yet another significant implication here: the possibility that what is sometimes called "the weaponization of data" might not be such a new phenomenon after all—at least not if we are drawing a comparison to the weaponization of *gifts* across the long arc of human history. Here, of course, I'm talking not about literal weaponization, but rather the transformation of data and gifts into tools for political struggles and power plays. There are perhaps no better examples of this than the cases of *moka* exchange in Papua New Guinea and the potlatch among Northwest Coast Indians in Washington State and British Columbia. In *moka* ceremonies, "big men" give away larger and larger gifts of pigs, often to their political rivals—and their prestige grows accordingly.

The potlatch functioned in a similar way historically: as a kind of economic battle among peers to win status and prestige by giving away prized copper shields and elaborately designed wool blankets. According to some accounts, rivals would sometimes throw copper shields into the sea as a gesture of lavishly flamboyant excess.

52. See Lemov 2016.

53. Even today, not nearly enough emphasis is given to ethics in engineering. A recently published collection of articles, edited by Sakellariou and Milleron (2018), does an impressive job of beginning to fill the gap.

54. Elshtain 1995.

CHAPTER 2. REQUIEM FOR A ROBOT

1. This account is a dramatization of events described in *The Atlantic* (see Garber 2013).

2. Several other remote-controlled robots are similar to the MARCbot, including the TALON series manufactured by Massachusetts-based Foster-

Miller, the ANDROS series manufactured by REMOTEC (a subsidiary of Northrop Grumman), and the PackBot series manufactured by iRobot.

3. These comments were posted to a 2014 Reddit thread ("Soldiers are developing relationships with their battlefield robots, naming them, assigning genders, and even holding funerals when they are destroyed"), at www.reddit.com/r/Military /comments/1mn6yl/soldiers_are_developing_relationships_with_their/. See also Short 2018.

4. Ibid.

5. Garber 2013.

6. See Reddit thread cited above and Kolb 2012, 137–38. "Johnny 5" is a reference to the cute robotic protagonist of the science-fiction comedy film *Short Circuit*. Other names for EOD robots included Hollywood actors and characters (Danny DeVito, Owen Wilson, the Godfather), cartoon characters (Scooby Doo, Snoopy, Tweek, Wall-E), and fictional robots and monsters (R2-D2, Terminator, Frankenstein). Tattooing has a precedent in the lavish "body art" applied to aircraft, tanks, and other machinery during World War II. Images such as these might render machines more human to those who operate them.

7. See Reddit thread cited above. This wasn't the only time American soldiers had sent an EOD robot on a suicide mission. One US Army unit stationed in Iraq reportedly outfitted its robots with antipersonnel mines, sent them into places where insurgents were thought to be hiding, and then detonated the explosives by remote control. See Singer 2009, 32.

8. See Allison 2006, 13.

9. A version of this question was posed by Short (2018).

10. US Department of Defense 2017, 21.

11. Rosenberg and Markoff 2016.

12. Klein 2018. By comparison, the NSF's budget for fiscal year 2019 was just under $7.5 billion. The DoD's budget for unmanned and robotic systems represents only 1.4 percent of the Pentagon's total budget, but it's growing rapidly.

13. Connor 2018.

14. Work quoted in Pellerin 2015b. For information about the F-35's costs, see Mizokami 2019.

15. Work quoted in Pellerin 2015b.

16. Wedel 2009.

17. Singer 2009, 1. Fans of the sci-fi TV series *Battlestar Galactica* will recognize the terms *frak* and *frakin'* as the program's faux expletives of choice.

18. Singer quoted in Suchman 2015, 12–13.

19. Ibid. Suchman notes that Gordon Moore himself refuted the notion that his hypothesis is a "law."

20. Etzioni and Etzioni 2017, 73–74.

21. Root quoted in Tadjdeh 2019.

22. Rosenberg and Markoff 2016.

23. Larson 2015.

24. Defense Science Board 2016, i.

25. Nader 1997, 733. History provides several important examples of societies that have been reticent about accepting new technologies. Noel Perrin's book *Giving Up the Gun: Japan's Reversion to the Sword, 1543–1879* is an account of how, after a century in which guns were widely used in Japan, they were gradually phased out over a three-hundred-year period. There are many cases of societies in which collective decisions are made about whether to accept or reject new technologies. See, for example, the case of the Amish, described in Wetmore 2007.

26. Eveleth 2019.

27. Bickford 2020, 60.

28. Singer 2009, 46–51. Although Singer's book *Wired for War* has important historical information, his enthusiasm for today's military robots gets in the way of his narrative.

29. Manson 2018.

30. Suchman 2015, 10.

31. Ibid., 2.

32. Hodder 2012.

33. Hodder 2014, 26–27.

34. Springer 2018.

35. Gibbs 2017.

36. US Department of Defense 2012a.

37. Cowan 2013.

38. Work quoted in Pellerin 2015b.

39. DARPA 2019a.

40. Freedberg 2015.

41. Scharre 2018, 323.

42. Inagaki and Itoh 2013; see also Lin 2016.

43. Defense Science Board 2016, 14. The report also listed six specific barriers to human trust in autonomous systems, including "lack of human-analog sensing and thinking by the machine," "lack of self- or environmental awareness by the machine," and "low mutual understanding of goals."

44. Gillis 2017; see also Hendrickson 2018.

45. Smith 2015.

46. Hawley 2011. By no means are these the only examples. There are numerous semi-autonomous anti-aircraft weapon systems (with "fire-and-forget" missile guidance) that have struck civilian airliners. Examples include Iran Air Flight 655 (downed by a US missile fired from the *USS Vincennes* in 1988) and Ukraine International Airlines Flight 752 (downed by an Iranian missile in 2020). I'm grateful to Andy Bickford and Hugh Gusterson for bringing these to my attention.

47. Cloud and Zucchino 2011. Another problem with drones (and automated systems more generally) is that hackers can potentially hijack them. Some reports have suggested that Iranian cyberwarfare specialists successfully landed a US drone on Iranian soil by jamming its communication links. See Peterson and Faramarzi 2011.

48. Quoted in Cloud 2011.

49. Quoted in ibid.

50. Defense Science Board 2004, 154.

51. Muchina and Merryman-Lotze 2019.

52. Gusterson 2016.

53. Zulaika 2020, 27. The legitimating rhetoric of drone operators is that unlike their colonial-era predecessors, they're able to discriminate "good guys" from "bad guys" and only target those who deserve to be killed. Several anthropologists have also critically examined drone warfare and its effects (see, for example, Sluka 2011; Gusterson 2016; Edney-Browne 2017). Akbar Ahmed's work on drones will be discussed in chapter 7.

54. See Bickford 2020, 65. Bickford's analysis cites the work of anthropologist Alfred Bell. As early as 1925, another anthropologist, Bronisław Malinowski, argued that magic, science, and religion often coexist within the same society. See Malinowski 1948 [1925].

55. Gregory 2011, 201.

56. The comments were posted to a Reddit thread ("Marine Corps testing remote controlled robot outfitted with M240 machine gun"), at www.reddit .com/r/USMC/comments/4tt7pu/marine_corps_testing_remote_controlled_ robot/.

57. Ibid.

58. An old Vietnam War–era quip went something like this: "Never forget that your weapon was made by the lowest bidder." I'm grateful to Andy Bickford for bringing this to my attention.

59. Soboleski 2018.

60. US Army Research Laboratory 2015.

61. Ibid.

62. US Army Research Laboratory 2018; see also Chen et al. 2017, 2018. Chen has suggested that at some point, real-time "bidirectional transparency" between humans and robots might be achieved. ARL is also exploring the inverse case: how human intentions might be made more transparent for robots—by relaying humans' brain activity to machines (see Miller 2019).

63. Wang, Pynadath, and Hill 2016.

64. Billings et al. 2012, 110.

65. Giroux 2007. Even at my own university (which is not considered an "R2" university), human factors researchers obtained a five-year, $100 million NASA grant in 2017 for a project on "human-automation interaction" and "individual

and team performance factors" with potential military applications. During my twenty years at San José State University, some of the largest grants awarded to researchers have come from the sprawling NASA Ames Research Center (see chapter 3).

66. Eddins 2017b.

67. US Air Force Research Laboratory 2015.

68. Draper quoted in Eddins 2017a.

69. Alarcon et al. 2018; Gallimore et al. 2019.

70. Zacharias 2019.

71. Johnson et al. 2018.

72. Aha and Coman 2017. This research was presented at a conference of the Association for the Advancement of Artificial Intelligence. Researchers from the Naval Research Laboratory have expressed great interest in the subject of trust in autonomous systems, and even published a book on the topic several years ago (see Mittu et al. 2016).

73. Jenkins quoted in Schehl 2016.

74. Jenkins quoted in Seck 2016.

75. Bainbridge 1983; see also Ganesh 2020.

76. Pineiro quoted in Brady 2016.

77. Tomczak quoted in Tadjdeh 2019.

78. Anthropologist David Price has noted that social science in the service of a militarized state can lead to unforeseen and troubling consequences. See Price 2016.

79. Mills 1958, 64.

80. Lee 2018; Thompson and Bremmer 2018; US Department of Defense 2018.

81. Mills 1958, 60.

82. Grossman 1996.

CHAPTER 3. PENTAGON WEST

1. For a discussion of "strategic partnerships," see Ivey 2018. For a discussion of "synergistic" relationships and "cross-pollination," see Pellerin 2015a. Anthropologist Ruth Benedict may have introduced the term *synergy* into modern English during the 1940s (see Maslow and Honigman 1970, 326).

2. Cook 2016; see also Fang 2018b.

3. Zegart and Childs 2018. Zegart is a senior fellow at the conservative-leaning Hoover Institution, and Childs is an air force officer, but their observations are frequently echoed by both military and civilian writers from a range of political perspectives.

4. Ibid.

5. See Turner 2006, chap. 4.

6. Brand 1972.

7. Levine 2018, 106.

8. Hafner and Lyon 1998; see also Turner 2006, chap. 4.

9. Brand 1972.

10. English-Lueck 2002.

11. Fox 2014; Frank 1997.

12. Balise 2015.

13. Kaplan 2016.

14. Mewhinney and Pederson 2008; Kastrenakes 2014.

15. Kaplan 2016.

16. Quoted in Hempel 2015.

17. Ibid.

18. Freedberg 2017.

19. Quoted in Mitchell 2018.

20. Quoted in Kuldell and Konkel 2018.

21. Williams 2018; Behrens 2019.

22. Yannuzzi 2000.

23. Quoted in Stanford University 2017.

24. O'Hara 2005.

25. Paletta 2016.

26. Cook 2016.

27. Shachtman 2010.

28. Levine 2018.

29. Kehaulani Goo and Klein 2007.

30. Page 2018.

31. Szoldra 2016.

32. Fang 2016.

33. Work 2017.

34. Allen 2017.

35. Ibid.

36. Ibid.

37. Quoted in Pellerin 2017. In reality, Google (like Facebook, Twitter, and many other tech firms) is primarily an advertising company. As noted in chapter 1, the vast majority of Google's revenue comes from online ads.

38. Fang 2019c.

39. Conger 2019.

40. Quoted in ibid.

41. Quoted in ibid.

42. Conger 2018.

43. Conger 2019; see also Pichai 2019. The Google statement included an important qualifier: the company would continue working with the military in

other areas, including "cybersecurity, training, military recruitment, veterans' healthcare, and search and rescue."

44. Fernández Campbell 2018.

45. Poulson 2019.

46. Bergen 2018.

47. Fang 2019a, 2019b; Hatmaker 2018. It's worth mentioning that Anduril Industries takes its name from a fictional sword, Andúril, described in J. R. R. Tolkien's 1954 fantasy novel *The Lord of the Rings*. In the fictional language of Quenya, Andúril means "Flame of the West," and the sword was a reforged weapon carried by the heroic protagonist Aragorn. The story's villain is the evil Sauron, from the eastern lands of Mordor. One can only speculate about the degree to which the company's executives view their enterprise as a weapon for countering the threat of enemies from the East. This isn't the only example of a high-tech defense firm donning the mantle of Tolkien's mythical world—see note 58 below.

48. Battelle 2005.

49. National Science Foundation 1994.

50. Hart 2004.

51. Nesbit 2017; see also Ahmed 2015.

52. Nesbit 2017.

53. Ullman 2000; Thuraisingham 2015.

54. Nesbit 2017.

55. Quoted in Menegus 2019.

56. Quoted in Kelly 2019.

57. Snow 2018. Despite these problems, the FBI was using Amazon's Rekognition in pilot tests by early 2019.

58. Biddle and Devereaux 2019. Palantir has received funding from both DIUx and In-Q-Tel. As in the case of Anduril Industries (see note 47 above), Palantir's name is inspired by Tolkien's *The Lord of the Rings*. In the book, the *palantír* are crystal stones that allow people to see past and future events. We might imagine some of the reasons that Silicon Valley's tech industry includes many devotees of Tolkien's work. Perhaps it's a way of romanticizing and aestheticizing what might otherwise be tedious, boring desk jobs—a magical metamorphosis of Dilbert into Aragorn. See Sapra 2020; Rodriguez 2020.

59. Quoted in Tiku 2018.

60. Quoted in Fang 2018a.

61. Amazon 2018.

62. Kim 2019; see also Oracle 2020. Even relatively minor players like Adobe Systems tried to get a piece of the action. Among other things, the company posted a blog titled "How the Department of Defense Will Benefit from New Adobe Software Solutions." See Lindgren 2016.

63. Kuldell and Konkel 2018.

64. Emmons 2019.

65. Conger, Sanger, and Shane 2019.

66. Price 2016, xiv–xviii.

67. O'Mara 2018; see also O'Mara 2019.

68. Tucker 2015. *National Defense* magazine has reported that the US Army is developing a program to integrate Google Earth with images of building interiors to create what researchers are calling "Google Earth on steroids." See Magnuson 2019.

69. Dastin 2019.

70. Quoted in Ferdinando 2018.

71. Price 2016.

72. O'Mara 2018. A clear example of the historical links between US military and intelligence agencies and Silicon Valley is the KH-11 Kennen satellite system, a group of reconnaissance satellites manufactured by Lockheed in Sunnyvale, California, and first launched in 1976. This system, often called the Key Hole series, still functions today.

73. Mehta 2019.

74. For an analysis of controlling processes as dynamic components of power, see Nader 1997.

75. Quoted in Mehta 2019. It appears that Stephens incorrectly referred to the Android Team Awareness Kit as ATAP. A US Department of Homeland Security white paper refers to the app as TAK, which presumably is pronounced "talk." See US Department of Homeland Security 2019.

76. Quoted in ibid.

77. Quoted in ibid.

78. Zegart and Childs 2018.

79. For abundant evidence, see Poulson 2020.

80. McCray 2018.

81. Heinrich 2002.

82. Ibid.

83. Jack Poulson, personal communication, June 19, 2019.

CHAPTER 4. THE DARK ARTS

1. Foucault 2003, 15. Michel Foucault was provocatively inverting a phrase attributed to Carl von Clausewitz, the great nineteenth-century military theorist and Prussian general, who famously wrote, "War is nothing more than the continuation of politics by other means . . . for political aims are the end and war is the means, and the means can never be conceived without the end."

2. Beinart 2018; see also Kinzer 2006.

3. Rouse n.d.

4. During World War II, influential twentieth-century anthropologist Gregory Bateson aided the war effort in Burma by creating "black propaganda" (messages that appear to come from one source but in fact come from another) that was disseminated as radio broadcasts. Bateson, whose theory of "schismogenesis" informed his work, sought to foster distrust and disunity among the Japanese troops that occupied the region by eroding morale. For example, some of the broadcasts communicated messages that exaggerated how poorly things were going at home. After the war, Bateson bitterly regretted his participation in the war effort. See Price 1998.

5. See, for example, Orwell 1946; Ellul 1962; Herman and Chomsky 1988.

6. Hodges 2018. See also Hodges 2019; Oddo 2018; Briant 2022. A timely example of the potentially dangerous effects of domestic propaganda is the US Capitol riot of January 6, 2021, led by right-wing extremists and conspiracy theorists fueled by social media messages and ultraconservative media outlets.

7. The reason the companies are opposed to regulation is that their business models rely on advertising sales (rather than, say, subscription or membership fees). See Sherman 2018.

8. Hodges 2018. On a related note, five billion people worldwide have cell phones, but only about half of these are smartphones (with internet access).

9. See, for example, Wylie 2019, 75–79.

10. Lane 2016.

11. See, for example, Lapowsky 2016; Tett 2017; Taggart 2017.

12. See Anderson and Horvath 2017; Foster 2016; Grassegger and Krogerus 2017.

13. Witt and Pasternack 2019a.

14. Knight 2018.

15. Bidlake 1992, 21.

16. Quoted in Laterza 2021, 130.

17. Wagstaff 2000.

18. Weinberger 2005.

19. Quoted in Morgan 2005.

20. See Witt and Pasternack 2019b; NATO STRATCOM 2015; Sarawak Report 2018; Knight 2018; Blumenthal 2018.

21. Hersh 2002.

22. Bamford 2005.

23. Mazzetti and Daragahi 2005.

24. Eng 2016.

25. Prendergast 2010; DeYoung and Pincus 2008.

26. Ewen 1996. Emma Briant's book *Propaganda and Counter-terrorism* (2015) includes a discussion of SCL Group and the way in which it blurred the boundaries between foreign and domestic targets.

27. Bernays quoted in ibid., 162–63. See also Bernays 1923, 1928.

28. Cutlip 1994, 164.

29. Quoted in Tye 2002, 111.

30. See Weiss 2018; Ghoshal 2018.

31. *Behavior change* is a term that has often been used in public health settings in impoverished countries—for example, HIV awareness campaigns to get people accustomed to the idea of using condoms, or anti-polio initiatives that convince people it's safe to get their children immunized.

32. Details of these encounters are presented in Wylie 2019.

33. Doward and Gibbs 2017.

34. Blakely 2016.

35. "Five-factor" traits were first proposed in the early 1960s (Tupes and Christal 1961) but weren't popularized in social psychology until the 1980s (see, for example, Goldberg 1981; McCrae and Costa 1983). The "Big Five" is the latest in a long line of psychometric instruments created over the past century. Critics within psychology include Samuel Juni, Jack Block, and Paul McAdams. For a summary of their work, see Paul 2005, 191–96. Anthropologists have scarcely shown interest in the topic, though research among the Tsimane of Bolivia indicates that "Big Five" traits are not universal (Gurven et al. 2013). OCEAN personality tests are big business and have been adopted by many organizations for hiring, career counseling, and marketing purposes.

36. Davies 2015.

37. Lapowsky 2018.

38. Kosinski 2013; Kosinski et al. 2016.

39. See Grassegger and Krogerus 2017. The claims made by Kosinski and his colleagues are remarkable: on the basis of sixty-eight Facebook "likes," they claim to be able to predict a user's skin color, sexual orientation, and political party affiliation. Cambridge Analytica reportedly developed similar tools after SCL Group hired psychologist Aleksandr Kogan to create a predictive personality instrument using Facebook "likes" from tens of thousands of users and their "friends" (Davies 2015).

40. Grassegger and Krogerus 2017.

41. Quoted in Kranish 2016. What is curious—and typical of comments made by big data's boosters—is the notion that bigger is better, that collecting enough "data points" will magically reveal the truth. Anthropologist Genevieve Bell calls this the "new empiricism," peddled by the custodians of big data, the "new priests and alchemists" of the digital era (see Bell 2015, 23–24).

42. Grassegger and Krogerus 2017. In the end, it appears that Cambridge Analytica may not have used psychographic techniques very widely in the 2016 Trump campaign, as its executives claimed. See Kaiser 2019; Laterza 2021, 134–36.

43. Wylie 2019, 49.

44. Ibid., 74. Cambridge Analytica's influence on the 2016 US presidential elections shouldn't be entirely dismissed, since Wylie's memoir describes at some length the ways in which psychometric methods complemented (rather than competed with) the company's immersive qualitative research. For an anthropologically informed analysis of Wylie's claims, see Laterza 2021. Wylie has never mentioned the names of any anthropologists or sociologists employed by Cambridge Analytica or SCL Group, so the degree to which social scientists were involved with Cambridge Analytica has yet to be confirmed.

45. Grasseger and Krogerus 2017.

46. BBC 2018.

47. Quoted in Auchard 2018.

48. Eckdale and Tully 2019; Pasternack 2017.

49. Epstein 2017.

50. Goldsmith 2017.

51. Ibid.

52. Ahmed and Hakim 2018.

53. See Cadwalladr 2020; Kaiser 2019.

54. In the early 2000s, Cabayan played an instrumental role in launching the precursor to the Human Terrain System, a US Army counterinsurgency effort that embedded anthropologists and other social scientists with US combat brigades in Iraq and Afghanistan. See Gezari 2013.

55. Rebala 2018.

56. Day and Braun 2017.

57. Flynn, Pottinger, and Batchelor 2010. Among other things, the publication advocated the use of social scientists embedded with military units "human terrain teams" as intelligence-gatherers.

58. Dreyfuss 2018.

59. Taggart 2017.

60. Quoted in Kranish 2016.

61. Condliffe 2017.

62. See Nader 1997. Vito Laterza (2021) argues that those who focus exclusively on Cambridge Analytica's "psychographic" techniques fail to consider the role of qualitative and perhaps even ethnographic methods in influencing Trump's victory in the 2016 US presidential election.

63. Koreh 2019.

64. Quoted in Cadwalladr 2020; see also Briant 2022.

65. Wylie 2019, 8.

66. Franceschi-Bicchierai 2018.

67. In 2012, Facebook famously engaged in an experiment to manipulate the moods of its users by means of its News Feed feature. One can only speculate about the extent to which Facebook and other social media firms have conducted similar experiments. See Meyer 2014.

68. Tufekci 2018.

69. See Hsu and Lutz 2020; Abril 2020.

70. McNamee 2018.

71. See Alter 2017; Bosker 2016. Stanford University's Persuasive Technology Laboratory, directed by psychologist B. J. Fogg, is an alarming example of how this influential new area of applied social science has quickly become normalized. Critics of these techniques include Tristan Harris, a computer scientist and former Google "design ethicist" who later founded the Center for Humane Technology (see Bosker 2016).

CHAPTER 5. JUGGERNAUT

1. See Price 2007. A crucial factor in understanding the militarization of science is the fact that nearly one-third of all funding for domestic research and development in the United States (more than $350 billion in 2009) comes from the federal government, and the majority of that funding—approximately 60 percent—is for defense spending. In other words, *almost 20 percent of all funding* for science research and development in the United States is channeled through the military. See Kennedy 2012, 9–13.

2. I'm not at all suggesting that Russell didn't follow the heavily regulated contracting processes that are involved in DARPA program management, or that he engaged in any kind of fiscal misconduct or ethical impropriety. It's difficult to know exactly how much money is managed by individual DARPA program managers. Projects that "cut metal" (in other words, create material objects such as drone prototypes or robotic systems) tend to be vastly more expensive than basic research contracts. In the current era of DARPA, program managers typically "pitch" their projects to agency directors, hoping to get approval. I'm grateful to Sharon Weinberger for explaining these details.

3. Duke University 1996.

4. Quoted in *Oxford Mail* 2002.

5. Quoted in Llewellyn 1998.

6. Russell 2003.

7. Quoted in Henderson 2002.

8. Russell 2003.

9. See Hewett 1999.

10. Ibid.; Glover 1995.

11. *Oxford Mail* 2002.

12. ESPN 2002.

13. *Oxford Mail* 2002.

14. Bolton 2007.

15. Nicolson 2003; Orwell 1945.

16. *Economist* 2003.

17. An entertaining and thoughtful article written by an anonymous gay rugby player points out the gender contradictions built into the game: "Rugby, taken out of its sporting context, is about as homoerotic as a platonic activity can get. Yet somehow, the game where thirty muscular (mostly) in-shape men hug each other has the reputation of being the pinnacle of masculinity." See Anonymous 2016.

18. Military men have made explicit connections between these contests over the years. "There are similarities between the harsh and legal demands of warfare and the thrill we get from a full-bodied contact sport like rugby," wrote Australian army general Sir Peter Cosgrove. British admiral Lord Jellicoe noted: "Rugby football, to my mind, above all games is one which develops the qualities which go to make good fighting men. It teaches unselfishness, esprit de corps, quickness of decision, and keeps fit those engaged in it." Quoted in Cooper 2016.

19. Quoted in DARPA 2017a. Russell's comments had an anthropological twist that might be interpreted as a nod to Bronisław Malinowski, a towering figure in modern British social anthropology, who stressed the importance of documenting the "imponderabilia of everyday life" when doing ethnographic work. Malinowski also played a crucial role in outlining the differences between magic, science, and religion. See Malinowski 1922, 1948 [1925].

20. Waddington and Smith 2009, 113–16. At least one study, published in 1993, surveyed students at a British university and found that nearly one in twenty males reported using anabolic steroids, particularly if active in bodybuilding or rugby, suggesting that "use of anabolic steroids may be widespread in the UK." See Williamson 1993.

21. One of Russell's cowritten SAIC publications (Russell, Bulkley, and Grafton 2005) has been cited in a number of journal articles and books. See, for example, Brown and Tvaryanas 2008, 43; Deuster et al. 2007; Matthews and Schnyer 2019, 264.

22. SAIC's website uses the term *lethality solutions* to describe its weapons systems. See www.saic.com/what-we-do/platforms/weapon-systems.

23. Russell, Bulkley, and Grafton 2005.

24. See, for example, Deuster et al. 2007; Brown and Tvaryanas 2008.

25. See Martindale 2006.

26. Quoted in Hawkins 2019.

27. See Hawkins 2019. For example, psychologist Leslie Sherlin—who, among other things, is cofounder of the company Neuro Therapeutics—has developed research partnerships with US Special Operations Forces, USA Track and Field, the National Football League's Seattle Seahawks, and other organizations. See also www.lesliesherlin.com/bio.

28. For a concise summary of the SAIC report by Russell, Bulkley, and Grafton, see Martindale 2006.

29. Russell, Bulkley, and Grafton 2005.

30. Deuster et al. 2007.

31. Russell 2003.

32. Bartlett Bulkley now goes by her married name, Bartlett Russell; her educational experience is summarized at www.linkedin.com/in/bartlett-russell-4634b1105.

33. Woo 2011.

34. See Rosalind Franklin Society 2013.

35. See *Cleveland Plain Dealer* 2015; *Delaware Cape Gazette* 2013; Singer and Russell 2012.

36. See MITRE Corporation 2008, 6; Defence Research and Development Canada 2009, 23. See also the LinkedIn profile of Bartlett Russell, cited in note 32 above. The description of Scitor Corporation is from Shorrock 2015.

37. Shorrock 2015. I am not implying that either Adam Russell or Bartlett Bulkley ever participated in covert operations or "black ops"—there's no evidence that they did any such work for Scitor Corporation, SAIC, or any other organization.

38. Hawkins 2019.

39. Russell and Bulkley 2007, 1–5, 9–13; see also Watts 2008, 29.

40. See Cognitive Engineering Research Institute 2008, 2; Shaffer 2008, 92.

41. MITRE Corporation 2008, 4–5.

42. Belfiore 2015.

43. Belfiore 2014.

44. IARPA 2014.

45. *FCW* 2014; see also US Office of the Director of National Intelligence 2014b.

46. Hurley 2014, 240.

47. Charles River Analytics 2014.

48. Soterix Medical 2014; Feyereisen 2016. Among the many subcontractors involved in the multiyear project was Simcoach Games, a small firm that develops "brain training" games. See http://sgschallenge.com/robot-factory/.

49. IARPA 2013.

50. Hunter 2015.

51. ARGFest 2013.

52. For example, the Defense Intelligence Agency has reportedly been monitoring the geospatial location of some cell phone users by purchasing commercially available data from weather and gaming apps. See Tau 2021.

53. IARPA 2013.

54. IARPA 2012.

55. Geertz 1973, 44.

56. Creative Technologies 2012.

57. For example, IARPA sponsored a project in which computer scientists from the University of Santa Cruz and BBN Technologies developed live-action role-playing games "for supporting an emic approach to understanding culture . . . [and] to gain cross-cultural awareness in a more internalized manner than what results from traditional etic description-based learning" (see Logas et al. 2014). Additional research funding came from the US Army Research Office; see Ferguson and Diller 2015. The emphasis on online gaming and virtual training tools may have been partly the legacy of Russell's predecessor, IARPA program manager and psychologist Rita Bush.

58. Weinberger 2017.

59. Sharon Weinberger, personal communication, June 14, 2019.

60. Weinberger 2017, 423. In an interview conducted prior to his 2009 departure, Tether was asked about whether DARPA had expanded into behavioral or anthropological studies. He replied: "Yes, we have a program starting up, and it's one of those programs that worries me. It could easily go south . . . in a real political sense. . . . [I]t has the potential to be a TIA [Total Information Awareness, a sweeping 2002 surveillance technology program that DARPA canceled following a public outcry], so I'm watching it very carefully, obviously" (see DARPA 2009, 415–16). Tether was almost certainly referring to ICEWS, the Integrated Conflict Early Warning System (see chapter 6), which was eventually contracted to the gargantuan defense firm Lockheed Martin.

61. Prabhakar 2013, 8.

62. Ibid., 7.

63. Immediately after leaving DARPA, Dugan accepted a position with Google to create its Advanced Technology and Projects group, and then left to direct Facebook's Building 8, the company's advanced research division.

64. The phrase "department of mad scientists" comes from the title of a book about DARPA. See Belfiore 2009.

65. For a summary of the principle of "limited tenure" at DARPA (as well as a great deal more information about the agency), see Congressional Research Service 2020.

66. Baker 2015; Yong 2018. By 2016, there were indications that the crisis might go far beyond psychology. See, for example, Baker 2016.

67. Physicist Richard Feynman lambasted "cargo cult science," by which he meant psychology and other disciplines whose practitioners held scientific pretensions. He commented on what's now fashionably called the "reproducibility crisis" nearly a half-century ago. See Feynman 1974.

68. DARPA 2016a, 2016b.

69. Mead 1973, 6–7.

70. DARPA 2016b. On the other hand, DARPA's interests might have been more prosaic. As a colleague with a good understanding of the political and cul-

tural context once mentioned to me, "they may have just been trying to latch onto the last vestiges of the culture money."

71. Suchow et al. 2016. It appears that the main project investigator is UC Berkeley psychologist Thomas Griffiths.

72. The co-principal investigators for this project include applied mathematician Joshua Plotkin and mathematical biologist Alexander Stewart, according to their curricula vitae (which are available online; see http://mathbio.sas.upenn .edu/Papers/Plotkin_CV.pdf and www.alexanderjstewart.org/Stewart_CV.pdf).

73. Micale 2017.

74. Ning et al. 2018.

75. See Ravindranath 2016. It's possible that Russell borrowed the supercollider concept from Microsoft engineer Duncan Watts, who suggested in 2014 that "a major breakthrough for computational social science . . . would be a 'social supercollider': a facility that combines multiple streams of data, creating richer and more realistic portraits of individual behavior and identity, while retaining the benefits of massive scale" (see Watts 2014). On the other hand, the similarity might be pure coincidence.

76. DARPA 2017b; see also Gera 2018. To put Ground Truth into motion, DARPA reportedly awarded a $3.7 million contract to the Johns Hopkins University Applied Physics Laboratory, in partnership with the University of Hawaii and an artificial intelligence company called Graphika. See Blinde 2018.

77. Social Science Space 2019; Rogers 2017.

78. DARPA 2019b; see also Atherton 2019.

79. Quoted in Scales 2018.

80. According to his LinkedIn profile, Adam Russell left DARPA in March 2020, after nearly five years with the agency. He had a relatively long stint at DARPA—as noted earlier, program managers are typically employed for three to five years. Russell moved on to serve as a chief scientist at the University of Maryland's Applied Research Laboratory for Intelligence and Security. See https:// linkedin.com/in/adam-russell-00868b162/. After his departure, Bartlett Russell took over management of Understanding Group Biases, according to DARPA's website (see www.darpa.mil/program/understanding-group-biases).

81. DARPA 2018.

82. Geertz 1973, 5. The phrase "webs of significance" is among Geertz's most memorable. It comes from the following sentence: "Believing, with Max Weber, that man is an animal suspended in webs of significance he himself has spun, I take culture to be those webs, and the analysis of it to be therefore not an experimental science in search of law but an interpretive one in search of meaning."

83. DARPA 2018.

84. SIFT n.d.

85. From SIFT 2019.
86. Lin and Hwa n.d.
87. Ibid.

CHAPTER 6. PRECOGS, INC.

1. Maybury 2010, 3.
2. Mark Maybury quoted in Shachtman 2012. Several of those using the term *social radar* are affiliated with the MITRE Corporation, a federally funded research and development center. See, for example, Costa and Boiney 2012.
3. Mathieu et al. 2012.
4. Contemporary modeling and simulation (M&S) methods were first developed in engineering and computer sciences and are now used in many fields, ranging from medicine to meteorology. For a historical perspective on M&S, see Sokolowski and Banks 2009, 7–14. DoD has used modeling and simulation for decades (flight simulators to train pilots, war games simulating nuclear attacks, etc.), but sociocultural modeling is relatively new.
5. Maybury 2010, 3. A number of social scientists, such as Laura McNamara and Jessica Turnley, have written about the challenges of sociocultural modeling, and their work may have shifted the thinking of some people within defense circles—at least for a time. See McNamara 2010; Turnley 2010.
6. Sociocultural modeling, simulation, and forecasting is a discourse with specialized terminology, academic journals (for example, *Journal of Artificial Societies* and *Social Simulation*), conferences, and so on. University laboratories specializing in this field include Carnegie Mellon University's Center for Computational Analysis of Social and Organizational Systems, University of Maryland's Laboratory for Computational Cultural Dynamics, University of Pennsylvania's Center for Human Modeling and Simulation, MIT's Media Center, and Dartmouth College's Laboratory for Human Terrain.
7. Flynn, Sisco, and Ellis 2015, 14.
8. Social scientists' participation in such projects will almost certainly be more ethically ambiguous than the US Army's Human Terrain System, an initiative that was condemned by the American Anthropological Association in 2007. Predictive modeling programs tend to place social scientists in the role of "subject matter experts" delivering (or translating) cultural knowledge from their offices, rather than in the role of ethnographers embedded in war zones.
9. See, for example, Ferguson 2012; Davis 2010; Lutz 2008. I don't mean to imply that these ethically problematic and ineffective initiatives represent the majority of what anthropologists or other social scientists are doing within the defense establishment. In fact, there are a significant number who serve as faculty in military colleges, as training instructors, and in many other roles. For

examples, see Rubenstein, Fosher, and Fujimura 2012; McNamara and Rubenstein, 2011; Albro and Ivey 2014; Fosher 2009.

10. See Boiney and Foster 2013.

11. HSCB 2009, 1.

12. Abella 2008; Krepivenich and Watts 2015.

13. For an example of how the Arab Spring has been used to justify DoD funding, see SBIR 2012.

14. These included Rebecca Goolsby, Richard Lobban, Patricia Partnow, and
Lawrence Kuznar. See Hartley 2008, 8, 12–13.

15. Ibid., 53, 55.

16. Schmorrow 2010, 15.

17. Aptima's company directory lists employees' credentials and publications.
See www.aptima.com/about/our-team/.

18. SBIR 2014. Despite these claims, it appears that SCIPR's architects relied
on social psychology (not cultural anthropology); see Grier et al. 2008.

19. SBIR 2014.

20. Quoted in Aptima 2012.

21. Ibid.

22. Circinus 2015.

23. In 2018, while Circinus was under the leadership of Elliott Briody, reports
revealed that the company had offered to sell "social media surveillance tools" to
repressive governments in Eastern Europe and the Middle East, including the
United Arab Emirates, Romania, and Tunisia. See Biddle 2018.

24. US Office of the Director of National Intelligence 2014a.

25. Beckman Institute 2014.

26. Fosher 2008, 54.

27. Tambayong and Carley 2013, 3.

28. Diesner et al. 2012, 337; Diesner 2012, 179–80.

29. Diesner 2012, 59. The Human Relations Area Files (HRAF) is a compila-
tion of thousands of ethnographic sources on hundreds of cultures, indexed to
facilitate cross-cultural comparisons. HRAF was created in 1949 with significant funding from American military and intelligence agencies, and originated
with Yale University's "Cross-Cultural Survey." See Price 2012.

30. Kuznar 2008, 20–21.

31. Fosher 2014.

32. Quoted in Weinberger 2011, 566, 568.

33. Quoted in Stockman 2010.

34. I'm grateful to an anonymous peer reviewer for suggesting this point. On
a related note, see Zulaika 2012.

35. Quoted in Smolan and Erwitt 2012.

36. Kitchin 2014, 24.

37. National Science Foundation 2006.

38. University of California, Los Angeles 2014a.

39. University of California, Los Angeles 2014b.

40. Quoted in Wolpert 2010.

41. Brantingham 2013.

42. See Marlowe 2010.

43. PredPol 2014.

44. Bond-Graham and Winston 2013.

45. Quoted in ibid.

46. Ibid.

47. Quoted in Bond-Graham and Winston 2014.

48. Quoted in Stockman 2010.

49. Goldstein 2006, 28.

50. Ackoff Collaboratory n.d.

51. Quoted in Goldstein 2006.

52. Quoted in Stockman 2010.

53. Ibid.

54. For information about ICEWS from the point of view of two developers, see Schmorrow and Nicholson 2012, 419–54.

55. US Federal Business Opportunities 2012.

56. Shachtman 2011b.

57. Software programs that analyze databases of news reports or social media must be able to distinguish between "real" news and "fake" news (for example, disinformation or propaganda). Not surprisingly, the Defense Department is funding research aimed at developing tools for "computational fact checking." See Ciampaglia et al. 2015.

58. Shachtman 2011b.

59. Lockheed-Martin 2014.

60. Anthropologist Andrew Bickford (2020, 6) reminds us: "Whether through war magic or technology, those concerned with warfare and violence have tried to devise ways to make their soldiers or warriors better than their enemies, or at least make their soldiers or warriors think they are better armed and armored than their enemies. . . . Just as mythology and folklore bring us tales of men and women made seemingly invincible through the application of magic or enchantment, the US military also trades in ideas and portrayals of the mythic warrior."

61. Shachtman 2011a.

62. US Department of Defense 2012b.

63. Gorman et al. 2013.

64. Ibid. See also Ackerman 2011.

65. Gorman et al. 2013.

66. Nakashima and Warrick 2013.

67. Woodward 2011, 7, 10.

68. Gorman et al. 2013.

69. Cockburn 2015, 244–60; see also Ambinder and Grady 2012.

70. Gorman et al. 2013.

71. The team included computer scientists Galen Pickard and Christopher White (MIT graduates and former students of Alex Pentland). See Shachtman 2011a.

72. Quoted in ibid.

73. Kilcullen 2010, 51–76.

74. Belcher 2013, 181.

75. Ibid., 190.

76. Pentland 2012.

77. Pentland 2011.

78. Belcher 2013, 189–90.

79. In an interview with Sharon Weinberger (with whom I communicated while researching this book), Prabhakar declined to provide any substantive details about the program, citing its classified nature.

80. US Department of Defense 2013, 2014.

81. US Department of Defense 2014, 125–29.

82. US Department of Defense 2015, 142–43. In an April 2013 press briefing, Prabhakar noted that Nexus7 provided part of the basis of XDATA. Apparently, XDATA's program manager is none other than Christopher White (one of the former MIT students sent to Kabul to work on Nexus7). The program was consistent with the Obama administration's support for big data initiatives.

83. Belcher 2013, 63.

84. US Office of the President 2012; Rossino 2020.

85. Hudson 2014.

86. The late Stephen Hawking, an internationally renowned physicist, famously sounded alarm bells in 2014, specifically citing the threat of autonomous weapons. Elon Musk (CEO of SpaceX and Tesla Motors) warned, "We should be careful about artificial intelligence. With artificial intelligence we are summoning the demon" (quoted in Cooper-White 2014). And in 2015, Clive Sinclair told the BBC: "Once you start to make machines that are rivalling and surpassing humans with intelligence, it's going to be very difficult for us to survive. It's just an inevitability" (quoted in BBC 2015). Perhaps the most influential movement to stop autonomous weapon systems is the Campaign to Stop Killer Robots, an international coalition of scientists and NGOs opposed to such systems.

CHAPTER 7. POSTDATA

1. For a discussion of militarization as a cultural process, see González and Gusterson 2009, 6–7. A full discussion of a "permanent state of war readiness" can

be found in Lutz 2001. For a thorough overview of the latest phase of American militarism, see Bacevich 2013. For a historical analysis of the topic, see Vine 2020.

2. Sideris 2020.

3. Metz 2012.

4. Even before the Facebook–Cambridge Analytica scandal, a "data rights" movement was taking shape. For an overview, see Tisne 2018.

5. It's possible that advertising had an effect. The VIC-20 was marketed aggressively, with the tagline "Why buy just a video game?"

6. I don't mean this as an insult—I'm speaking largely from my own experiences, including conversations with friends and relatives in the tech industry. Four decades ago, Langdon Winner proposed the idea that artifacts have politics, a notion that has influenced my thinking over the years. See Winner 1980.

7. See Buolamwini and Gebru 2018; Hardesty 2018.

8. See Hao 2019b.

9. Quoted in Wood 2020. There's a rapidly growing body of work that documents different forms of racial, sexual, and class bias in algorithms (see, for example, O'Neil 2016; Eubanks 2017; Wachter-Boettcher 2017; Noble 2018).

10. Here I'm not just referring to the pitifully low numbers of women, African Americans, and Latinos working as executives and AI researchers in companies like Facebook, Google, and Amazon (Bogost 2019; Harrison 2019) or to the widely publicized scandals in which tech executives tolerated and sometimes encouraged racist and sexist work environments (Pao 2017; Chang 2018). I'm also talking about the reluctance of Facebook and other social media companies to rein in white supremacists (see, for example, Newton 2019; Wong 2019).

11. Taleb 2010, 135–36.

12. As noted in chapter 1, a dramatic example was the US Army's Phoenix Program, which used IBM mainframe computers to create "kill lists" in Vietnam during the 1960s (Valentine 1990, 258–59). David Kilcullen (2004) proposed "a global Phoenix program . . . [that] would provide a useful start point" for "a new strategic approach to the Global War on Terrorism."

13. For critiques of big data analysis, digital positivism, and "predictive analytics," see Kitchin 2014 and Mosco 2014. For a collection of anthropologically informed essays that reframe and contextualize big data, see Boellstorff and Maurer 2015.

14. It's important to recognize that ethnography is neither a mere tool nor only a descriptive method. Ethnography is a theory about how we might make sense of the world around us. A compelling argument for ethnography as theory can be found in Nader 2011.

15. Montgomery McFate, quoted in Price 2009. Once again, this doesn't represent the bulk of what social scientists are doing within the defense establishment. For example, see Rubenstein, Fosher, and Fujimura 2012; McNamara and Rubenstein 2011; Albro and Ivey 2014; Fosher 2009.

16. Ahmed 2013, 9–10.

17. Ibid., 19.

18. It remains to be seen whether the administration of President Joseph Biden will pursue an aggressive strategy of drone warfare as did his predecessors, but his appointment of Avril D. Haines as director of national intelligence isn't encouraging—she played a key role in Obama's drone program. See Barnes 2020.

19. Ahmed 2013, 19. David Price, in a prescient commentary written just weeks after the 9/11 attacks, warned that the war on terror would almost certainly become a war on indigenous peoples (see Price 2001).

20. Ahmed 2013, 19.

21. Ahmed isn't alone in his analysis. Counterinsurgency expert David Kilcullen, who was a staunch advocate of General Petraeus's surge strategy in Iraq, cowrote a scathing critique of drone warfare in a *New York Times* commentary during the height of the so-called war on terror. See Kilcullen and Exum 2009.

22. Quoted in Bartlett 2016.

23. Ibid.

24. Atran 2003.

25. Atran 2016.

26. Atran 2010.

27. Quoted in Bartlett 2016.

28. Price 2008. Perhaps more significantly, many anthropologists would consider Atran's ethics highly questionable—especially his interviews with captive ISIS soldiers. Among the foundational ethical concepts in anthropology is that of voluntary informed consent: the notion that an anthropologist should only conduct research among people who have freely granted him or her permission to do so, after being informed of potential risks. Since Atran's research participants included prisoners captured on a battlefield who were being monitored by armed guards, it is difficult to imagine how Atran would have been able to obtain truly voluntary consent.

29. Aside from any quibbles about Atran's timing, his analyses of white nationalism have been compelling and incisive. See Atran 2017, 2019.

30. Gusterson 2017, 210.

31. Ibid., 212.

32. Ibid., 211.

33. Ibid., 213.

34. Ibid., 214.

35. Tett 2010.

36. For a detailed description of controlling processes—the dynamic components of power—see Nader 1997.

37. Price 2011.

38. Zinn 2012, 46–47. I recognize the fact that there are people working in the defense and intelligence establishments who are seeking to make long-term

changes. However, the extent to which they can transform these institutions within the framework of the US national security state is greatly limited. Efforts to bring about much broader, sweeping changes across the entire society must continue. We all have our roles to play.

APPENDIX

1. I'm using the term *secretive* metaphorically, as a way of indicating that these publicly funded organizations conduct much of their work behind closed doors. Within military and intelligence agencies, terms such as *secret, covert, clandestine,* and *classified* have very specific meanings, and so I have tried to avoid using these terms.

2. Gusterson 1997, 115.

3. Nader 1969, 307.

4. Ibid., 308.

5. See Federation of American Scientists at www.fas.org.

6. González 2009, 86–87.

7. Ibid., 13–18.

8. Access the Internet Archive at www.archive.org.

9. Price 1997.

10. Ibid., 14.

11. See Public Intelligence at www.publicintelligence.net and the Snowden Archive at https://www.cjfe.org/snowden.

12. Singer 1999.

13. Allison 2010.

14. Mills 1959, 218.

References

Abella, Alex. 2008. *Soldiers of Reason: The RAND Corporation and the Rise of the American Empire*. New York: Mariner Books.

Abril, Danielle. 2020. The Facebook Ad Boycott Ended Months Ago, but Some Big Companies Continue the Fight. *Fortune,* November 7. https://fortune.com/2020/11/07/facebook-ad-boycott-big-brands-lego-clorox-verizon-microsoft-hp/.

Ackerman, Spencer. 2011. How Special Ops Copied al-Qaida to Kill It. *Wired,* September 9. www.wired.com/2011/09/mcchrystal-network/all/.

Ackoff Collaboratory. n.d. NonKin Village. www.acasa.upenn.edu/nonKin/nonkin-description.htm.

Aha, David, and Alexandra Coman. 2017. *The AI Rebellion: Changing the Narrative.* Proceedings of the 31st AAAI Conference on Artificial Intelligence, 4826–30. Menlo Park, CA: Association for the Advancement of Artificial Intelligence.

Ahmed, Akbar. 2013. *The Thistle and the Drone: How America's War on Terror Became a Global War on Tribal Islam.* Washington, DC: Brookings Institution Press.

Ahmed, Azam, and Danny Hakim. 2018. Mexico's Hardball Politics Get Even Harder as PRI Fights to Hold On to Power. *New York Times,* June 24. www.nytimes.com/2018/06/24/world/americas/mexico-election-cambridge-analytica.html.

Ahmed, Nafeez. 2015. How the CIA Made Google. *Medium,* January 22. https://
medium.com/insurge-intelligence/how-the-cia-made-google-e836451a959e.

Alarcon, Gene, Joseph Lyons, James Christensen, and Margaret Bowers. 2018.
The Role of Propensity to Trust and the Five Factor Model across the Trust
Process. *Journal of Research in Personality* 75 (August): 69–82.

Albro, Robert, and Bill Ivey. 2014. *Cultural Awareness in the Military: Developments and Implications for Future Humanitarian Cooperation.* London:
Palgrave.

Allen, Gregory. 2017. Project Maven Brings AI to the Fight against ISIS. *Bulletin
of the Atomic Scientists,* December 21. https://thebulletin.org/2017/12
/project-maven-brings-ai-to-the-fight-against-isis/.

Allen, Roberson. 2017. *America's Digital Army: Games at Work and War.*
Lincoln: University of Nebraska Press.

Allison, Anne. 2006. *Millennial Monsters: Japanese Toys and the Global
Imagination.* Berkeley: University of California Press.

Allison, John. 2010. The Leavenworth Diary. *Zero Anthropology,* December 5.
http://zeroanthropology.net/all-posts/the-leavenworth-diary-double-agent-
anthropologist-inside-the-human-terrain-system/.

Alter, Adam. 2017. *Irresistible: The Rise of Addictive Technology and the
Business of Keeping Us Hooked.* New York: Penguin.

Amazon. 2018. Amazon Web Services for the Warfighter. Video, August 9.
www.youtube.com/watch?v=HHbBizyTet4.

Ambinder, Marc, and D. B. Grady. 2012. *The Command: Inside the President's
Secret Army.* Hoboken, NJ: Wiley.

American Anthropological Association. 2007. Executive Board Statement on
the Human Terrain System. October 31. www.aaanet.org/issues/policy-
advocacy/statement-on-HTS.cfm.

Amnesty International. 2020. Bahrain, Kuwait, and Norway Contact Tracing
Apps among Most Dangerous for Privacy. June 16. www.amnesty.org/en
/latest/news/2020/06/bahrain-kuwait-norway-contact-tracing-apps-danger-
for-privacy/.

Anderson, Berit, and Brett Horvath. 2017. The Rise of the Weaponized AI
Propaganda Machine. *Scout,* February 9. https://medium.com/join-scout
/the-rise-of-the-weaponized-ai-propaganda-machine-86dac61668b.

Anonymous. 2016. Is Rugby as Gay as It Looks? A CURUFC Player's Perspective. *Varsity,* October 28. www.varsity.co.uk/sport/11127.

Aptima. 2012. Aptima Develops E-MEME to Track Infectiousness of Ideas
across Groups and Geography. Press release, January 23. www.aptima.com
/news/2012/aptima-develops-e-meme-track-infectiousness-ideas-across-
groups-and-geography.

ARGFest. 2013. ARGFest-o-Con. Conference schedule. http://2013.argfestocon
.com/schedule/.

Arkin, Ronald, Patrick Ulam, and Alan R. Wagner. 2012. Moral Decision-Making in Autonomous Systems: Enforcement, Moral Emotions, Dignity, Trust and Deception. *Proceedings of the IEEE* 100(3): 571–89.

Atherton, Kelsey. 2019. DARPA Wants AI to Make Soldiers Fitter, Happier, More Productive. *C4ISRnet,* May 3. www.c4isrnet.com/c2-comms/2019 /05/02/darpa-wants-ai-to-improve-human-performance/.

Atran, Scott. 2003. The Genesis of Suicide Terrorism. *Science* 299: 1534–39.

———. 2010. *Talking to the Enemy: Faith, Brotherhood, and the (Un)making of Terrorists.* New York: HarperCollins.

———. 2016. The Devoted Actor: Unconditional Commitment and Intractable Conflict across Cultures. *Current Anthropology* 57(S13): 192–203.

———. 2017. Radical Islam and the Alt-Right Are Not So Different. *Aeon.co,* November 16. https://aeon.co/essays/radical-islam-and-the-alt-right-are-not-so-different.

———. 2019. Terrorism and the Crisis of Deliberative Democracy. *In Gods We Trust* (blog). *Psychology Today,* August 13. www.psychologytoday.com/us /blog/in-gods-we-trust/201908/terrorism-and-the-crisis-deliberative-democracy.

Atwan, Abdel Bari. 2019. *Islamic State: The Digital Caliphate.* Oakland: University of California Press.

Auchard, Eric. 2018. Cambridge Analytica Stage-Managed Kenyan President's Campaigns. *Reuters,* March 19. https://uk.reuters.com/article/uk-facebook-cambridge-analytica-kenya/cambridge-analytica-stage-managed-kenyan-presidents-campaigns-uk-tv-idUKKBN1GV302.

Bacevich, Andrew J. 2013. *The New American Militarism: How Americans Are Seduced by War.* Oxford: Oxford University Press.

Bainbridge, Lisanne. 1983. Ironies of Automation. *Automatica* 19(6): 775–79.

Baker, Monya. 2015. Over Half of Psychology Studies Fail Reproducibility Test. *Nature,* August 27. www.nature.com/news/over-half-of-psychology-studies-fail-reproducibility-test-1.18248.

———. 2016. 1,500 Scientists Lift the Lid on Reproducibility. *Nature* 533: 452–54. www.nature.com/news/1-500-scientists-lift-the-lid-on-reproducibility-1.19970.

Baker, Stephanie, David Kocieniewski, and Michael Smith. 2017. Trump Data Gurus Leave Long Trail of Subterfuge, Dubious Dealing. *Bloomberg News,* March 23. www.bloomberg.com/news/articles/2017-03-23/trump-data-gurus-leave-long-trail-of-subterfuge-dubious-dealing.

Balise, Julie. 2015. Office Space: Google's Campus Feels as Big as the Internet Itself. *San Francisco Chronicle,* January 5. www.sfgate.com/business/article /Office-Space-Google-s-campus-feels-as-big-as-5992389.php.

Bamford, James. 2005. The Man Who Sold the War. *Rolling Stone,* November 17.

Barnes, John A. 1954. Class and Committees in a Norwegian Island Parish. *Human Relations* 7: 39–58.

Barnes, Julian E. 2020. Biden Pick to Lead Spy Agencies Played Key Role in Drone Strike Program under Obama. *New York Times,* November 23. www.nytimes.com/2020/11/23/us/politics/biden-haines-national-intelligence.html.

Bartlett, Tom. 2016. The Scientists Who Talks to ISIS. *Chronicle of Higher Education,* May 20. www.chronicle.com/article/the-road-to-isis/.

Battelle, John. 2005. The Birth of Google. *Wired,* August 1. www.wired.com/2005/08/battelle/.

BBC. 2015. Out of Control AI Will Not Kill Us, Believes Microsoft Research Chief. January 28. www.bbc.com/news/technology-31023741.

———. 2018. Cambridge Analytica's Kenya Election Role "Must Be Investigated." March 20. www.bbc.com/news/world-africa-43471707.

Beckman Institute. 2014. Leading Innovation in the Science of Brain Training. Press release, February 6. http://beckman.illinois.edu/news/2014/02/insight.

Behrens, Jonathan. 2019. FY 2020 Budget Request: DoD Science and Technology. *American Institute of Physics News,* March 28. www.aip.org/fyi/2019/fy20-budget-request-dod-science-and-technology.

Beinart, Peter. 2018. The US Needs to Face Up to Its Long History of Electoral Meddling. *Atlantic,* July 22. www.theatlantic.com/ideas/archive/2018/07/the-us-has-a-long-history-of-election-meddling/565538/.

Belcher, Oliver. 2013. The Afterlives of Counterinsurgency: Postcolonialism, Military Social Science, and Afghanistan 2006–2012. PhD dissertation, University of British Columbia.

Belfiore, Michael. 2009. *The Department of Mad Scientists: How DARPA Is Remaking Our World, from the Internet to Artificial Limbs.* New York: Harper Perennial.

———. 2014. Your Guide to the Wacky Bond-Villian Jargon of DARPA. *Popular Mechanics,* July 17. www.popularmechanics.com/military/a10917/the-wacky-bond-villain-jargon-of-darpa-16994679/.

———. 2015. What They're Building inside America's Secret Spy Tech Lab. *Popular Mechanics,* September 23. www.popularmechanics.com/technology/security/a17451/iarpa-americas-secret-spy-lab/.

Bell, Genevieve. 2015. The Secret Life of Big Data. In *Data, Now Bigger and Better!,* edited by Tom Boellstorff and Bill Maurer, 7–26. Chicago: Prickly Paradigm Press.

Bergen, Mark. 2018. Google Engineers Refused to Build Security Tool to Win Military Contracts. *Bloomberg News,* June 21. www.bloomberg.com/news/articles/2018-06-21/google-engineers-refused-to-build-security-tool-to-win-military-contracts.

Bernays, Edward. 1923. *Crystallizing Public Opinion.* New York: H. Liveright.

———. 1928. *Propaganda*. New York: H. Liveright.

Besteman, Catherine, and Hugh Gusterson (eds.). 2019. *Life by Algorithms: How Roboprocesses Are Remaking Our World*. Chicago: University of Chicago Press.

Bickford, Andrew. 2020. *Chemical Heroes: Pharmacological Supersoldiers in the US Military*. Durham, NC: Duke University Press.

Biddle, Sam. 2018. Trump Insider Wanted to Sell Social Media Surveillance Tools to Abusive Governments, Leaked Documents Suggest. *Intercept*, June 22. https://theintercept.com/2018/06/22/broidy-circinus-spying-tunisia-romania-uae/.

———. 2020. Privacy Experts Say Responsible Coronavirus Surveillance Is Possible. *Intercept*, April 2. https://theintercept.com/2020/04/02/coronavirus-covid-19-surveillance-privacy/.

Biddle, Sam, and Ryan Devereaux. 2019. Peter Thiel's Palantir Was Used to Bust Relatives of Migrant Children, New Documents Show. *Intercept*, May 2. https://theintercept.com/2019/05/02/peter-thiels-palantir-was-used-to-bust-hundreds-of-relatives-of-migrant-children-new-documents-show/.

Bidlake, Suzanne. 1992. Scents of Real Purpose: Behavioral Dynamics. *Marketing*, October 15, 21.

Billings, Deborah, Kristin Schaefer, Jessie Y. C. Chen, and Peter Hancock. 2012. Human-Robot Interaction: Developing Trust in Robots. *Proceedings of the 7th ACM/IEEE International Conference on Human-Robot Interaction*. https://ieeexplore.ieee.org/xpl/mostRecentIssue.jsp?punumber=6243995.

Blakely, Rhys. 2016. Data Scientists Target 20 Million New Voters for Trump. *Times* (UK), September 22.

Blinde, Loren. 2018. APL Wins DARPA Contract to Uncover Hidden Ground Truth in Social Phenomena. *Intelligence Community News*, May 20. https://intelligencecommunitynews.com/apl-wins-darpa-contract-to-uncover-hidden-ground-truth-in-social-phenomena/.

Blumenthal, Max. 2018. Exclusive Leaked Docs Expose Yemen-Based Counterinsurgency Program by Cambridge Analytica Parent Company SCL. *Grayzone*, May 28. https://thegrayzone.com/2018/05/23/scl-group-yemen-surveillance-cambridge-analytica/.

Boellstorff, Tom, and Bill Maurer (eds.). 2015. *Data, Now Bigger and Better!* Chicago: Prickly Paradigm Press.

Bogost, Ian. 2019. The Problem with Diversity in Computing. *Atlantic*, June 25. www.theatlantic.com/technology/archive/2019/06/tech-computers-are-bigger-problem-diversity/592456/.

Bohannon, John. 2010. Should Social Scientists Help the US Fight Terror? *Science*, March 11. www.sciencemag.org/news/2010/03/should-social-scientists-help-us-fight-terror.

Boiney, John, and David Foster. 2013. Progress and Promise: Research and Engineering for Human Sociocultural Behavior Capability in the US Department of Defense. Bedford, MA: MITRE Corporation.

Bolton, Paul. 2007. American Hero's Rugby Legacy. *Telegraph*, October 24. www.telegraph.co.uk/sport/rugbyunion/2324022/American-heros-rugby-legacy.html.

Bond-Graham, Darwin, and Ali Winston. 2013. All Tomorrow's Crimes: The Future of Policing Looks a Lot Like Good Branding. *SF Weekly*, October 30. www.sfweekly.com/sanfrancisco/all-tomorrows-crimes-the-future-of-policing-looks-a-lot-like-good-branding/Content?oid=2827968.

———. 2014. From Fallujah to the San Fernando Valley. *TruthOut.org*, March 12. www.truth-out.org/news/item/22357-predictive-policing-from-fallujah-to-the-san-fernando-valley-military-grade-software-used-to-wage-wars-abroad-is-making-its-impact-on-americas-streets.

Bosker, Bianca. 2016. The Binge Breaker. *Atlantic*, November. www.theatlantic.com/magazine/archive/2016/11/the-binge-breaker/501122/.

Brady, Terry. 2016. Marine Corps Warfighting Lab Tests Autonomous Reconnaissance. Marine Corps press release, April 29. www.marines.mil/News/News-Display/Article/746745/marine-corps-warfighting-lab-tests-autonomous-reconnaissance/.

Brand, Stewart. 1972. Spacewar: Fanatic Life and Symbolic Death among the Computer Bums. *Rolling Stone*, December 7, 50–55.

Brantingham, Jeffrey. 2013. Prey Selection among Los Angeles Car Thieves. *Crime Science Journal* 2(3): 1–11.

Briant, Emma L. 2015. *Propaganda and Counter-terrorism: Strategies for Global Change*. Manchester, UK: Manchester University Press.

———. 2022. *Propaganda Machine: Inside Cambridge Analytica and the Digital Influence Industry*. New York: Bloomsbury.

Brown, Keith. 2008. "All They Understand Is Force": Debating Culture in Operation Iraqi Freedom. *American Anthropologist* 110(4): 443–53.

Brown, Lex, and Anthony P. Tvaryanas. 2008. Human Performance Enhancement: Uberhumans or Ethical Morass? *Air & Space Power Journal* 22(4): 39–43. https://apps.dtic.mil/dtic/tr/fulltext/u2/a491179.pdf.

Brynjolfsson, Eric, and Andrew McAfee. 2016. *The Second Machine Age: Work, Progress, and Prosperity in a Time of Brilliant Technologies*. New York: W. W. Norton.

Buolamwini, Joy, and Timnit Gebru. 2018. Gender Shades: Intersectional Accuracy Disparities in Commercial Gender Classification. *Proceedings of Machine Learning Research* 81: 1–15.

Cadwalladr, Carole. 2017a. Revealed: How US Billionaire Helped to Back Brexit. *Guardian*, February 25.

———. 2017b. Robert Mercer: The Big Data Billionaire Waging War on Mainstream Media. *Guardian*, February 26.

———. 2020. Fresh Cambridge Analytica Leak "Shows Global Manipulation Is Out of Control." *Guardian*, January 4. www.theguardian.com/uk-news/2020/jan/04/cambridge-analytica-data-leak-global-election-manipulation.

Cain, Geoffrey. 2021. *The Perfect Police State: An Undercover Odyssey into China's Terrifying Surveillance Dystopia of the Future*. New York: PublicAffairs.

Carpenter, Julie. 2016. *Culture and Human-Robot Interaction in Militarized Spaces: A War Story*. Abingdon, UK: Ashgate/Taylor & Francis.

Chang, Emily. 2018. *Brotopia: Breaking Up the Boys' Club of Silicon Valley*. New York: Penguin.

Charles River Analytics. 2014. Charles River Analytics Announces IARPA Contract to Improve Adaptive Reasoning and Problem Solving. Press release, March 17. www.cra.com/company/news/charles-river-analytics-announces-iarpa-contract-improve-adaptive-reasoning-and-problem.

Chen, Jessie Y. C., Shan G. Lakhmani, Kimberly Stowers, Anthony R. Selkowitz, Julia L. Wright, and Michael Barnes. 2018. Situation Awareness-Based Agent Transparency and Human-Autonomy Teaming Effectiveness. *Theoretical Issues in Ergonomics Science* 19(3): 259–82.

Chen, Jessie Y. C., Anthony R. Selkowitz, Kimberly Stowers, Shan G. Lakhmani, and Michael J. Barnes. 2017. Human-Autonomy Teaming and Agent Transparency. *Proceedings of the Companion of the 2017 ACM/IEEE International Conference on Human-Robot Interaction*, 91–92. https://dl.acm.org/citation.cfm?id=3038339.

Ciampaglia, Giovanni Luca, Prashant Shiralkar, Luis M. Rocha, Johan Bollen, Filippo Menczer, and Alessandro Flammini. 2015. Computational Fact Checking from Knowledge Networks. *PLOS ONE* 10(10): e0141938.

Circinus. 2015. Current Contracts. www.circinus-llc.com/index-2.html.

Cleveland Plain Dealer. 2015. Floyd D. Loop, M. D. (obituary). https://obits.cleveland.com/obituaries/cleveland/obituary.aspx?n=floyd-d-loop&pid=175069322&fhid=2337.

Clinton, Hillary. 2011. America's Pacific Century. *Foreign Policy*, October 11. https://foreignpolicy.com/2011/10/11/americas-pacific-century/.

Cloud, David. 2011. Anatomy of an Afghan War Tragedy. *Los Angeles Times*, April 10. www.latimes.com/archives/la-xpm-2011-apr-10-la-fg-afghanistan-drone-20110410-story.html.

Cloud, David, and David Zucchino. 2011. Multiple Missteps Led to Drone Killing US Troops in Afganistan. *Los Angeles Times*, November 5. www.latimes.com/archives/la-xpm-2011-nov-05-la-fg-drone-attack-20111106-story.html.

Cockburn, Andrew. 2015. *Kill Chain: The Rise of the High-Tech Assassins*. New York: Verso.

Cockerell, Isobel. 2019. Inside China's Massive Surveillance Operation. *Wired,* May 9. www.wired.com/story/inside-chinas-massive-surveillance-operation/.

Cognitive Engineering Research Institute. 2008. Readiness & Performance: Optimizing the 21st Century Warfighter. Conference schedule. http://cerici .org/documents/2008_workshop/Readiness%20and%20Performance%20 Agenda.pdf.

Condliffe, Jamie. 2017. The Right-Wing Propaganda Machine May Not Be as Smart as You Think. *MIT Technology Review,* February 27.

Confessore, Nicholas, and Danny Hakim. 2017. Data Firm Says "Secret Sauce" Aided Trump; Many Scoff. *New York Times,* March 6.

Conger, Kate. 2018. Google Employees Resign in Protest against Pentagon Contract. *Gizmodo,* May 14. https://gizmodo.com/google-employees-resign-in-protest-against-pentagon-con-1825729300.

———. 2019. Google Plans Not to Renew Its Contract for Project Maven, a Controversial Pentagon Drone AI Imaging Program. *Gizmodo,* June 1. https://gizmodo.com/google-plans-not-to-renew-its-contract-for-project-mave-1826488620.

Conger, Kate, David Sanger, and Scott Shane. 2019. Microsoft Wins Pentagon's $10 Billion JEDI Contract, Thwarting Amazon. *New York Times,* October 25. www.nytimes.com/2019/10/25/technology/dod-jedi-contract.html.

Congressional Research Service. 2020. Defense Advanced Research Projects Agency: Overview and Issues for Congress. https://fas.org/sgp/crs/natsec /R45088.pdf.

Connor, Roger. 2018. The Predator, a Drone That Transformed Military Combat. Smithsonian National Air and Space Museum, March 9. https:// airandspace.si.edu/stories/editorial/predator-drone-transformed-military-combat.

Cook, Cynthia. 2016. DIUx: Capturing Technological Innovation. *The RAND Blog,* November 23. www.rand.org/blog/2016/11/diux-capturing-technological-innovation.html.

Cook, Joana, and Gina Vale. 2018. From Daesh to Diaspora: Tracing the Women and Minors of Islamic State. London: International Centre for the Study of Radicalisation/King's College. https://icsr.info/wp-content/uploads/2018/07 /ICSR-Report-From-Daesh-to-%E2%80%98Diaspora%E2%80%99-Tracing-the-Women-and-Minors-of-Islamic-State.pdf.

Cooper, Stephen. 2016. War by Other Means: Rugby and Warfare. *The History Press* (blog). www.thehistorypress.co.uk/articles/war-by-other-means-rugby-and-warfare/.

Cooper-White, Macrina. 2014. Musk Issues Big Warning about Artificial Intelligence. *Huffington Post,* October 27.

Correll, John T. 2019. The Counter-Revolution in Military Affairs. *Air Force Magazine,* July 1. www.airforcemag.com/article/the-counter-revolution-in-military-affairs/.

Costa, Barry, and John Boiney 2012. Social radar. McLean, VA: MITRE Corporation. www.mitre.org/sites/default/files/pdf/12_0581.pdf.

Cowan, Tyler. 2013. *Average Is Over: Powering America beyond the Age of the Great Stagnation.* New York: Dutton.

Creative Technologies. 2012. Press release. https://cretecinc.com/iarpa-selects-cti-to-participate-in-emic-workshop/.

Cutlip, Scott. 1994. *The Unseen Power: Public Relations. A History.* Hove, UK: Lawrence Erlbaum.

DARPA. 2009. Tony Tether. Interview. www.esd.whs.mil/Portals/54/Documents /FOID/Reading%20Room/DARPA/15-F-0751_DARPA_Director_Tony_ Tether.pdf.

———. 2016a. Accelerating Discovery with New Tools and Methods for Next Generation Social Science. Press release. www.darpa.mil/news-events/2016–03–04.

———. 2016b. Next Generation Social Science (NGS2). Program announcement. www.darpa.mil/program/next-generation-social-science.

———. 2017a. The DARPAnthropologist. *Voices from DARPA,* Episode 15. Podcast. www.youtube.com/watch?v=uskbkBiDXEY.

———. 2017b. Putting Social Science Modeling through Its Paces. Press release, April 7. www.darpa.mil/news-events/2017–04–07.

———. 2018. Disruption Opportunity Special Notice—Understanding Group Biases. Program solicitation. www.fbo.gov/?s=opportunity&mode=form&id =459f4739616fd0e9f72e311baa52e471&tab=core&_cview=0.

———. 2019a. Competency-Aware Machine Learning. Program announcement. www.darpa.mil/program/competency-aware-machine-learning.

———. 2019b. Teaching AI to Leverage Overlooked Residuals. Program solicitation. www.fbo.gov/index?s=opportunity&mode=form&id=6c87b62aa 825afd497f0cca6436edfdb&tab=core&_cview=1.

Dastin, Jeffrey. 2019. US Border Patrol Eyeing Facial Recognition for Body Cams. *Reuters,* October 17. www.reuters.com/article/us-usa-immigration-facialrecognition/u-s-border-patrol-eyeing-facial-recognition-for-body-cams-idUSKBN1WW33J.

Davies, Harry. 2015. Ted Cruz Using Firm That Harvested Data on Millions of Unwitting Facebook Users. *Guardian,* December 11. www.theguardian .com/us-news/2015/dec/11/senator-ted-cruz-president-campaign-facebook-user-data.

Davis, Rochelle. 2010. Culture as a Weapon System. *Middle East Report* 255 (Summer). www.merip.org/mer/mer255/culture-weapon.

Day, Chad, and Stephen Braun. 2017. Flynn Files New Financial Form Report-ing Ties to Data Firm. *AP News*, August 4. https://apnews.com/bfc2de11c52f 40929f24d42e56014014.

Defence Research and Development Canada. 2009. Understanding the Human Dimension in 21st Century Conflict/Warfare. Symposium summary. https:// cradpdf.drdc-rddc.gc.ca/PDFS/unc103/p532345_A1b.pdf.

Defense Science Board (US Department of Defense). 2004. Summer Study on Transition to and from Hostilities. Washington, DC: Office of the Undersec-retary of Defense for Acquisition, Technology and Logistics.

———. 2012. The Role of Autonomy in DoD Systems. Washington, DC: Office of the Undersecretary of Defense for Acquisition, Technology and Logistics.

———. 2016. Summer Study on Autonomy. Washington, DC: Office of the Undersecretary of Defense for Acquisition, Technology and Logistics.

Delaware Cape Gazette. 2013. Browseabout to Hold Book Signing with Philoso-pher Dog and Co-authors May 11. May 9. www.capegazette.com/node/46350.

Del Monte, Louis A. 2018. *Genius Weapons: Artificial Intelligence, Autonomous Weaponry, and the Future of Warfare*. Buffalo, NY: Prometheus Books.

Democracy Now! 2020. Meet Brittany Kaiser, Cambridge Analytica Whistle-blower. January 7. www.democracynow.org/2020/1/7/the_great_hack_ cambridge_analytica.

Der Derian, James. 2009. *Virtuous War: Mapping the Military-Industrial-Media-Entertainment Network*. New York: Routledge.

Der Derian, James, David Udris, and Michael Udris. 2010. *Human Terrain: War Becomes Academic*. Bullfrog Films. 84 minutes. www.bullfrogfilms .com/catalog/humt.html.

Deuster, Patricia, Francis O'Connor, Kurt Henry, Valerie Martindale, Laura Talbot, Wayne Jonas, and Karl Friedl. 2007. Human Performance Optimiza-tion: An Evolving Charge to the Department of Defense. *Military Medicine* 172(11): 1133–37.

DeYoung, Karen, and Walter Pincus. 2008. US to Fund Pro-American Publicity in Iraqi Media. *Washington Post*, October 3. www.washingtonpost.com /wp-dyn/content/article/2008/10/02/AR2008100204223.html?nav= emailpage.

Diesner, Jana. 2012. Uncovering and Managing the Impact of Methodological Choices for the Computational Construction of Socio-technical Networks from Texts. PhD dissertation, Carnegie Mellon University.

Diesner, Jana, Kathleen M. Carley, and Laurent Tambayong. 2012. Extracting Socio-cultural Networks of the Sudan from Open-Source, Large-Scale Text Data. *Journal of Computational and Mathematical Organization Theory* 18(3): 328–39.

Doward, Jamie, and Alice Gibbs. 2017. Did Cambridge Analytica Influence the Brexit Vote and the US Election? *Guardian*, March 4. www.theguardian

.com/politics/2017/mar/04/nigel-oakes-cambridge-analytica-what-role-brexit-trump.

Dreyfuss, Bob. 2018. Cambridge Analytica's Psy-ops Warriors. *Rolling Stone,* March 21. www.rollingstone.com/politics/politics-news/cambridge-analyticas-psy-ops-warriors-204230/.

Duke University. 1996. Bound for Oxford. *Duke Magazine,* January–February. https://alumni.duke.edu/magazine/articles/gazette.

Eckdale, Brian, and Melissa Tully. 2019. African Elections as a Testing Ground: Comparing Coverage of Cambridge Analytica in Nigerian and Kenyan Newspapers. *African Journalism Studies* 40(4): 27–43.

Economist. 2003. A Question of Class. December 9. www.economist.com /unknown/2003/12/09/a-question-of-class.

———. 2015. Planet of the Phones. February 26. www.economist.com/leaders /2015/02/26/planet-of-the-phones.

———. 2016. Automation and Anxiety. June 23. www.economist.com/special-report/2016/06/23/automation-and-anxiety.

Eddins, J. M. 2017a. Creating Synthetic Teammates. *Airman,* October 2. https://airman.dodlive.mil/2017/10/02/creating-synthetic-teammates/.

———. 2017b. Optimizing the Data Loop: Fusion Warfare and the Future Digital Battlefield. *Airman,* September 21. https://airman.dodlive.mil/2017 /09/21/optimizing-the-data-loop/.

Edney-Browne, Alex. 2017. Embodiment and Affect in a Digital Age: Understanding Mental Illness among Military Drone Personnel. *Krisis* 2017(1): 18–32.

Ellul, Jacques. 1962. *Propaganda: The Formation of Men's Attitudes.* New York: Vintage.

Elshtain, Jean Bethke. 1995. The Compassionate Warrior: Wartime Sacrifice. In *Women and War,* edited by Jean Bethke Elshtain, 205–10. Chicago: University of Chicago Press.

Emmons, Alex. 2019. Amazon Offered Job to Pentagon Official Involved with $10 Billion Contract It Sought. *Intercept,* June 3. https://theintercept.com /2019/06/03/amazon-defense-department-jedi-contract/.

Eng, Dinah. 2016. How One Immigrant Made It Big in America. *Fortune,* January 27. https://fortune.com/2016/01/27/immigrant-sosi-setian-sos-international/.

English-Lueck, Jan. 2002. *Cultures@SiliconValley.* Stanford, CA: Stanford University Press.

Epstein, Helen. 2017. Kenya: The Election and the Cover-up. *New York Review ofBooks,* August 30. www.nybooks.com/daily/2017/08/30/kenya-the-election-and-the-cover-up/.

ESPN. 2002. Cambridge Take Varsity Glory. December 10. www.espn.com /rugby/story/_/id/15364347/cambridge-take-varsity-glory.

Etzioni, Amitai, and Oren Etzioni. 2017. Pros and Cons of Autonomous Weapons Systems. *Military Review* (May–June): 72–81.

Eubanks, Virginia. 2017. *Automating Inequality: How High-Tech Tools Profile, Police, and Punish the Poor.* New York: St. Martin's Press.

Eveleth, Rose. 2019. When Futurism Led to Fascism—and Why It Could Happen Again. *Wired,* April 18. www.wired.com/story/italy-futurist-movement-techno-utopians/.

Ewen, Stuart. 1996. *PR! A Social History of Spin.* New York: Basic Books.

Fang, Lee. 2016. The CIA Is Investing in Firms That Mine Your Tweets and Instagram Photos. *Intercept,* April 14. https://theintercept.com/2016/04/14/in-undisclosed-cia-investments-social-media-mining-looms-large/.

———. 2018a. Amazon Promises "Unwavering" Commitment to Police, Military Clients Using AI Technology. *Intercept,* July 30. https://theintercept.com/2018/07/30/amazon-facial-recognition-police-military/.

———. 2018b. Former Obama Officials Help Silicon Valley Pitch the Pentagon for Lucrative Defense Contracts. *Intercept,* July 22. https://theintercept.com/2018/07/22/google-westexec-pentagon-defense-contracts/.

———. 2019a. Defense Tech Startup Founded by Trump's Most Prominent Silicon Valley Supporters Wins Secretive Military AI Contract. *Intercept,* March 9. https://theintercept.com/2019/03/09/anduril-industries-project-maven-palmer-luckey/.

———. 2019b. Google Hedges on Promise to End Controversial Involvement in Military Drone Contract. *Intercept,* March 1. https://theintercept.com/2019/03/01/google-project-maven-contract/.

———. 2019c. Google Hired Gig Economy Workers to Improve Artificial Intelligence in Controversial Drone-Targeting Project. *Intercept,* February 4. https://theintercept.com/2019/02/04/google-ai-project-maven-figure-eight/.

FCW. 2014. Jedi Mind Tricks, Virginia Tech, and Ebola Modeling. *FCW.com,* October 10. https://fcw.com/articles/2014/10/10/news-in-brief-oct.-10.aspx.

Ferdinando, Lisa. 2018. DoD Officials Highlight Role of Cloud Infrastructure in Supporting Warfighters. Press release, March 14. https://dod.defense.gov/News/Article/Article/1466699/dod-officials-highlight-role-of-cloud-infrastructure-in-supporting-warfighters/igphoto/2001888747/.

Ferguson, Andrew G. 2017. *The Rise of Big Data Policing: Surveillance, Race, and the Future of Law Enforcement.* New York: NYU Press.

Ferguson, R. Brian. 2012. Anthropology as We Know It: A Casualty of War? In *War, Technology, Anthropology,* edited by Koen Stroeken. New York: Berghahn Books.

Ferguson, William, and David Diller. 2015. IMMERSE: Interactive Mentoring for Multimodal Experiences in Realistic Social Encounters. Final Report. https://apps.dtic.mil/dtic/tr/fulltext/u2/a625663.pdf.

Fernández Campbell, Alexia. 2018. How Tech Employees Are Pushing Silicon
Valley to Put Ethics before Profit. *Vox*, October 18. www.vox.com/technology
/2018/10/18/17989482/google-amazon-employee-ethics-contracts.

Feyereisen, Thea. 2016. *The Pilot's Brain* (blog), April 7. https://aerospace
.honeywell.com/en/blogs/2016/april/the-pilot-brain/.

Feynman, Richard. 1974. Cargo Cult Science. *Engineering and Science* 37(7):
10–13.

Financial Times. n.d. The AI Arms Race. www.ft.com/content/21eb5996–89a3–
11e8-bf9e-8771d5404543.

Flynn, Michael, Matt Pottinger, and Paul Batchelor. 2010. Fixing Intel: A
Blueprint for Making Intelligence Relevant in Afghanistan. Washington,
DC: Center for a New American Security.

Flynn, Michael, James Sisco, and David Ellis. 2015. Left of Bang: The Value of
Sociocultural Analysis in Today's Environment. *Prism* 3(4): 13–21. www
.enodoglobal.com/wp-content/uploads/2015/02/Prism-Left-of-Bang.pdf.

Fosher, Kerry. 2008. Illuminating Competing Discourses in National Security
Organizations. *Anthropology News* 49(8): 54–55.

———. 2009. *Under Construction: Making Homeland Security at the Local
Level*. Chicago: University of Chicago Press.

———. 2014. Cautionary Tales from the US Department of Defense's Pursuit of
Cultural Expertise. In *Cultural Awareness in the Military*, edited by Robert
Albro and Bill Ivey, 15–29. London: Palgrave Macmillan.

Foster, Peter. 2016. The Mind-Reading Software That Could Provide the
"Secret Sauce" for Trump to Win the White House. *Telegraph*, November 4.

Foucault, Michel. 2003. *Society Must Be Defended: Lectures at the Collège de
France*, edited by Mauro Bertani and Alessandro Fontana, translated by
David Macey. New York: Picador.

Fox, Justin. 2014. How Silicon Valley Became the Man. *Harvard Business
Review*, January 9. https://hbr.org/2014/01/how-silicon-valley-became-the-
man.

Franceschi-Bicchierai, Lorezo. 2018. Why We're Not Calling the Cambridge
Analytica Story a "Data Breach." *Motherboard*, March 19. www.vice.com
/en_us/article/3kjzvk/facebook-cambridge-analytica-not-a-data-breach.

Frank, Thomas. 1997. *Commodify Your Dissent: The Business of Culture in the
New Gilded Age*. New York: W. W. Norton.

Freedberg, Sydney, Jr. 2015. Centaur Army: Bob Work, Robotics, & the Third
Offset Strategy. *Breaking Defense*, November 9. https://breakingdefense
.com/2015/11/centaur-army-bob-work-robotics-the-third-offset-strategy/.

———. 2017. "DIUx Is Here to Stay": Mattis Embraces Obama Tech Outreach.
Breaking Defense, August 11. https://breakingdefense.com/2017/08/diux-is-
here-to-stay-mattis-embraces-obama-tech-outreach/.

Freeman, Linton C. 2004. *The Development of Social Network Analysis: A Study in the Sociology of Science*. Vancouver: University of British Columbia Press.

Gallimore, Darci, Joseph Lyons, Thy Vo, and Sean Mahoney. 2019. Trusting Robocop: Gender-Based Effects on Trust of an Autonomous Robot. *Frontiers in Psychology* 10: 482.

Galtung, Johan. 1967. Scientific Colonialism. *Transitions* 30 (April–May): 10–15.

Ganesh, Maya Indira. 2020. The Ironies of Autonomy. *Humanities and Social Sciences Communications* 7: article 157.

Garber, Megan. 2013. Funerals for Fallen Robots. *Atlantic*, September 20. www.theatlantic.com/technology/archive/2013/09/funerals-for-fallen-robots/279861/.

Garreau, Joel. 2007. Bots on the Ground. *Washington Post*, May 6. www.washingtonpost.com/wp-dyn/content/article/2007/05/05/AR2007050501009_pf.html.

Geertz, Clifford. 1973. *The Interpretation of Cultures*. New York: Basic Books.

Gentile, Gian. 2013. *Wrong Turn: America's Deadly Embrace of Counterinsurgency*. New York: The New Press.

Gera, Emily. 2018. Sim Society: DARPA, Serious Simulation, and the Model That Stopped a Flood. *Eurogamer*, February 24. www.eurogamer.net/articles/2018-02-24-sim-society-darpa-serious-simulation-and-the-model-that-stopped-a-flood.

Gezari, Vanessa. 2013. The Human Terrain System Sought to Transform the Army from Within. *Newsweek*, August 16. www.newsweek.com/2013/08/16/human-terrain-system-sought-transform-army-within-237818.html.

Ghoshal, Devjyot. 2018. Mapped: The Breathtaking Global Reach of Cambridge Analytica's Parent Company. *Quartz*, March 28. https://qz.com/1239762/cambridge-analytica-scandal-all-the-countries-where-scl-elections-claims-to-have-worked/.

Gibbs, Samuel. 2017. Elon Musk Leads 116 Experts Calling for Outright Ban of Killer Robots. *Guardian*, August 20. www.theguardian.com/technology/2017/aug/20/elon-musk-killer-robots-experts-outright-ban-lethal-autonomous-weapons-war.

Gillis, Jonathan. 2017. Warfighter Trust in Autonomy. *DSIAC Journal* 4(4): 23–30. www.dsiac.org/resources/journals/dsiac/fall-2017-volume-4-number-4/warfighter-trust-autonomy.

Giroux, Henry A. 2007. *The University in Chains: Confronting the Military-Industrial-Academic Complex*. Boulder, CO: Paradigm.

Glover, Tim. 1995. The Heady Mix of Style That Means Varsity. *Independent*, December 11. www.independent.co.uk/sport/the-heady-mix-of-style-that-means-varsity-1525162.html.

Gluckman, Max. 1954. *Rituals of Rebellion in South-east Africa.* Manchester, UK: Manchester University Press.

Goldberg, Lewis R. 1981. Language and Individual Differences. In *Review of Personality and Social Psychology, vol. 2,* edited by L. Wheeler, 141–65. Beverly Hills, CA: Sage.

Goldsmith, Paul. 2017. Enter Cambridge Analytica—Public Asks, Kabila Gani? *Elephant,*July20.www.theelephant.info/features/2017/07/20/enter-cambridge-analytica-public-asks-kabila-gani/.

Goldstein, Harry. 2006. Modeling Terrorists. *IEEE Spectrum* 43(9): 26–34.

González, Roberto J. 2009. *American Counterinsurgency: Human Science and the Human Terrain.* Chicago: Prickly Paradigm Press.

González, Roberto J., and Hugh Gusterson. 2019. Introduction. In *Militarization: A Reader,* edited by Roberto J. González, Hugh Gusterson, and Gustaaf Houtman, 1–28. Durham, NC: Duke University Press.

Goo, Sara Kehaulani, and Alec Klein. 2007. Google Makes Its Pitch to Expand Federal Business. *Washington Post,* February 28. www.washingtonpost.com /archive/business/2007/02/28/google-makes-its-pitch-to-expand-federal-business/.

Gorman, Siobhan, Adam Entous, and Andrew Dowell. 2013. Technology Emboldened the NSA. *Wall Street Journal,* June 9. www.wsj.com/articles /SB10001424127887323495604578535290627442964.

Gould, Stephen Jay. 1981. *The Mismeasure of Man.* New York: W. W. Norton.

Grassegger, Hannes, and Mikael Krogerus. 2017. The Data That Turned the World Upside Down. *Motherboard,* January 28. www.vice.com/en_us /article/mg9vvn/how-our-likes-helped-trump-win?.

Greenwald, Glenn. 2014. *No Place to Hide.* New York: Metropolitan.

Gregory, Derek. 2011. From a View to a Kill: Drones and Late Modern War. *Theory, Culture & Society* 28(7–8): 188–215.

Grier, Rebecca, et al. 2008. SCIPR: A Computational Model to Simulate Cultural Identities for Predicting Reactions to Events. Dayton, OH: Air Force Research Laboratory.

Grossman, Dave. 1996. *On Killing: The Psychological Cost of Learning to Kill in War and Society.* New York: Back Bay Books.

Gurven, Michael, Christopher von Rueden, Maxim Massenkoff, Hillard Kaplan, and Marino Lero Vie. 2013. How Universal Is the Big Five? *Journal of Personality and Social Psychology* 104(2): 354–70.

Gusterson, Hugh. 1997. Studying Up Revisted. *PoLAR* 20(1): 114–19.

———. 2016. *Drone: Remote Control Warfare.* Cambridge, MA: MIT Press.

———. 2017. From Brexit to Trump: Anthropology and the Rise of Nationalist Populism. *American Ethnologist* 44(2): 209–14.

Hafner, Katie, and Matthew Lyon. 1998. *Where Wizards Stay Up Late: The Origins of the Internet.* New York: Simon & Schuster.

Hao, Karen. 2019a. Inside Amazon's Plan for Alexa to Run Your Entire Life. *MIT Technology Review*, November 5. www.technologyreview.com/2019 /11/05/65069/amazon-alexa-will-run-your-life-data-privacy/.

———. 2019b. A US Government Study Confirms Most Face Recognition Systems Are Racist. *MIT Technology Review*, December 20. www.technologyreview .com/2019/12/20/79/ai-face-recognition-racist-us-government-nist-study/.

Hardesty, Larry. 2018. Study Finds Gender and Skin-Type Bias in Commercial Artificial Intelligence Systems. *MIT News*, February 11. http://news.mit.edu /2018/study-finds-gender-skin-type-bias-artificial-intelligence-systems-0212.

Harris, Shane. 2015. *@War: The Rise of the Military-Internet Complex*. Boston: Eamon Dolan/Mariner Books.

Harrison, Sara. 2016. Silicon Valley Tech Bros Want to Trick Us into Thinking Capitalism Is Revolutionary. *Quartz*, October 3. https://qz.com/797778 /silicon-valley-thinks-its-the-heir-to-1960s-counterculture-but-theres- no-revolution-here/.

———. 2019. Five Years of Tech Diversity Reports—and Little Progress. *Wired*, October 1. www.wired.com/story/five-years-tech-diversity-reports-little- progress/.

Hart, David. 2004. On the Origins of Google. *National Science Foundation News*, August 17. www.nsf.gov/discoveries/disc_summ.jsp?cntn_id=100660.

Hartley, D. S. (ed.). 2008. *Human Social Culture Behavior Modeling Workshop I*. Washington, DC: National Defense University. www.dtic.mil/get-tr-doc /pdf?AD=ADA489736.

Hatmaker, Taylor. 2018. Palmer Luckey's Defense Company Anduril Is Already Leading to Arrests at the Southern Border. *Techcrunch*, June 11. https:// techcrunch.com/2018/06/11/anduril-lattice-sentry-palmer-luckey/.

Hawking, Stephen. 2014. Transcendence Looks at the Implications of Artificial Intelligence—But Are We Taking AI Seriously Enough? *Independent*, March 1. www.independent.co.uk/news/science/stephen-hawking-transcendence- looks-at-the-implications-of-artificial-intelligence—but-are-we-taking-ai- seriously-enough-9313474.html.

Hawkins, Ed. 2019. *The Men on Magic Carpets: Searching for the Superhuman Sports Star*. New York: Bloomsbury.

Hawley, John K. 2011. Not by Widgets Alone: The Human Challenge of Technology-Intensive Military Systems. *Armed Forces Journal*, February 1. http://armedforcesjournal.com/not-by-widgets-alone/.

Heinrich, Thomas. 2002. Cold War Armory: Military Contracting in Silicon Valley. *Enterprise & Society* 3(2): 247–84.

Hempel, Jessi. 2015. DoD Head Ashton Carter Enlists Silicon Valley to Trans- form the Military. *Wired*, November 18. www.wired.com/2015/11/secretary- of-defense-ashton-carter/.

Henderson, Jon. 2002. Ornamental Masculinity: Twickers to a T. *Observer,*
    December 8. http://wesclark.com/rrr/om.html.

Hendrickson, Katherine. 2018. Overcoming the Barriers to Human-Machine
    Teams. *DSIAC Journal* 5(4). www.dsiac.org/resources/journals/dsiac
    /fall-2018-volume-5-number-4/overcoming-barriers-human-machine-
    teams.

Herman, Edward S., and Noam Chomsky. 1988. *Manufacturing Consent: The
    Political Economy of the Mass Media.* New York: Pantheon.

Hersh, Eitan D. 2015. *Hacking the Electorate: How Campaigns Perceive Voters.*
    Cambridge: Cambridge University Press.

Hersh, Seymour. 2002. The Debate Within: The Objective Is Clear—Topple
    Saddam, but How? *New Yorker,* March 3. www.newyorker.com/magazine
    /2002/03/11/the-debate-within.

Hewett, Chris. 1999. Rugby Union: Beer Is the Toast of Dark Blues. *Independ-
    ent,* December 8. www.independent.co.uk/sport/rugby-union-beer-is-the-
    toast-of-dark-blues-1131116.html.

Hodder, Ian. 2012. *Entangled: An Archaeology of the Relationships between
    People and Things.* Hoboken, NJ: Wiley-Blackwell.

———. 2014. The Entanglements of Humans and Things: A Long-Term View.
    New Literary History 45(1): 19–36.

Hodges, Adam. 2018. A Theory of Propaganda for the Social Media Age.
    Anthropology News, April 9.

———. 2019. *When Words Trump Politics: Resisting a Hostile Regime of
    Language.* Stanford, CA: Stanford University Press.

Human Social Cultural Behavioral Modeling Program. 2009. *HSCB Newsletter,*
    vol. 1. https://web.archive.org/web/20130124081055/www.dtic.mil/biosys
    /files/HSCB-news-spring-2009.pdf.

Hsu, Tiffany, and Eleanor Lutz. 2020. More than 1000 Companies Boycotted
    Facebook. Did It Work? *New York Times,* August 1. www.nytimes.com/2020
    /08/01/business/media/facebook-boycott.html.

Hudson, Adam. 2014. How Google and the Big Tech Companies Are Helping
    Maintain America's Empire. *AlterNet,* August 19. www.alternet.org/news-
    amp-politics/how-google-and-big-tech-companies-are-helping-maintain-
    americas-empire.

Human Rights Watch. 2018. China: Big Data Fuels Crackdown in Minority
    Region. *HRW.org,* February 26. www.hrw.org/news/2018/02/26/china-big-data-
    fuels-crackdown-minority-region.

Hunter, Lindsay. 2015. This Is Not a Threat: Conspiracy for Good. *International
    Journal of Performance Arts and Digital Media* 11(2): 185–201.

Huntington, Samuel P. 1996. *The Clash of Civilizations and the Remaking of
    World Order.* New York: Simon & Schuster.

Hurley, Dan. 2014. *Smarter: The New Science of Building Brain Power*. New York: Plume.

IARPA. 2012. EMIC. Request for information. www.iarpa.gov/index.php/working-with-iarpa/requests-for-information/emic.

———. 2013. Using Alternate Reality Environments to Help Enrich Research Efforts (UAREHERE). Request for information. www.iarpa.gov/index.php /working-with-iarpa/requests-for-information/using-alternate-reality-environments-to-help-enrich-research-efforts.

———. 2014. INSTINCT-IARPA's Trustworthiness Challenge. Press release. www.iarpa.gov/index.php/working-with-iarpa/prize-challenges/218-instinct-iarpa-s-trustworthiness-challenge.

Ignatieff, Michael. 2001. *Virtual War: Kosovo and Beyond*. New York: Metropolitan Books.

Inagaki, Toshiyuki, and Makoto Itoh. 2013. Human Overtrust in and Overreliance on Advanced Driver Assistance Systems. *International Journal of Vehicular Technology* 2013: article 951762.

Ingram, Mathew. 2017. How Google and Facebook Have Taken Over the Digital Ad Industry. *Fortune*, January 4. https://fortune.com/2017/01/04/google-facebook-ad-industry/.

Issenberg, Sasha. 2015. Cruz-Connected Data Miner Aims to Get inside US Voters' Heads. *Bloomberg*, November 12. www.bloomberg.com/news /features/2015-11-12/is-the-republican-party-s-killer-data-app-for-real-.

Ivey, Matthew. 2018. Cementing Silicon Valley Partnerships: A National Security Imperative. *National Defense*, June 18.

Johnson, Benjamin, Michael Floyd, Alexandra Coman, Mark Wilson, and David Aha. 2018. Goal Reasoning and Trusted Autonomy. In *Foundations of Trusted Autonomy*, edited by Hussein Abbass, Jason Scholz, and Darryn Reid, 47–66. New York: Springer.

Jorgensen, Joseph, and Eric Wolf. 1970. Anthropology on the Warpath in Thailand. *New York Review of Books*, November 19, 26–35.

Kaiser, Brittany. 2019. *Targeted: My Inside Story of Cambridge Analytica and How Trump and Facebook Broke Democracy*. New York: HarperColllins.

Kanaan, Michael. 2020. *T-Minus AI: Humanity's Countdown to Artificial Intelligence and the New Pursuit of Global Power*. Dallas, TX: BenBella Books.

Kaplan, Fred. 2016. The Pentagon's Innovation Experiment. *MIT Technology Review*, December 19. www.technologyreview.com/s/603084/the-pentagons-innovation-experiment/.

Kaplan, Robert D. 2019. A New Cold War Has Begun. *Foreign Policy*, January 7. https://foreignpolicy.com/2019/01/07/a-new-cold-war-has-begun/.

Kastrenakes, Jacob. 2014. Google Signs 60-Year Lease on NASA Airfield and Hangars. *Verge*, November 10. www.theverge.com/2014/11/10/7190057 /nasa-leases-moffett-airfield-to-google-60-years.

Kelly, Makena. 2019. Microsoft CEO Defends Pentagon Contract Following Employee Outcry. *Verge*, February 25. www.theverge.com/2019/2/25 /18240300/microsoft-ceo-defends-pentagon-contract-ar-headsets-employee-outcry.

Kennedy, Joseph V. 2012. The Sources and Uses of U.S. Science Funding. *New Atlantis* (Summer): 3–22.

Khalid, Amrita. 2020. Digital Privacy Is Being Threatened as Governments Attempt to Stop Coronavirus. *Quartz*, May 2. https://qz.com/1849518 /contract-tracing-threatens-digital-privacy-during-coronavirus/.

Kilcullen, David. 2004. Countering Global Insurgency. *Journal of Strategic Studies* 28(4): 597–617.

———. 2009. *The Accidental Guerrilla: Fighting Small Wars in the Midst of a Big One*. New York: Oxford University Press.

———. 2010. *Counterinsurgency*. New York: Oxford University Press.

Kilcullen, David, and Andrew McDonald Exum. 2009. Death from Above, Outrage Down Below. *New York Times*, May 16. www.nytimes.com/2009/05 /17/opinion/17exum.html.

Kim, Lily. 2019. Announcing Azure Government Secret Private Preview and Expansion of DoD IL5. *Microsoft Azure* (blog), April 17. https://azure .microsoft.com/en-us/blog/announcing-azure-government-secret-private-preview-and-expansion-of-dod-il5/.

Kim, Max S. 2020. Seoul's Radical Experiment in Digital Contact Tracing. *New Yorker*, April 17. www.newyorker.com/news/news-desk/seouls-radical-experiment-in-digital-contact-tracing.

Kinzer, Steve. 2006. *Overthrow: America's Century of Regime Change from Hawaii to Iraq*. New York: Times Books.

Kitchin, Rob. 2014. *The Data Revolution: Big Data, Open Data, Data Infrastructures and Their Consequences*. Los Angeles: Sage.

Klein, David. 2018. Unmanned Systems and Robotics in the FY2019 Budget. *AUVSI Breaking News*, August 14. www.auvsi.org/%E2%80%8Bunmanned-systems-and-robotics-fy2019-defense-budget.

Knight, Sam. 2018. Life inside S.C.L., Cambridge Analytica's Parent Company. *New Yorker*, March 26. www.newyorker.com/news/letter-from-the-uk/life-inside-scl-cambridge-analyticas-parent-company.

Koerner, Brendan I. 2016. #jihad: Why ISIS Is Winning the Social Media War. *Wired*, December.

Kolb, Michael. 2012. Soldier and Robot Interaction in Combat Environments. PhD dissertation, University of Oklahoma.

Kollanyi, Bence, Philip N. Howard, and Samuel C. Woolley. Bots and Automation over Twitter during the U.S. Election. Data Memo 2016.4. Oxford, UK: Project on Computational Propaganda. www.politicalbots.org.

Koreh, Raya. 2019. Congress Should Strengthen Laws Outlawing Domestic Government Propaganda. *Hill*, October 20. https://thehill.com/opinion /technology/466647-congress-should-strengthen-laws-outlawing-domestic-government-propaganda#bottom-story-socials.

Kosinski, Michal, David Stillwell, and Thore Graepel. 2013. Private Traits and Attributes Are Predictable from Digital Records of Human Behavior. *Proceedings of the National Academy of Sciences USA* 110(15): 5802–5.

Kosinski, Michal, Yilun Wang, Himabindu Lakkaraju, and Jure Leskovec. 2016. Mining Big Data to Extract Patterns and Predict Real-Life Outcomes. *Psychological Methods* 21(4): 493–506.

Kowalski, Robin M. 2012. *Cyberbullying*, 2nd ed. Malden, MA: Wiley-Blackwell.

Kranish, Michael. 2016. Trump's Plan for a Comeback Includes Building a "Psychographic" Profile of Every Voter. *Washington Post*, October 27.

Krepinevich, Andrew F., and Barry D. Watts. 2015. *The Last Warrior: Andrew Marshall and the Shaping of Modern American Defense Strategy*. New York: Basic Books.

Kroenig, Matthew. 2020. *The Return of Great Power Rivalry: Democracy versus Autocracy from the Ancient World to the US and China*. New York: Oxford University Press.

Kroll, Andy. 2018. Cloak and Data: The Real Story behind Cambridge Analytica's Rise and Fall. *Mother Jones*, May–June. www.motherjones.com /politics/2018/03/cloak-and-data-cambridge-analytica-robert-mercer/.

Kuldell, Heather, and Frank Konkel. 2018. JEDI: One Year in the Pentagon's Push for a Revolutionary Cloud. *Nextgov*. www.nextgov.com/feature/jedi-contract/.

Kuznar, Lawrence. 2008. Anthropological Perspectives on Rare Event Prediction. In *Anticipating Rare Events*, edited by Nancy Chesser, 17–24. DoD white paper. Washington, DC: US Department of Defense.

Lane, Justin. 2016. Big Data and Anthropology: Concerns for Data Collection in a New Research Context. *Journal of the Anthropological Society of Oxford* 3(1): 74–88.

Lapowsky, Issie. 2016. Trump's Big Data Mind Explains How He Knew Trump Could Win. *Wired*, November 9.

———. 2018. Facebook Exposed 87 Million Users to Cambridge Analytica. *Wired*, April 4. www.wired.com/story/facebook-exposed-87-million-users-to-cambridge-analytica/.

Larson, Erik. 2015. Questioning the Hype about Artificial Intelligence. *Atlantic*, May 14. www.theatlantic.com/technology/archive/2015/05/the-humanists-paradox/391622/.

Laterza, Vito. 2021. Could Cambridge Analytica Have Delivered Donald
Trump's 2016 Presidential Victory? An Anthropologist's Look at Big Data
and Political Campaigning. *Public Anthropologist* 3(1): 119–47.

Latiff, Robert H. 2017. *Future War: Preparing for the New Global Battlefield.*
New York: Vintage.

Lee, Kai-Fu. 2018. *AI Superpowers: China, Silicon Valley and the New World
Order.* New York: Houghton Mifflin Harcourt.

Lemov, Rebecca. 2016. "Big Data Is People!" *Aeon.co,* June 16. https://aeon.co
/essays/why-big-data-is-actually-small-personal-and-very-human.

Leung, A., D. Diller, L. Ji, R. Slitt, R. Strauss, K. Cushner, D. Shaprio, M.
Mateas, H. Logas, and J. Garbe. 2014. Emic Training to Improve Cross
Cultural Prediction: Final Report. Technical Report sponsored by DOI
Contract Number D13PC00246, 20 May 2014.

Levine, Barry. 2016. Marketers, Welcome to the World of Emotional Analytics.
MartechToday, January 12. https://martechtoday.com/marketers-welcome-
to-the-world-of-emotional-analytics-159152.

Levine, Yasha. 2018. *Surveillance Valley: The Secret Military History of the
Internet.* New York: Public Affairs.

Lin, Patrick. 2016. Relationships with Robots: Good or Bad for Humans?
Fortune, February 1. www.forbes.com/sites/patricklin/2016/02/01
/relationships-with-robots-good-or-bad-for-humans/#44d60b707adc.

Lin, Yu-Ru, and Rebecca Hwa. n.d. TRIBAL: A Tripartite Model for Group Bias
Analytics. University of Pittsburgh webpage. www.momacs.pitt.edu/process
/tribal-a-tripartite-model-for-group-bias-analytics/.

Lindgren, Lisa. 2016. How the Department of Defense Will Benefit from New
Adobe Software Solutions. *Adobe Blog,* December 14. https://blog.adobe
.com/en/2016/12/14/how-the-department-of-defense-will-benefit-from-new-
adobe-software-solutions.html#gs.lwb67u7.

Llewellyn, David. 1998. Russell Is Ready to Live Out an American Dream.
Independent, December 8. www.independent.co.uk/sport/russell-is-ready-to-
live-out-an-american-dream-1190104.html.

Lockheed-Martin. 2014. Worldwide Integrated Crisis Early Warning System.
www.lockheedmartin.com/us/products/W-ICEWS.html.

Logas, Heather, Jacob Garbe, Dan Shapiro, and Michael Mateas. 2014. Emic
Experience Design: Becoming a Member of Another Culture through Live
Action Role-Play. *Proceedings of the Digital Games Research Association
2014 Conference.* www.researchgate.net/publication/311308405_Emic_
Experience_Design_Becoming_a_Member_of_Another_Culture_through_
Live_Action_Role-Play.

Lu, Leqi, Daniel Preotiuc-Pietro, Zahra Riahi Samani, Mohsen Moghaddam,
and Lyle Ungar. 2016. Analyzing Personality through Social Media Profile
Picture Choice. http://wwbp.org/papers/persimages16icwsm.pdf.

Lutton, Jonathan. 2015. DARPA Is Spending Big on Big Data. *FCW.com*, April 15. http://fcw.com/articles/2015/04/15/snapshot-data-programs.aspx.

Lutz, Catherine. 2001. *Homefront: A Military City and the American 20th Century*. Boston: Beacon Press.

———. 2008. The Perils of Pentagon Funding for Anthropology and the Other Social Sciences. Social Science Research Council, November 6. http://essays .ssrc.org/minerva/2008/11/06/lutz/.

Machi, Vivienne. 2017. Data Fusion Central to the Future of Air Warfare. *National Defense*, March 2. www.nationaldefensemagazine.org/articles /2017/3/2/goldfein-data-fusion-central-to-the-future-of-air-warfare.

Magnuson, Stew. 2019. Army's "Google Earth on Steroids" to Include Inside of Buildings. *National Defense*, May 17. www.nationaldefensemagazine.org /articles/2019/5/17/news-from-itec-armys-google-earth-on-steroids-to-include-inside-of-buildings.

Malinowski, Bronisław. 1922. *Argonauts of the Western Pacific*. London: G. Routledge and Sons.

———. 1948 [1925]. *Magic, Science and Religion and Other Essays*. Boston: Beacon Press.

Manson, Katrina. 2018. Robot-Soldiers, Stealth Jets and Drone Armies: The Future of War. *Financial Times*, November 15. www.ft.com/content /442de9aa-e7a0-11e8-8a85-04b8afea6ea3.

Marlowe, Frank. 2010. *The Hadza: Hunter-Gatherers of Tanzania*. Berkeley: University of California Press.

Martindale, Valerie E. 2006. Human Performance Optimization in Aviation. *Aviation, Space, and Environmental Medicine* 77(9): 996. www.asma.org /getmedia/aa08868b-4321-4930-925a-76667a74ad93/Sept06BoB.

Maslow, Abraham, and John Honigman. 1970. Synergy: Some Notes of Ruth Benedict. *American Anthropologist* 72: 320–33.

Mathieu, Jennifer, Michael Fulk, Martha Lorber, Gary Klein, Barry Costa, and Dylan Schmorrow. 2012. Social Radar Workflows, Dashboards and Environments. McLean, VA: MITRE Corporation. www.mitre.org/sites/default/files /pdf/12_0567.pdf.

Matthews, Michael D., and David M. Schnyer (eds.). 2019. *Human Performance Optimization: The Science and Ethics of Enhancing Human Capabilities*. New York: Oxford University Press.

Mauss, Marcel. 1990 [1925]. *The Gift: Forms and Functions of Exchange in Archaic Societies*. London: Routledge.

Maybury, Mark. 2010. Social Radar for Smart Power. McLean, VA: MITRE Corporation. www.mitre.org/publications/technical-papers/social-radar-for-smart-power.

Mazarr, Michael J., Ryan Michael Bauer, Abigail Casey, Sarah Heintz, and Luke J. Matthews. 2019. The Emerging Risk of Virtual Societal Warfare: Social

Manipulation in a Changing Information Environment. Santa Monica, CA: RAND Corporation. www.rand.org/pubs/research_reports/RR2714.html.

Mazzetti, Mark, and Borzou Daragahi. 2005. US Military Covertly Pays to Run Stories in Iraq Press. *Los Angeles Times*, November 30. www.latimes.com /archives/la-xpm-2005-nov-30-fg-infowar30-story.html.

McCormack, Robert, and William Salter. 2010. An Application of Epidemiological Modeling to Information Diffusion. *Advances in Social Computing*, edited by Sun-Ki Chai, John Salerno, and Patricia L. Mabry, 382–89. New York: Springer.

McCrae, Robert R., and Paul T. Costa 1983. Social Desirability Scales: More Substance Than Style. *Journal of Counseling and Clinical Psychology* 51: 882–88.

McCray, Patrick. 2018. @margaretomara's op-ed about the Pentagon's relation with Silicon Valley made me recall the region's long engagement with technology and patrons (including the military). Twitter, October 27. https://twitter .com/LeapingRobot/status/1056318026033709056 @LeapingRobot.

McCurry, Justin. 2020. Test, Trace, Contain: How South Korea Flattened Its Coronavirus Curve. *Guardian*, April 22. www.theguardian.com/world/2020 /apr/23/test-trace-contain-how-south-korea-flattened-its-coronavirus-curve.

McNamara, Laura A. 2010. Why Models Don't Forecast. In *Sociocultural Data to Accomplish Department of Defense Missions*, edited by Robert Pool. Washington, DC: National Academies Press. https://sites.nationalacademies. org/cs/groups/dbassesite/documents/webpage/dbasse_071326.pdf.

McNamara, Laura A., and Robert A. Rubenstein (eds.). 2011. *Dangerous Liaisons: Anthropologists and the National Security State*. Santa Fe, NM: SAR Press.

McNamee, Roger. 2018. How to Fix Facebook—Before It Fixes Us. *Washington Monthly*, January–March. https://washingtonmonthly.com/magazine /january-february-march-2018/how-to-fix-facebook-before-it-fixes-us/.

Mead, Margaret. 1973. Changing Styles of Anthropological Work. *Annual Review of Anthropology* 2: 1–27.

Mehta, Aaron. 2019. Cultural Divide: Can the Pentagon Crack Silicon Valley? *Defense News*, January 28. www.defensenews.com/pentagon/2019/01/28 /cultural-divide-can-the-pentagon-crack-silicon-valley/.

Menegus, Bryan. 2019. Microsoft Employees Demand Company End $480 Million Contract with US Army. *Gizmodo*, February 22. https://gizmodo .com/microsoft-employees-demand-company-end-480-million-con-1832815683.

Metz, Cade. 2012. Paul Baran, the Link between Nuclear War and the Internet. *Wired*, September 4. www.wired.co.uk/article/h-bomb-and-the-internet.

Mewhinney, Michael, and Andrew Pederson. 2008. NASA and Google Announce Lease at Ames Research Center. NASA press release, August 5. www.nasa.gov/centers/ames/news/releases/2008/08_51AR.html.

Meyer, Robinson. 2014. Everything We Know about Facebook's Secret Mood Manipulation Experiment. *Atlantic*, June 28. www.theatlantic.com /technology/archive/2014/06/everything-we-know-about-facebooks-secret-mood-manipulation-experiment/373648/.

Micale, Barbara. 2017. Virginia Tech Leads DARPA Project to Develop Tools for Next Generation Social Science. Press release. www.bi.vt.edu/news /virginia-tech-leads-darpa-project-to-develop-tools-for-next-generation-soci.

Miller, Susan. 2019. AI May Read Soldiers' Intents, Anticipate Their Needs. *GCN.com*, April 5. https://gcn.com/articles/2019/04/05/ai-brain-waves-soldier-assist.aspx.

Mills, C. Wright. 1958. *The Causes of World War Three*. New York: Ballantine Books.

———. 1959. *The Sociological Imagination*. New York: Oxford University Press.

Mitchell, Billy. 2018. "No Longer an Experiment"—DIUx Becomes DIU, Permanent Pentagon Unit. *Fedscoop*, August 9. www.fedscoop.com/diu-permanent-no-longer-an-experiment/.

MITRE Corporation. 2008. Human Performance (Report for Office of Defense Research and Engineering), Report No. JSR-07–625. McLean, VA: MITRE Corporation. https://fas.org/irp/agency/dod/jason/human.pdf.

Mittu, Ranjeev, Donald Sofge, Alan Wagner, and W. F. Lawless (eds.). 2016. *Robust Intelligence and Trust in Autonomous Systems*. New York: Springer.

Mizokami, Kyle. 2019. The F-35 Is Cheap to Buy (but Not to Fly). *Popular Mechanics*, October 30. www.popularmechanics.com/military/aviation /a29626363/f-35-cheap/.

Molla, Rani. 2020. Tech Companies Tried to Help Us Spend Less Time on Our Phones—It Didn't Work. *Vox*, January 6. www.vox.com/recode/2020/1/6 /21048116/tech-companies-time-well-spent-mobile-phone-usage-data.

Morgan, Oliver. 2005. Lobby Firm Goes to War. *Guardian*, September 10. www .theguardian.com/business/2005/sep/11/theobserver.observerbusiness4.

Mosco, Vincent. 2014. *To the Cloud: Big Data in a Turbulent World*. Boulder, CO: Paradigm.

Mozur, Paul, Raymond Zhong, and Aaron Krolik. 2020. In Coronavirus Fight, China Gives Citizens a Color Code, with Red Flags. *New York Times*, March 1. www.nytimes.com/2020/03/01/business/china-coronavirus-surveillance .html.

Muchina, Pauline, and Mike Merryman-Lotze. 2019. The U.S. Has Killed Thousands of People with Lethal Drones—It's Time to Put a Stop to It.

American Friends Service Committee Blog, May 16. www.afsc.org/blogs /news-and-commentary/us-has-killed-thousands-people-lethal-drones.

Nader, Laura. 1969. Up the Anthropologist: Perspectives Gained from Studying Up. In *Reinventing Anthropology,* edited by Dell Hymes, 284–311. New York: Random House.

———. 1986. The Drift to War. In *War and Peace: Cross-cultural Perspectives,* edited by Mary Lecron Foster and Robert A. Rubinstein, 185–92. New Brunswick, NJ: Transaction Books.

———. 1997. Controlling Processes: Tracing the Dynamic Components of Power. *Current Anthropology* 38(5): 711–37.

———. 2011. Ethnography as Theory. *HAU: Journal of Ethnographic Theory* 1(1): 211–19.

Naik, Ravi. 2017. Let's Take Back Control of Our Data: It's Too Precious to Leave to the Tech Giants. *Guardian,* October 3. www.theguardian.com /commentisfree/2017/oct/03/data-tech-giants-trail-digital-age.

Nakashima, Ellen, and Joby Warrick 2013. For NSA Chief, Terrorist Threat Drives Passion to Collect It All. *Washington Post,* July 14. www.washington post.com/world/national-security/for-nsa-chief-terrorist-threat-drives-passion-to-collect-it-all/2013/07/14/3d26ef80-ea49-11e2-a301-ea5a8116d211_story.html.

National Science Foundation. 1994. Award Abstract #9411306: The Stanford Integrated Digital Library Project. www.nsf.gov/awardsearch/showAward? AWD_ID=9411306.

———. 2006. Mathematical and Simulation Modeling of Crime Hot Spots. www.nsf.gov/awardsearch/showAward?AWD_ID=0527388.

NATO STRATCOM. 2015. Countering Propaganda: NATO Spearheads Use of Behavioural Change Science. Press release, May 12. https://stratcomcoe.org /countering-propaganda-nato-spearheads-use-behavioural-change-science.

Nebehay, Stephanie. 2018. UN Says It Has Credible Reports That China Holds Million Uighurs in Secret Camps. *Reuters,* August 10. www.reuters.com /article/us-china-rights-un/u-n-says-it-has-credible-reports-that-china-holds-million-uighurs-in-secret-camps-idUSKBN1KV1SU.

Nesbit, Jeff. 2017. Google's True Origin Partly Lies in CIA and NSA Research Grants for Mass Surveillance. *Quartz,* December 8. https://qz.com/1145669 /googles-true-origin-partly-lies-in-cia-and-nsa-research-grants-for-mass-surveillance/.

Newton, Casey. 2019. How White Supremacists Evade Facebook Bans. *The Verge,* May 31. www.theverge.com/interface/2019/5/31/18646525 /facebook-white-supremacist-ban-evasion-proud-boys-name-change.

Nicas, Jack, and Daisuke Wakabayashi. 2020. Apple and Google Team Up to "Contact Trace" the Coronavirus. *New York Times,* April 10. www.nytimes .com/2020/04/10/technology/apple-google-coronavirus-contact-tracing.html.

Nicolson, Adam. 2003. Rugby Is War Continued by Other Means. *Telegraph,* October 14. www.telegraph.co.uk/comment/personal-view/3597600/Rugby-is-war-continued-by-other-means.html.

Ning, Yue, Sathappan Muthiah, Huzefa Rangwala, David Mares, and Naren Ramakrishnan. 2018. When Do Crowds Turn Violent? Uncovering Triggers from Media. *Proceedings of the 2018 IEEE/ACM International Conference on Advances in Social Network Analysis and Mining.* http://people.cs.vt.edu/naren/papers/RP-ASONAM_2018_paper_139.pdf.

Noble, Safiya. 2018. *Algorithms of Oppression: How Search Engines Reinforce Racism.* New York: New York University Press.

O'Brien, Sean P. 2010. Crisis Early Warning and Decision Support: Contemporary Approaches and Thoughts on Future Research. *International Studies Review* 12(1): 87–104.

Oddo, John. 2018. *The Discourse of Propaganda: Case Studies from the Persian Gulf War and the War on Terror.* University Park, PA: Penn State University Press.

O'Hara, Terence. 2005. In-Q-Tel, CIA's Venture Arm, Invests in Secrets. *Washington Post,* August 15. www.washingtonpost.com/wp-dyn/content/article/2005/08/14/AR2005081401108.html.

O'Mara, Margaret. 2018. Silicon Valley Can't Escape the Business of War. *New York Times,* October 26. www.nytimes.com/2018/10/26/opinion/amazon-bezos-pentagon-hq2.html.

———. 2019. *The Code: Silicon Valley and the Remaking of America.* New York: Penguin.

O'Neil, Cathy. 2016. *Weapons of Math Destruction: How Big Data Increases Inequality and Threatens Democracy.* New York: Crown.

Oracle. 2020. Oracle Public Sector—Defense (webpage). www.oracle.com/industries/public-sector/defense.html.

Orwell, George. 1945. The Sporting Spirit. *London Tribune,* December. www.orwellfoundation.com/the-orwell-foundation/orwell/essays-and-other-works/the-sporting-spirit/.

———. 1946. Politics and the English Language. In *A Collection of Essays,* edited by George Orwell, 156–70. London: Horizon.

Osnos, Evan. 2015. The Fearful and the Frustrated. *New Yorker,* August 31.

Oxford Mail. 2002. An American in Oxford. December 4. www.oxfordmail.co.uk/news/6583792.an-american-in-oxford/.

Page, Holden. 2018. What Big Tech Has Acquired from In-Q-Tel, the CIA's VC Arm. *Crunchbase,* June 8. https://news.crunchbase.com/news/what-big-tech-has-acquired-from-in-q-tel-the-cias-vc-arm/.

Paletta, Damian. 2016. The CIA's Venture-Capital Firm, Like Its Sponsor, Operates in the Shadows. *Wall Street Journal,* August 30. www.wsj.com/articles/the-cias-venture-capital-firm-like-its-sponsor-operates-in-the-shadows-1472587352.

Pao, Ellen. 2017. *Reset: My Fight for Inclusion and Lasting Change.* New York: Random House.

Pasternack, Alex. 2017. Cambridge Analytica Quietly Worked on Fake News-Fueled Kenyan Election. *Fast Company,* August 10. www.fastcompany.com /40450037/trumps-big-data-firm-worked-on-the-kenyan-election-amid-concerns-over-fake-news-and-hacking-allegations.

Paul, Annie M. 2005. *The Cult of Personality Testing.* New York: Free Press.

Pellerin, Cheryl. 2015a. DoD's Silicon Valley Innovation Experiment Begins. *DoD News,* October 29. https://dod.defense.gov/News/Article/Article/626602 /dods-silicon-valley-innovation-experiment-begins/.

———. 2015b. Work Details the Future of War at Army Defense College. *DoD News,* April 8. https://dod.defense.gov/News/Article/Article /604420/.

———. 2015c. Work: Human-Machine Teaming Represents Defense Technology Future. *DoD News,* November 8. https://dod.defense.gov/News/Article /Article/628154/work-human-machine-teaming-represents-defense-technology-future/.

———. 2017. Project Maven to Deploy Computer Algorithms to War Zone by Year's End. *DoD News,* July 21. https://dod.defense.gov/News/Article/Article /1254719/project-maven-to-deploy-computer-algorithms-to-war-zone-by-years-end/.

Pentland, Alex. 2011. Computational COIN: Sensing, Characterization, and Shaping Human Behavior. Presentation delivered at Rensselaer Polytechnic Institute, March 2. http://scnarc.rpi.edu/content/scnarc-seminar-computational-coin-sensing-characterization-and-shaping-human-social-behavior.

———. 2012. Reinventing Society in the Wake of Big Data. *Edge,* August 30. www.edge.org/conversation/reinventing-society-in-the-wake-of-big-data.

Perrin, Noel. 1979. *Giving Up the Gun: Japan's Reversion to the Sword, 1543–1879.* New York: David Godine.

Peterson, Scott, and Payam Faramarzi. 2011. Iran Hijacked US Drone, Says Iranian Engineer. *Christian Science Monitor,* December 15. www.csmonitor .com/World/Middle-East/2011/1215/Exclusive-Iran-hijacked-US-drone-says-Iranian-engineer.

Pfautz, Stacy L., and Michael Salwen. 2010. A Hybrid Model of Ethnic Conflict, Repression, Insurgency and Strife. In BRIMS Committee (ed.), *Proceedings of the 19th conference of behavior representation in modeling and simulation,* 211–15. Red Hook, NY: Curran Associates.

Phelps, Timothy. 2014. Holder Announces Task Force on "Homegrown" Terrorists. *Los Angeles Times,* June 2. www.latimes.com/la-na-nn-holder-terrorism-task-force-20140601-story.html.

Pichai, Sundar. 2019. AI at Google: Our Principles (blog post). June 7. https:// blog.google/technology/ai/ai-principles/.

Posner, Sarah, and David Neiwert 2016. How Trump Took Hate Groups Mainstream. *Mother Jones,* October 14. www.motherjones.com/politics /2016/10/donald-trump-hate-groups-neo-nazi-white-supremacist-racism/.

Poulson, Jack. 2019. I Used to Work for Google. I Am a Conscientious Objector. *New York Times,* April 23. www.nytimes.com/2019/04/23/opinion/google-privacy-china.html.

———. 2020. Reports of a Silicon Valley/Military Divide Have Been Greatly Exaggerated. Report published by Tech Inquiry, July 7. https://techinquiry .org/SiliconValley-Military/.

Prabhakar, Arati. 2013. Statement to the US House of Representatives Subcommittee on Intelligence, Emerging Threats, and Capabilities, April 16. https:// docs.house.gov/meetings/AS/AS26/20130416/100657/HHRG-113-AS26-Wstate-PrabhakarA-20130416.pdf.

Prasso, Sheridan. 2020. Counterterrorism Tools Deployed against Virus Spur Privacy Fears. *Bloomberg Law,* April 6. https://news.bloomberglaw.com /privacy-and-data-security/counterterrorism-tools-deployed-against-virus-spur-privacy-fears.

PredPol. 2014. Scientifically Proven Field Results. www.predpol.com/results/.

Prendergast, Mark J. 2010. Behind the Media Contractors' Veil. *Ombudsman* (blog). *Stars and Stripes,* July 12. www.stripes.com/blogs-archive/ombudsman /ombudsman-blog-archive-1.8931/behind-the-media-contractors-veil-1 .110840#.Xv5shChKhPa.

Price, David. 1997. Anthropological Research and the Freedom of Information Act. *CAM Journal* 9(1): 12–15.

———. 1998. Gregory Bateson and the OSS: World War II and Bateson's Assessment of Applied Anthropology. *Human Organization* 57(4): 379–84.

———. 2001. Terror and Indigenous Peoples. *CounterPunch,* November 3. www .counterpunch.org/2001/11/03/terror-and-indigenous-peoples/.

———. 2007. Buying a Piece of Anthropology, Part 1: Human Ecology and Unwitting Anthropological Research for the CIA. *Anthropology Today* 23(3): 8–13.

———. 2008. Social Science in Harness. *CounterPunch,* June 24. www .counterpunch.org/2008/06/24/social-science-in-harness/.

———. 2009. Human Terrain Systems, Anthropologists, and the War in Afghanistan. *CounterPunch,* December 1. www.counterpunch.org/2009/12/01 /human-terrain-systems-anthropologists-and-the-war-in-afghanistan/.

———. 2011. *Weaponizing Anthropology: Social Science in the Service of the Militarized State.* Petrolia, CA: CounterPunch-AK Press.

———. 2012. Counterinsurgency and the M-VICO System: Human Relations Area Files and Anthropology's Dual-Use Legacy. *Anthropology Today* 28(1): 16–20.

————. 2016. *Cold War Anthropology: The CIA, the Pentagon, and the Growth of Dual Use Anthropology*. Durham, NC: Duke University Press.

Ravindranath, Mohana. 2016. DARPA Wants a "Social Supercollider" to Help It Understand Humans. *Nextgov.com*, September 9. www.nextgov.com /cio-briefing/2016/09/darpa-wants-build-social-supercollider/131416/.

Rebala, Pratheek. 2018. The State Department Hired Cambridge Analytica's Parent Company to Target Terrorist Propaganda. *Time*, August 21. https://time.com/5372923/cambridge-analytica-state-department-terrorist-propaganda/.

Reinert, John T. 2013. In-Q-Tel: The Central Intelligence Agency as Venture Capitalist. *Northwestern Journal of International Law and Business* 33(3): 677–709.

Rodriguez, Salvador. 2020. Why Silicon Valley Is Obsessed with "The Lord of the Rings." *CNBC.com*, February 22. www.cnbc.com/2020/02/22/why-silicon-valley-is-obsessed-with-the-lord-of-the-rings.html.

Rogers, Adam. 2017. DARPA Wants to Build a BS Detector for Science. *Wired*, June 30. www.wired.com/story/darpa-bs-detector-science/.

Rohde, Joy. 2009. Gray Matters: Social Scientists, Military Patronage, and Democracy in Cold War. *Journal of American History* 96(1): 99–122.

Rosalind Franklin Society. 2013. In My Genes: The Legacy of Bernadine Healy, M.D. Video, January 28. www.youtube.com/watch?v=V9BrS-McaLk.

Rosenberg, Matthew, and John Markoff. 2016. The Pentagon's "Terminator Conundrum": Robots That Could Kill on Their Own. *New York Times*, October 26. www.nytimes.com/2016/10/26/us/pentagon-artificial-intelligence-terminator.html.

Rossino, Alex. 2020. Big Data in DoD's FY 2021 Procurement and RDT&E Budget Programs. *GovWin.com*, September 23. https://iq.govwin.com/neo /marketAnalysis/view/Big-Data-in-DODs-FY-2021-Procurement-and-RDTE-Budget-Programs/4504.

Rouse, Ed. n.d. Psywarrior (website). www.psywarrior.com/psyhist.html.

Rubenstein, Robert A., Kerry Fosher, and Clementine Fujimura (eds.). 2012. *Practicing Military Anthropology: Beyond Traditional Boundaries and Expectations*. Bloomfield, CT: Kumarian Press.

Russell, Adam. 2003. Nurturing Nature: Men, Steroids, and Anthropology. PhD dissertation, University of Oxford.

Russell, Adam, and Bartlett Bulkley. 2007. *Human Performance Modification Primer*. Herndon, VA: Scitor Corporation.

Russell, Adam, Bartlett Bulkley, and Christine Grafton. 2005. *Human Performance Optimization and Military Missions*. Washington, DC: Office of Net Assessment. Publication no. GS-10F-0297K.

Sakellariou, Nicholas, and Rania Milleron (eds.). 2018. *Ethics, Politics, and Whistleblowing in Engineering*. Boca Raton, FL: CRC Press.

Sapra, Bani. 2020. Silicon Valley Loves "Lord of the Rings," but Why? *Business Insider,* February 8. www.businessinsider.com/lord-of-the-rings-palantir-anduril-salesforce-tower-sauron-2020-1.

Sarawak Report. 2018. Najib Lied about UMNO Links to SCL/Cambridge Analytica. May 8. www.sarawakreport.org/2018/05/najib-lied-about-umno-links-to-sclcambridge-analytica/.

SBIR. 2012. Intuitive Information Fusion and Visualization. www.sbir.gov/node/374165.

———. 2014. Aptima, Inc. http://sbir.gov/sbirsearch/detail/95053.

Scahill, Jeremy, and Glenn Greenwald. 2014. The NSA's Secret Role in the US Assassination Program. *Intercept,* February 10. https://theintercept.com/2014/02/10/the-nsas-secret-role/.

Scales, Bob. 2018. Mattis's Infantry Task Force: Righting "a Generational Wrong." *Breaking Defense,* November 26.

Scharre, Paul. 2018. *Army of None: Autonomous Weapons and the Future of War.* New York: W. W. Norton.

Schehl, Matthew. 2016. Marines Are on the Hunt for Robots That Can Follow Their Orders. *Defense News,* May 17. www.defensenews.com/digital-show-dailies/sea-air-space/2016/05/17/the-marines-are-on-the-hunt-for-robots-that-can-follow-their-orders/.

Schmorrow, Dylan. 2010. A View of Defense Department Science and Technology. Slide presentation. Retrieved from www.navalengineers.org/.

Schmorrow, Dylan, and Denise Nicholson (eds). 2013. *Advances in Design for Cross-cultural Activities.* Boca Raton, FL: Taylor & Francis.

Schrader, Stuart. 2019. *Badges without Borders: How Global Counterinsurgency Transformed American Policing.* Oakland: University of California Press.

Schubarth, Cromwell. 2020. Palantir Emerges in US, Europe as a COVID-19 Tracker. *Silicon Valley Business Journal,* April 1. www.bizjournals.com/sanjose/news/2020/04/01/palantir-covid-19-tracking.html.

Seaver, Nick. 2015. Bastard Algebra. In *Data, Now Bigger and Better!,* edited by Tom Boellstorff and Bill Maurer, 27–45. Chicago: Prickly Paradigm Press.

Seck, Hope H. 2016. Corps Sees Hurdle in Getting Marines to Bond with Robotic Battle Buds. *Military.com,* May 18. www.military.com/daily-news/2016/05/18/corps-sees-hurdle-in-getting-marines-to-bond-robotic-battle-buds.html.

Shachtman, Noah. 2010. Google, CIA Invest in "Future" of Web Monitoring. *Wired,* July 28. www.wired.com/2010/07/exclusive-google-cia/.

———. 2011a. Inside DARPA's Secret Afghan Spy Machine. *Wired,* July 21. www.wired.com/2011/07/darpas-secret-spy-machine/all/.

———. 2011b. Pentagon's Prediction Software Didn't Spot Egypt Unrest. *Wired,* February 11. www.wired.com/2011/02/pentagon-predict-egypt-unrest/.

———. 2012. Air Force's Top Brain Wants a Social Radar to See into Hearts and Minds. *Wired,* January 19. www.wired.com/2012/01/social-radar-sees-minds/.

Shaffer, Al. 2008. Department of Defense Science and Technology Program: A Time of Continued Change. Slide presentation. https://ndiastorage.blob.core .usgovcloudapi.net/ndia/2008/science/Day1/07Shaffer.pdf.

Sherman, Len. 2018. Why Facebook Will Never Change Its Business Model. *Forbes,* April 16. www.forbes.com/sites/lensherman/2018/04/16/why-facebook-will-never-change-its-business-model/#133a752864a7.

Shorrock, Tim. 2015. A Major Defense Contractor Buys Its Way Back into the Spying Business. *Nation,* May 11. www.thenation.com/article/biggest-corporation-youve-never-heard-helping-government-spy-you.

Short, Elliot. 2018. What Happens to Us When Robots Fight Our Wars? *War Is Boring* (blog), March 15. https://warisboring.com/what-happens-to-us-when-robots-fight-our-wars/.

Sideris, Lisa H. 2020. American Techno-Optimism. In *Theologies of American Exceptionalism,* edited by Winnifred Fallers Sullivan and Elizabeth Shakman Hurd. Bloomington: Indiana University Press.

SIFT. 2019. Sonja Schmer-Galunder. www.sift.net/staff/sonja-schmer-galunder.

———. n.d. MARGARET: Multidimensional Algorithm Generated Anthropological Recording and Ethnographic Tool. www.sift.net/research /computational-social-science/margaret.

Singer, Merrill. 1999. Studying Hidden Populations. In *Mapping Social Networks, Spatial Data, and Hidden Populations,* edited by Jean J. Schensul, Margaret LeCompte, Robert Trotter, and Merrill Singer. Walnut Creek, CA: AltaMira Press.

Singer, Natasha, and Choe Sang-Hun. 2020. As Coronavirus Surveillance Escalates, Personal Privacy Plummets. *New York Times,* March 23. www .nytimes.com/2020/03/23/technology/coronavirus-surveillance-tracking-privacy.html.

Singer, Paris S., and Adam Russell. 2012. *Lunch with Diogenes.* Washington, DC: PhilosopherDog.

Singer, P. W. 2009. *Wired for War: The Robotics Revolution and Conflict in the 21st Century.* New York: Penguin.

Singer, P. W., and Emerson T. Brooking. 2019. *LikeWar: The Weaponization of Social Media.* Boston: Mariner Books.

Sluka, Jeffrey. 2011. Death from Above: UAVs and Losing Hearts and Minds. *Military Review* (May–June): 70–76.

Smith, Greg. 2015. Trusting Autonomous Systems: It's More Than Technology. *CIMSEC,* September 18. http://cimsec.org/trusting-autonomous-systems-its-more-than-technology/18908.

Smolan, Rick, and Jennifer Erwitt 2012. *The Human Face of Big Data.* New York: Sterling.

Snow, Jacob. 2018. Amazon's Face Recognition Falsely Matched 28 Members of Congress with Mugshots. *ACLU Free Future* (blog), July 26. www.aclu.org /blog/privacy-technology/surveillance-technologies/amazons-face-recognition-falsely-matched-28.

Soboleski, Courtney. 2018. The Social Science of Soldier-Machine Teaming. *C4ISRNET*, August 6. www.c4isrnet.com/opinion/2018/08/06/the-social-science-of-soldier-machine-teaming/.

Social Science Space. 2019. DARPA Aims to Score Social and Behavioral Research (blog post). March 6. www.socialsciencespace.com/2019/03/darpa-aims-to-score-social-and-behavioral-research/.

Sokolowski, John, and Catherine Banks (eds). 2009. *Principles of Modeling and Simulation: A Multidisciplinary Approach*. Hoboken, NJ: Wiley.

Solomon, Salem. 2018. Cambridge Analytica Played Roles in Multiple African Elections. *VOANews*, March 22. www.voanews.com/africa/cambridge-analytica-played-roles-multiple-african-elections.

Soterix Medical. 2014. Beckman Institute Initiates Study Using Soterix Medical HD-tDCS for Fluid Intelligence. Press release, March 24. www.soterixmedical .com/painx/news/2014/03/beckman-institute-initiates-study-using-soterix-medical/14.

Springer, Paul. 2018. *Outsourcing War to Machines: The Military Robotics Revolution*. Santa Barbara, CA: Praeger Security International.

Srinivasan, Ramesh. 2019. *Beyond the Valley: How Innovators around the World Are Overcoming Inequality and Creating the Technologies of Tomorrow*. Cambridge, MA: MIT Press.

Stanford University. 2017. Gilman Louie: In-Q-Tel and Funding Startups for the Government. Video. www.youtube.com/watch?v=DfUm0RxXWxI.

Stockman, Farah. 2010. Knowing the Enemy, One Avatar at a Time. *Boston Globe*, May 3. www.boston.com/news/nation/washington/articles/2010 /05/30/knowing_the_enemy_one_avatar_at_a_time/.

Suchman, Lucy. 2015. Situational Awareness: Deadly Bioconvergence at the Boundaries of Bodies and Machines. *MediaTropes* 5(1): 1–24.

Suchman, Lucy, and Jutta Weber. 2015. Human-Machine Autonomies Revised. Conference paper from the symposium "Autonomous Weapons Systems." www.researchgate.net/publication/272173538_Human-Machine_ Autonomies_Revised.

Suchow, Jordan, et al. 2016. Culture on a Chip (project website). https://osf.io /nfd5c/.

Szoldra, Paul. 2016. 14 Cutting Edge Firms Funded by the CIA. *Business Insider*, September 21. www.businessinsider.com/companies-funded-by-cia-2016-9#heres-how-its-chameleon-software-works-16.

Tadjdeh, Yasmin. 2015. Seeing, Thinking Robots to Assist Troops. *National Defense*, February 6. www.nationaldefensemagazine.org/articles/2018/2/6 /seeing-thinking-robots-to-assist-troops.

———. 2019. Marine Corps Eyeing Modular, Interoperable Robotic Systems. *National Defense*, April 2. www.nationaldefensemagazine.org/articles /2019/4/2/marine-corps-eyeing-modular-interoperable-robotic-systems.

Taggart, Kendall. 2017. The Truth about the Trump Data Team That People Are Freaking Out About. *BuzzFeed*, February 16. www.buzzfeednews.com /article/kendalltaggart/the-truth-about-the-trump-data-team-that-people- are-freaking.

Taibbi, Matt. 2018. How to Survive America's Kill List. *Rolling Stone*, July 19. www.rollingstone.com/politics/politics-features/how-to-survive-americas-kill- list-699334/.

Taleb, Nassim Nicholas. 2010. *The Black Swan: The Impact of the Highly Improbable*, 2nd ed. New York: Random House.

Tambayong, Laurent, and Kathleen Carley. 2013. Network Text Analysis in Computer-Intensive Rapid Ethnography Retrieval. *Journal of Social Structure* 13(2): 1–24.

Tau, Byron. 2021. Military Intelligence Agency Says It Monitored US Cellphone Movements without Warrant. *Wall Street Journal*, January 22. www.wsj .com/articles/military-intelligence-agency-says-it-monitored-u-s-cellphone- movements-without-warrant-11611350374.

Taylor, Adam. 2015. The US Keeps Killing Americans in Drone Strikes, Mostly by Mistake. *Washington Post*, April 23. www.washingtonpost.com/news /worldviews/wp/2015/04/23/the-u-s-keeps-killing-americans-in-drone- strikes-mostly-by-accident/.

Tett, Gillian. 2010. Silence and Silos: The Problems of Fractured Thought in Finance. Presented at the 109th annual meeting of the American Anthropo- logical Association, New Orleans, LA. http://vimeo.com/17854712.

———. 2017. Donald Trump's Campaign Shifted Odds by Making Big Data Personal. *Financial Times*, January 26. www.ft.com/content/bee3298c- e304-11e6-9645-c9357a75844a.

———. 2018. Language Matters: The Real Meaning of Big Data. *Financial Times*, November 14. www.ft.com/content/bd88b9f2-e79f-11e8-8a85- 04b8afea6ea3.

Thompson, Nicholas, and Ian Bremmer. 2018. The AI Cold War with China That Threatens Us All. *Wired*, October 23. www.wired.com/story/ai-cold- war-china-could-doom-us-all/.

Thuraisingham, Bhavani. 2015. Big Data: Have We Seen It Before? January 25. www.utdallas.edu/~bxt043000/Motivational-Articles/Big_Data-Have_we_ seen_it_before.pdf.

Tiku, Nitasha. 2018. Amazon's Jeff Bezos Says Tech Companies Should Work with the Pentagon. *Wired,* October 15. www.wired.com/story/amazons-jeff-bezos-says-tech-companies-should-work-with-the-pentagon/.

Tisne, Martin. 2018. It's Time for a Data Bill of Rights. *MIT Technology Review,* December 14. www.technologyreview.com/2018/12/14/138615/its-time-for-a-bill-of-data-rights/.

Tucker, Patrick. 2015. How US Special Forces Uses Google Maps. *Defense One,* January 7. www.defenseone.com/technology/2015/01/how-us-special-forces-uses-google-maps/102396/.

———. 2016. The Other Michael Flynn. *Defense One,* November 21. www.defenseone.com/policy/2016/11/other-michael-flynn/133337/.

Tufekci, Zeynep. 2017. *Twitter and Tear Gas: The Power and Fragility of Networked Protest.* New Haven, CT: Yale University Press.

———. 2018. Twitter comment, March 17. https://twitter.com/zeynep/status/975076957485457408.

Tupes, Ernest, and Raymond Christal. 1961. Recurrent Personality Factors Based on Trait Ratings (USAF ASD Tech. Rep. No. 61–97). Lackland Air Force Base, TX: US Air Force.

Turner, Fred. 2006. *From Counterculture to Cyberculture: Stewart Brand, the Whole Earth Network, and the Rise of Digital Utopianism.* Chicago: University of Chicago Press.

Turnley, Jessica Glicken. 2010. The Dangers of Rushing to Data: Constraints on Data Types and Targets on Computational Modeling and Simulation. In *Sociocultural Data to Accomplish Department of Defense Missions,* edited by Robert Pool. Washington, DC: National Academies Press.

Tye, Larry. 2002. *The Father of Spin: Edward L. Bernays and the Birth of Public Relations.* New York: Picador.

Ullman, Jeffrey D. 2000. NSF Grant IRI-96–31952 Data Warehousing and Decision Support. Summary report. db.cs.pitt.edu/idm/reports/2000/9631952.html.

University of California, Los Angeles. 2014a. Andrea Bertozzi Prior Research Funding. www.math.ucla.edu/~bertozzi/past-grants.html.

———. 2014b. Andrea Bertozzi Research Group. www.math.ucla.edu/~bertozzi/research.html.

US Air Force Research Laboratory. 2015. Trust in Autonomy for Human Machine Teaming. Solicitation. https://govtribe.com/opportunity/federal-contract-opportunity/trust-in-autonomy-for-human-machine-teaming-baaafrlrqkh 20150008.

US Army Research Laboratory. 2015. ARL Researcher Recognized for Work in Robotics and Automation. Press release. www.arl.army.mil/www/?article = 2624.

———. 2018. Army Scientists Improve Human-Machine Teaming by Making AI Agents More Transparent. Press release, January 11. www.eurekalert.org/pub_releases/2018–01/uarl-asi011118.php.

US Department of Defense. 2012a. Autonomy in Weapon Systems (Directive 3000.09), November 21. https://fas.org/irp/doddir/dod/d3000_09.pdf.

———. 2012b. DARPA Funding List. www.dod.gov/pubs/foi/Reading_Room/DARPA/12-F-1039_2012-DARPA-Funding-List.pdf.

———. 2013. Fiscal Year 2014 Budget Estimates: DARPA, vol. 1. www.darpa.mil/.

———. 2014. Fiscal Year 2015 Budget Estimates: DARPA, vol. 1. www.darpa.mil/.

———. 2015. Fiscal Year 2016 Budget Estimates: DARPA, vol. 1. www.darpa.mil/.

———. 2017. Unmanned Systems Integrated Roadmap, 2017–2042. Washington, DC: Department of Defense.

———. 2018. Assessment on US Defense Implications of China's Expanding Global Access. https://media.defense.gov/2019/Jan/14/2002079292/-1/-1/1/EXPANDING-GLOBAL-ACCESS-REPORT-FINAL.PDF.

US Department of Homeland Security. 2019. Tactical Awareness Kit (TAK): Enhancing Homeland Security Enterprise Collaboration. White paper. www.dhs.gov/sites/default/files/publications/tactical_awareness_kit_508.pdf.

US Federal Business Opportunities. 2012. Worldwide Integrated Crisis Early Warning System. www.fbo.gov/index?s=opportunity&mode=form&tab=core&id=58d0e5c2ac017648980ca573374d644e.

US Office of the Director of National Intelligence. 2014a. IARPA Launches New Research Program to Significantly Improve Adaptive Reasoning and Problem-Solving. Press release, January 27. www.dni.gov/index.php/newsroom/press-releases/198-press-releases-2014/1003-iarpa-launches-new-research-program-to-significantly-improve-adaptive-reasoning-and-problem-solving.

———. 2014b. JEDI MIND Wins IARPA's INSTINCT Challenge. Press release, October 9. www.dni.gov/index.php/newsroom/press-releases/press-releases-2014/item/1124-jedi-mind-wins-iarpa-s-instinct-challenge.

US Office of the President. 2012. Fact Sheet: Big Data across the Federal Government. https://obamawhitehouse.archives.gov/the-press-office/2015/12/04/fact-sheet-big-data-across-federal-government.

Valentine, Douglas. 1990. *The Phoenix Program*. New York: William Morrow.

Vine, David. 2020. *The United States of War: A Global History of America's Endless Conflicts, from Columbus to the Islamic State*. Oakland: University of California Press.

Vogel, Kenneth P., and Tarini Parti. 2015. Cruz Partners with Donor's "Psychographic" Firm. *Politico*, July 7. www.politico.com/story/2015/07/ted-cruz-donor-for-data-119813.

Wachter-Boettcher, Sara. 2017. *Technically Wrong: Sexist Apps, Biased Algorithms, and Other Threats of Toxic Tech*. New York: W. W. Norton.

Waddington, Ivan, and Andy Smith. 2009. *An Introduction to Drugs in Sport: Addicted to Winning?* London: Routledge.

Wagstaff, Jeremy. 2000. Indonesia's Wahid Hires Consultant to Help Boost His Tarnished Image. *Wall Street Journal*, August 2. www.wsj.com/articles /SB965108975998990678.

Wang, Maya. 2019. China's Algorithms of Repression. Human Rights Watch, May 2. www.hrw.org/report/2019/05/02/chinas-algorithms-repression /reverse-engineering-xinjiang-police-mass.

Wang, Ning, David Pynadath, and Susan Hill. 2016. Trust Calibration within a Human-Robot Team: Comparing Automatically Generated Explanations. *HRI '16: The Eleventh ACM/IEEE International Conference on Human Robot Interaction*, 109–16. http://people.ict.usc.edu/~pynadath/Papers /hri16.pdf.

Ward, Antonia. 2018. ISIS's Use of Social Media Still Poses a Threat to Stability in the Middle East and Africa. *The RAND Blog*, December 11. www.rand .org/blog/2018/12/isiss-use-of-social-media-still-poses-a-threat-to-stability .html.

Warrick, Joby. 2015. *Black Flags: The Rise of ISIS*. New York: Doubleday.

Watts, Barry D. 2008. US Combat Training, Operational Art, and Strategic Competence: Problems and Opportunities. Washington, DC: Center for Strategic and Budgetary Assessments.

Watts, Duncan. 2014. Computational Social Science: Exciting Progress and Future Directions. In *Frontiers of Engineering: Reports on Leading-Edge Engineering from the 2013 Symposium*. www.nap.edu/read/18558 /chapter/6.

Wedel, Janine. 2009. *The Shadow Elite: How the World's New Power Brokers Undermine Democracy, Government, and the Free Market*. New York: Basic Books.

Weinberger, Sharon. 2005. You Can't Handle the Truth—Psyops Propaganda Goes Mainstream. *Slate*, September 19. https://slate.com/news-and-politics /2005/09/psy-ops-propaganda-goes-mainstream.html.

———. 2008. Introducing IARPA: It's Like DARPA, but for Spies. *Wired*, March 24. www.wired.com/2008/03/st-alphageek-10/.

———. 2011. Web of War. *Nature* 471: 566–68.

———. 2017. *The Imagineers of War: The Untold Story of DARPA, the Pentagon Agency That Changed the World*. New York: Vintage.

Weisgerber, Marcus. 2017. The Pentagon's New Algorithmic Warfare Cell Gets Its First Mission: Hunt ISIS. *Defense One*, May 14. www.defenseone.com /technology/2017/05/pentagons-new-algorithmic-warfare-cell-gets-its- first-mission-hunt-isis/137833/.

Weiss, Brennan. 2018. New Details Emerge about Steve Bannon's Ties to Cambridge Analytica. *Business Insider,* March 24. www.businessinsider.com/steve-bannon-ties-to-cambridge-analytica-facebook-data-run-deep-2018-3.

Wetmore, Jameson. 2007. Amish Technology: Reinforcing Values, Building Community. *IEEE Technology & Society* 26(2): 10–21.

Whitehead, Neil, and Sverker Finnstrom. 2013. *Virtual War and Magical Death: Technologies and Imaginaries for Terror and Killing.* Durham, NC: Duke University Press.

Williams, Lauren C. 2018. DIUx Gets a Big Boost in FY2019 Budget. *FCW.com,* February 12. https://fcw.com/articles/2018/02/12/budget-williams-dod.aspx.

Williamson, D. J. 1993. Anabolic Steroid Use among Students at a British College. *British Journal of Sports Medicine* 27(3): 200–201. www.ncbi.nlm.nih.gov/pubmed/8242280.

Winner, Langdon. 1980. Do Artifacts Have Politics? *Daedalus* 109(1): 121–36.

Witt, Jesse, and Alex Pasternack. 2019a. Before Trump, Cambridge Analytica Quietly Built "Psyops" for Militaries. *Fast Company,* September 25. www.fastcompany.com/90235437/before-trump-cambridge-analytica-parent-built-weapons-for-war.

———. 2019b. The Strange Afterlife of Cambridge Analytica and the Mysterious Fate of Its Data. *Fast Company,* July 26. www.fastcompany.com/90381366/the-mysterious-afterlife-of-cambridge-analytica-and-its-trove-of-data.

Wolpert, Stuart. 2010. Can Math and Science Help Solve Crimes? *US News & World Report,* March 2. www.usnews.com/science/articles/2010/03/02/can-math-and-science-help-solve-crimes.

Wong, Julia Carrie. 2019. White Nationalists Are Openly Operating on Facebook. The Company Won't Act. *Guardian,* November 21. www.theguardian.com/technology/2019/nov/21/facebook-white-nationalists-ban-vdare-red-ice.

Woo, Elaine. 2011. Bernadine Healy Dies at 67; Doctor Led Red Cross after 9/11. *Los Angeles Times,* August 9. www.latimes.com/archives/la-xpm-2011-aug-09-la-me-bernadine-healy-20110809-story.html.

Wood, Molly. 2020. Why the Racism in Facial Recognition Software Probably Can't Be Fixed. *Marketplace,* June 29. www.marketplace.org/shows/marketplace-tech/facial-recognition-software-racism-people-of-color-wrongful-arrests-algorithmic-bias/.

Woodward, Bob. 2011. *Obama's Wars.* New York: Simon & Schuster.

Work, Robert O. 2017. Establishment of an Algorithmic Warfare Cross-Functional Team (Project Maven). Memo dated April 26. www.govexec.com/media/gbc/docs/pdfs_edit/establishment_of_the_awcft_project_maven.pdf.

Wylie, Christopher, 2019. *Mindf*ck: Cambridge Analytica and the Plot to Break America.* New York: Random House.

Yannuzzi, Rick. 2000. In-Q-Tel: A New Partnership between the CIA and the Private Sector. *Defense Intelligence Journal* 9(1): 25–37.

Yong, Ed. 2018. Psychology's Replication Crisis Is Running Out of Excuses. *Atlantic*, November 19. www.theatlantic.com/science/archive/2018/11 /psychologys-replication-crisis-real/576223/.

Zacharias, Greg L. 2019. *Autonomous Horizons: The Way Forward*. Montgomery, AL: Air Force University Press.

Zarkadakis, George. 2015. *In Our Own Image: Savior or Destroyer? The History and Future of Artificial Intelligence*. New York: Pegasus.

Zastrow, Mark. 2020. South Korea Is Reporting Intimate Details of COVID-19 Cases: Has It Helped? *Nature*, March 18. www.nature.com/articles /d41586-020-00740-y.

Zegart, Amy, and Kevin Childs. 2018. The Divide between Silicon Valley and Washington Is a National Security Threat. *Atlantic*, December 13. www .theatlantic.com/ideas/archive/2018/12/growing-gulf-between-silicon-valley-and-washington/577963/.

Zinn, Howard. 2012. *The Historic Unfulfilled Promise*. San Francisco: City Lights Books.

Zulaika, Joseba. 2012. Drones, Witches, and Other Flying Objects: The Force of Fantasy in US Counterterrorism. *Critical Studies in Counterterrorism* 5(1): 51–68.

———. 2020. *Hellfire from Paradise Ranch: On the Frontlines of Drone Warfare*. Oakland: University of California Press.

Index

INDEX

autonomous systems (continued)
42, 44–46, 48, 151, 184n43, 186n72.
See also robots
Awlaki, Abdulrahman al-, 6–7

battlefields, 26–27, 38, 40, 70, 163, 203n28
BDI (Behavioural Dynamics Institute), xiv,
82. *See also* SCL Group
biases, 119, 150–53
big data, 2, 4, 16, 34, 58, 191n41, 201n82;
and autonomous systems, 44; and Cambridge Analytica, 21; and counterinsurgency, 92, 139; and counterterrorism,
134; critical analysis of, 202n13; and
DARPA, 22, 111, 113–14, 118, 122,
143, 146; definition of, 179–80n3; and
military, 61–62, 146, 151–52; and politics, 137–38; and predictive modeling,
157–58; and robotics, 29, 31; weaponization of, 148. *See also* data
Big Five, 45, 86, 88, 191n35
Big Tech, 6, 19, 52, 55, 70, 170. *See also* Silicon Valley; tech industry
blogs, 84, 121, 123, 126, 175
bodybuilding, 98–100, 194n20
Bulkley, Bartlett. *See* Russell, Bartlett
businesses, 7, 64, 73, 83, 95, 111, 122. *See
also* companies; corporations; defense
contractors

Cambridge Analytica, 21, 81–82, 86–95,
191n39, 192n44, 202n4. *See also* SCL
Group
centaurs. *See* human-machine teaming
Charles River Analytics, 109, 127–28, 131
China, 8; contact tracing in, 12; surveillance
in, 14–16; and United States, 10, 28, 49,
124
CIA (Central Intelligence Agency), xiv, 4, 21,
77, 84, 107; and Freedom of Information
Act, 175–76; and Google, 67; and In-Q-
Tel, 58–60
Circinus, 130–31, 199n23
civilians, 4, 7, 9, 34, 39, 57, 177; and drone
warfare, 156–58
cloud computing, 34, 63, 65, 70
Cold War, 21, 49, 63, 71, 75, 140
companies, 107, 165, 187n37, 188n47;
political consulting, 21–22, 81–87, 89,
91–97; predictive modeling, 131–32,
135–36, 141–42; public relations, 78;
robotics, 24; surveillance, 13, 15–16;
technology, 54, 60–67, 72–74, 80, 90.

See also businesses; corporations; defense
contractors
computer programmers, 19, 21, 93, 115,
119, 133, 150; in Silicon Valley, 59,
73–75
computers, 20, 36, 52, 112, 120; for counterinsurgency, 9, 118, 133–35, 140, 146,
163; for predictive modeling, 133, 137,
143; and Silicon Valley, 66, 71; for surveillance, 15, 17; in Vietnam War, 4
computer scientists, 2–3, 10, 22, 110,
193n71, 196n57; and predictive modeling, 119–20, 122; and robots, 46; in
Silicon Valley, 51, 65
conflict, 1–2, 85, 114, 138, 153–54, 159;
armed, 77, 113, 119, 160, 163; prediction of, 22, 114, 138, 153–54
control: of citizens, 13, 164; of data, 5, 95,
166; of knowledge, 72; over robots, 34,
41; social, 4, 164
corporate executives, 51, 75, 80, 165
corporations, 5, 54, 68, 96–97, 105, 173,
178. *See also* businesses; companies;
defense contractors
counterinsurgency, 92, 122, 145, 159, 174;
computational, 9, 118, 133–35, 140,
146, 163
CPI (Committee on Public Information), xiv,
85
Creech Air Force Base, 39–40
cultural knowledge, 78, 80, 122–23, 153,
177, 180n17, 198n8
culture, 7, 111–12, 118–19, 197n82,
199n29; and biases, 151; and predictive
modeling, 115, 131–33; and technology,
20; weaponization of, 123–24
cyberwarfare, 9, 11, 59, 179n2, 181n30

DARPA (Defense Advanced Research
Projects Agency), xiv, 22, 99, 104, 193n2,
194n19, 196n60; and autonomous systems, 33; and counterinsurgency, 139–
46; and predictive modeling, 121; programs, 108–9, 112–19
data, 81, 90, 180n3; and algorithms, 6; personal, 18–19, 78, 80, 86–87, 94, 97,
148; positional, 15; qualitative, 22, 118,
153; quantitative, 22, 118, 153. *See also*
big data
databases, 4, 124, 133, 141, 200n57
data scientists, 6, 9, 86, 88, 141
defense contractors, 4, 10, 16, 21, 107, 123,
173, 181n27; and predictive modeling,

Founded in 1893,
UNIVERSITY OF CALIFORNIA PRESS
publishes bold, progressive books and journals
on topics in the arts, humanities, social sciences,
and natural sciences—with a focus on social
justice issues—that inspire thought and action
among readers worldwide.

The UC PRESS FOUNDATION
raises funds to uphold the press's vital role
as an independent, nonprofit publisher, and
receives philanthropic support from a wide
range of individuals and institutions—and from
committed readers like you. To learn more, visit
ucpress.edu/supportus.